THE GLOBAL FINANCIAL SYSTEM

THE GLOBAL FINANCIAL SYSTEM

A Functional Perspective

GLOBAL FINANCIAL SYSTEM PROJECT
HARVARD BUSINESS SCHOOL

Dwight B. Crane   Robert C. Merton
Kenneth A. Froot   Zvi Bodie
Scott P. Mason   Erik R. Sirri
André F. Perold   Peter Tufano

Harvard Business School Press
Boston, Massachusetts

Library of Congress Cataloging-in-Publication Data

The global financial system: a functional perspective /
  Dwight B. Crane . . . [et al.].
    p. cm.
  Includes biographical references and index.
  ISBN 0-87584-622-X
  1. International finance.   2. Financial institutions, International.
I. Crane, Dwight B.
HG3881.G5753   1995
332'.042—dc20   95-14396
                                                           CIP

The paper used in this publication meets the requirements of the American
National Standard for Permanence of Paper for Printed Library Materials
Z39.49-1984.

CONTENTS

PREFACE

The Global Financial System: A Functional Perspective is the first research monograph produced as part of the Global Financial System Project at the Harvard Business School. Our interest in the challenges facing managers of financial institutions and public policy officials led us to initiate this project. Rapidly changing boundaries—geopolitical, regulatory, and technological—have rendered strategic and public policy decision making more difficult. Regulation, framed by traditional institutions and geographic territories, has become increasingly problematic as financial activities have moved outside conventional institutions and transactions now easily cross geographic boundaries. Furthermore, decades of unprecedented financial innovation have significantly increased the complexity of managing financial firms, including the recurring problems of risk measurement and management, capital allocation, and performance measurement.

A key element of our research project, and this book, is the use of a functional perspective to study the financial system. Rather than taking existing institutions and organizational structures as givens, we anchor our research on the underlying functions of financial systems. Basic financial functions, such as payments, are required in all economies, whether past or present, East or West. In contrast, organizational arrangements used to fulfill these functions are less constant, generally changing over time and differing across national boundaries.

Even when the outward identities are the same, the functions financial institutions perform often differ dramatically. For example, insurance companies today perform a broader set of functions and underwrite a wider array of risks than did insurance companies of forty years ago. And banks in the United States in 1995 are very different from those in 1925 or in 1955, just as they are distinct from the institutions called "banks" in Germany or the United Kingdom today. Finally, the present financial markets in New York, London, or Tokyo are very different from what they were as recently as 1980—before the widespread introduction of securitization and the trading in fixed-income and index futures, options, and swap contracts.

We contend that the underlying financial functions, however, have changed little. We focus on six of them in this book, believing that they form the core needs served by the financial system. These functions provide:

- Methods of *clearing and settling payments*
- Mechanisms for *pooling of resources*
- Ways to *transfer economic resources* through time and across distances
- Methods of *managing risk*
- Price *information* to help coordinate decentralized decision-making in various sectors of the economy
- Ways of *dealing with incentive problems* created when one party to a transaction has information that another party does not or when one party acts as agent for another

Each of these functions meets a basic need. The ability to pool resources, for example, is required because the wealth of an individual household is not sufficient to fund large-scale efficient enterprises. Pooling mechanisms break the link between household wealth and enterprise scale. They permit individuals to invest in large firms and, correspondingly, permit firms to reach an efficient scale that would be unattainable if funded by single households.

While the set of financial functions is stable, the way each need is met varies from location to location depending upon regulations, the level of technology, and other factors. In some environments, for example, traditional financial institutions play a dominant role in providing the pooling function, while in others the issuance of securities directly to investors provides an important pooling mechanism. Furthermore, the performance of the function changes over time as product innovation, improved technology, and competitive forces lead to more efficient performance. This is illustrated by the development and growth of asset-backed securities in some markets. Loans that are relatively homogeneous in nature and do not require substantial ongoing monitoring are packaged and sold as securities to investors, bypassing the traditional pooling and intermediation role of lending institutions.

A key premise of our research is that the dynamic performance of the functions leads to new institutional arrangements; in other words, institutional form follows function. Thus, it is important to understand how the functions are performed and how the performance is changing if one wishes to consider how financial institutions may evolve over time.

This book explains the functional perspective and puts it to work, testing its usefulness as a new tool for understanding the fundamental changes underway in the financial system. Some parts of the book emphasize an historical perspective, providing an understanding of why institutional arrangements took the form they did in the past. Other sections look at the present situation, using a functional perspective to develop a different or deeper understanding of current changes in the financial markets. Some parts of the book speculate about the future, asking the reader to imagine a world in the future when, for example, a new financial instrument might replace some of the risk management functions performed by insurance companies. The point of these speculations is not to make specific predictions but to illustrate that old institutional labels, and the regulatory structures based on them, will continue to be challenged as competitors search for more efficient ways to perform the financial functions.

The Global Financial System begins with an explanation of the functional framework for studying the financial system and a discussion of the six major functions the system performs. Chapter 1 also illustrates how the functional perspective can be used to explore a variety of topics from financial system issues, to issues faced by individual financial institutions, to specific financial activities such as lending. Each of the six succeeding chapters discusses one underlying function, providing the basis for understanding of the forces affecting the performance of the functions and the financial system. Finally, Chapter 8 applies the functional perspective to regulation and public policy issues.

We believe the functional perspective provides a new and helpful way of looking at financial institutions and markets. An important purpose of the book is to show that this perspective can be constructively used to frame questions and seek answers about public policy issues, the strategy of financial institutions, the prospective structure of the industry, and so on. Thus, its intent is to lay the foundation for future work.

We and other faculty involved in the Global Financial System Project have begun to study a number of issues using the functional perspective developed in this book. Current research efforts are focused on the challenges that financial systems will face in providing retirement income, the changing structure of the property and casualty insurance industry, the problems institutions face in allocating capital and measuring performance, and corporate risk management. Our hope is that others at academic institutions, financial organizations, and regulatory authorities will find the functional perspective helpful as they think carefully about the issues they face.

The work represented by this book and our ongoing research efforts have profited greatly from the involvement and support of a group of major financial institutions from around the world. They have generously provided major financial support, as well as the time and perspective of top management. They have also answered questions, provided data, and offered constructive criticism. We are very grateful to these organizations for their continuing support and involvement in our efforts:

American International Group, Inc. and The Starr Foundation
Bancomer, S.A.
Dean Witter, Discover & Company
Deutsche Bank and The Deutsche Bank Research Foundation
GE Capital
HSBC Holdings plc
The Industrial Bank of Japan, Limited
Mercury Asset Management Group plc
Mitsui Marine & Fire Insurance Co., Ltd.
J.P. Morgan & Co. Incorporated
Morgan Stanley Group Inc.
Prudential Insurance Company of America
Reuters Holdings and The Reuter Foundation
State Street Bank and Trust Company
S.G. Warburg Group plc

The Division of Research of the Harvard Business School has also strongly backed our research efforts. We thank our colleagues and the School for their support.

We have benefited immensely from advice and contributions by other individuals. In particular, we would like to thank our colleagues Carliss Y. Baldwin and Jerry R. Green, who provided excellent advice on the research manuscript. Patricia Peat was an extremely helpful editor who met the challenge of dealing with numerous authors. Joanne Segal played a significant role in helping us work with the institutions participating in the research project.

We received valuable research assistance from Kendall Backstrand, Mihir Desai, Arnout Eikeboom, Philip T. Hamilton, Jonathon S. Headley, Barbara Kyrillos, Wai Lee, Bhanu Narasimhan, Kuljot Singh, W. James Whalen, and Ann Zeitung. We would also like to acknowledge the helpful contributions of our assistants, Linda Arricale, Debbie Hannon, Elaine Hetu, Dee Luther, and Janice Wright.

Finally, we would like to express a special word of appreciation to two individuals who were there at the start of the project and who have been very important to its progress since then. A significant impetus to begin this project came from William S. Edgerly, former chairman of State Street Bank and Trust. Several conversations with Mr. Edgerly about his interests in research on the financial system encouraged us to begin the project and helped to frame our efforts. We were also honored to receive one of the "200th Anniversary Grants" awarded by Mr. Edgerly and his colleagues in recognition of State Street Bank and Trust's two-hundredth anniversary in 1992.

One of the many things Dean John H. McArthur does well is to bring people together and encourage them to look for ways to make progress on important issues. He brought us together in 1992 and has provided continuing encouragement and support. We are very grateful.

THE GLOBAL FINANCIAL SYSTEM

CHAPTER ONE

A Conceptual Framework for Analyzing the Financial Environment

ROBERT C. MERTON AND ZVI BODIE

Financial markets and intermediaries today are globally linked through a vast international telecommunications network, so that the trading of securities and the transfer of payments go on virtually around the clock. The financial markets include the foreign exchange, fixed-income, and equity markets, as well as the new and growing markets for "derivative" securities such as futures, options, and swaps. Capital market functions are also performed by financial intermediaries such as banks and insurance companies, which provide customized products and services—the kind that do not lend themselves to the standardization necessary to support a liquid market.

For a variety of reasons—including differences in size, complexity, and available technology, as well as differences in political, cultural, and historical backgrounds—financial institutions generally differ across borders. They also change over time. Even when the names of institutions are the same, the functions they perform often differ dramatically. For example, banks in the United States today are very different from what

---

The conceptual framework set forth in this chapter is a synthesis and extension of work presented by the authors in Merton (1989; 1990; 1992a; 1992b, Ch.14; 1994; 1995), Bodie and Merton (1992; 1993), and Merton and Bodie (1992a; 1992b; 1993).

they were in 1925 or in 1955, and they are very different from the institutions called banks in Germany or the United Kingdom today.

This monograph is an attempt to improve the understanding of how and why the institutional structure of the financial system changes and how it is likely to evolve in the future. In this opening chapter, we try our hand at setting forth a unifying conceptual framework.[1]

The key element in the framework is its focus on *functions* rather than on *institutions* as the conceptual "anchor." Hence, we call it the *functional perspective.* It rests on two basic premises:

- Financial functions are more stable than financial institutions—that is, functions change less over time and vary less across borders.

- Institutional form follows function—that is, innovation and competition among institutions ultimately result in greater efficiency in the performance of financial system functions.[2]

The chapter develops the functional perspective and gives an overview of its range of application. Applicability of this perspective ranges widely, from analysis of the entire financial system to individual business strategy decisions and specific public policy choices. We distinguish four levels of analysis: system-level, institution-level, activity-level, and product-level.

The evolution of the financial system is described as an *innovation spiral,* in which organized markets and intermediaries compete with each other in a *static* sense and complement each other in a *dynamic* sense. The functional perspective views financial innovation as driving the financial system toward the goal of greater economic efficiency.[3] Technological advances that have already resulted in dramatically reduced transactions costs, and

---

1. In the economics literature, the closest analogue is the work of Schumpeter (1911), Williamson (1985), and North (1994). These authors, however, focus on the economic system as a whole; we focus on the financial system only.

2. The functional perspective adopted here is similar in spirit to the functional approach in sociology pioneered by Robert K. Merton (1957). There are a number of others whose work fits comfortably within this framework. In the area of financial innovation, see Black and Scholes (1974), Benston and Smith (1976), Ross (1989), and Scholes (1994). In the intermediation literature, the analytical approaches of Black, Miller, and Posner (1978), Black (1985), Pierce (1991, 1993), Gorton and Pennacchi (1992), and Brennan (1993), are aligned with the functional perspective. In the case of finance practitioners, the perspective is perhaps best exemplified in Sanford (1993).

3. Theories of financial innovation that are consistent with this view are espoused by: Ross (1973, 1976, 1989), Benston and Smith (1976), Fama (1980), Diamond and Verrecchia (1982), Diamond (1984), Barnea, Haugen, and Senbet (1985), Fama and Jensen (1985), Williamson (1985), Strong and Walker (1987), Allen and Gale (1988, 1990, 1994), Duffie and Jackson (1989), Merton (1989, 1992b, Ch. 14), Townsend (1990), and Milgrom and Roberts (1992).

advances in the theory and practice of finance that rely on low transactions costs, are likely to produce wide-ranging institutional changes in the future. We sketch the broad outlines of some of those changes.

From the most aggregated level of the single *primary* function of resource allocation, we distinguish six basic or *core* functions performed by the financial system:

- To provide ways of *clearing and settling payments* to facilitate trade.
- To provide a mechanism for the *pooling of resources* and for the *subdividing* of shares in various enterprises.
- To provide ways to *transfer economic resources* through time, across borders, and among industries.
- To provide ways of *managing risk.*
- To provide *price information* to help coordinate decentralized decision-making in various sectors of the economy.
- To provide ways of *dealing with the incentive problems* created when one party to a transaction has information that the other party does not or when one party acts as agent for another.

The six chapters to follow offer in-depth descriptions, analyses, and illustrations of each of the core functions of the financial system. A final chapter discusses the evolving infrastructure and regulation of the global financial system in the future.

Change and Diversity in the Global Financial System

We know that people have engaged in financial transactions since the dawn of recorded history. Sumerian documents reveal the systematic use of credit for agricultural and other purposes in Mesopotamia around 3000 BC. Barley and silver served as a medium of exchange—i.e., money. Even regulation of financial contracts existed in ancient times. Hammurabi's Code contains many sections relating to the regulation of credit in Babylon around 1800 BC.[4]

Banking institutions arose in the city-state of Genoa in the twelfth century AD, and flourished there and in Florence and Venice for several centuries. These banks took demand deposits and made loans to merchants, princes, and towns. Security issues similar to the modern form also originated in the Italian city-states in the late Middle Ages. Long-term loans floated by the Republic of Venice, called the *prestiti,* were a popular

---

4. See Homer (1977).

form of investment in the thirteenth and fourteenth centuries, and their market price was a matter of public record. Even organized exchanges for trading financial futures contracts and other financial derivatives, which some see as an innovation of the 1980s, are not entirely new. Similar contracts were widely traded on the Amsterdam securities exchange in the 1600s.[5]

As this little bit of history makes clear, some things have not changed. Financial activities, such as borrowing, investing in securities, and other forms of financial contracting, are very old indeed. The ways in which these activities are carried out, however, have changed through the ages.

In the past few decades, in particular, the pace of financial innovation has greatly accelerated.[6] Think of round-the-clock trading in Tokyo-London-New York, financial futures, swaps, mortgage-backed securities, exchange-traded options, "junk" bonds, shelf registration, electronic funds transfer and security trading, automated teller machines, asset-based financing, and LBO, MBO, and all the other acronymic approaches to corporate restructuring. And this is but a small sampling.

While it may be hard to believe that the pace of general financial innovation during the past few decades can sustain itself into the future, there are reasons to believe it can, because it is rooted in fundamental economic factors.[7] Technological advances in telecommunications, data processing, and computation, which began in the 1960s, have resulted in dramatically reduced transactions costs for the financial services industry. In addition to lower transactions costs due to technological advances, there is also the learning curve: When one has created nine new markets, the tenth one becomes a lot easier.

The decision to implement an innovation involves a trade-off between its benefit and its cost. With lower transactions costs, the threshold benefit to warrant implementing financial innovations drops. If we continue to see the same pace of change in the underlying fundamentals as in the past, the implementation of financial innovation is likely to remain rapid, as the threshold for change is lower.

With much lower costs of change, it becomes profitable not only to introduce new products and create new markets, but also to change entire institutional arrangements (including geographical and political locations) in response to much smaller shifts in customer tastes or operating costs than in the past. Thus, technological advances, lower costs, and the prospect of greater global competition in financial services all form the basis for

---

5. See de la Vega (1688).
6. See Finnerty (1992) and Miller (1992).
7. See Remolona (1992) for evidence on the rate of growth of financial derivatives markets.

predicting substantial increases in both the frequency and the magnitude of institutional changes for private sector and government financial intermediaries and for regulatory bodies alike.[8]

As an illustration of both the change and the diversity in institutional structures around the world, consider the financing of retirement income for older people. For much of the world's population, the extended family is the main institution to perform this function. Elderly family members live and work with younger members of the agrarian family, and all draw a common livelihood from it. But in much of the industrialized world, urbanization and other fundamental economic and social changes have led to new institutional structures for the care and support of the elderly.

An often-used metaphor for describing a country's retirement income system is the "three-legged stool." The first leg is government-provided pension and welfare programs (such as Social Security in the United States); the second is employer- or labor union-provided pensions; and the third is direct individual savings. There is substantial variation across countries in the mix of the three sources of retirement income.

Table 1-1 illustrates these national differences. The first column shows Social Security replacement rates of final salary for 12 different countries in 1992. The replacement rate is given for two levels of final salary—$20,000 (low income) and $50,000 (middle income).

Table 1-1 also shows the proportion of the labor force that is covered by a private pension plan. At one extreme is Italy, where the government-run social security system provides a replacement rate greater than 70% for both low- and middle-income workers. It is therefore not surprising to see that in Italy only 5% of the labor force is covered by an employer pension plan. At the other extreme is Australia, where the social security replacement rate is quite low, but 92% of workers are covered by a compulsory employer-based pension plan.

Table 1-1 is a snapshot at a point in time. It therefore fails to convey the dramatic changes that have occurred in national retirement income systems and the changes that are bound to come in the decades ahead.[9]

For example, the high proportion of Australian workers covered by a private pension plan shown in the last column of Table 1-1 is a very recent phenomenon. Only in July 1992 did the Australian government implement a major pension reform that introduced a system of mandatory employer-based pensions similar to those in Chile and Switzerland.[10]

Pension reform is currently a high-priority issue in several European

8. This is also the conclusion drawn by Hayes (1993).
9. See, for example, the study sponsored by the World Bank (1994).
10. See Bateman and Piggott (1993).

Table 1-1 International Social Security Replacement Rates and Pension Coverage in 1992

Country	Social Security Retirement Benefit as a *Percentage* of Final Earnings (based on final salary of $20,000 and $50,000)	Percentage of Labor Force Covered by a Private Pension Plan
United States	65%–40%	46%
United Kingdom	50–26	50
Germany	70–59	42
Japan	54	50
Canada	34	41
Netherlands	66–26	83
Sweden	69–49	90
Denmark	83–33	50
Switzerland	82–47	90 (compulsory)
Australia	28–11	92 (compulsory)
France	67–45	100 (compulsory)
Italy	77–73	5

Source: Davis (1995).

Notes: 1. The social security replacement rates in column 2 are given for two different levels of final salary—$20,000 and $50,000. For example, in the United States the replacement rate is 65% for someone with a final salary of $20,000 and 40% for someone with a final salary of $50,000. Where only a single replacement rate is given (e.g., Japan), the rate is the same for both salary levels.

2. The pension plan coverage rates in column 3 only include pensions provided by employers or labor unions. They do not include voluntary retirement savings accounts for individuals such as IRAs in the United States.

countries (e.g., Italy, Germany, France) that have relied heavily on pay-as-you-go systems of retirement income provision in the past. As the proportion of the elderly in these populations increases in the next few decades, these systems will come under tremendous strains that are likely to lead to institutional change. And in the developing nations of Asia and Africa, some of which have had no formal pension system at all, institutional reforms are being considered to supplement the informal systems of family provision of old-age income.

The example of retirement finance clearly demonstrates that the financial system encompasses a broader set of institutions than just financial markets and intermediaries. The family and government play an important role everywhere. In many countries—even those with fully developed financial markets and intermediaries—the family is still an important institutional mechanism for financing education, housing, care of the elderly, and even start-ups of new businesses.[11]

Government's role in supporting the infrastructure of the financial system is fundamental. It includes establishing and enforcing property rights and other laws affecting contracts as well as regulating financial markets and intermediaries. Governmental bodies often substitute for or supplement private sector intermediaries, providing cash loans, subsidized interest rates, and loan guarantees.

The roles of family, government, and private sector markets and intermediaries, and the regulatory structures governing them, vary considerably from country to country and from financing activity to activity. The relations among all of these institutions are typically both competitive and complementary. This applies to both the relations between financial intermediaries and markets and the relations between those private sector institutions and the family and government.

Why a Functional Perspective?

As illustrated by the example of systems for providing retirement income, institutional change in the financing of economic activity is today a dominant theme around the world in both the private and the public sector. Among other policy issues of current concern are the following:

- What regulatory or other institutional arrangements are most efficient for dealing with over-the-counter markets for derivatives such as forward contracts, options, and swaps?[12]

- Is there a way to improve the institutional mechanisms that support investment in business innovation?[13]

---

11. We use the term "family" in a technical sense to mean any group of people with strongly interdependent utility functions. It is thus not necessarily the same as a "household." If within a household such interdependent utility is not present, then the legal or biological family does not function as "family."

12. For example, Financial Derivatives . . . (1994), a report by the United States General Accounting Office, recommends that "Congress require federal regulation of the safety and soundness of all major U.S. OTC derivatives dealers."

13. Porter (1994), for example, believes that the institutional structure of the United States financial system tends to create a problem of insufficient investment in business innovation.

To tackle such questions, one requires a tool of analysis that explicitly deals with the dynamics of institutional change. The *neoclassical economics perspective* addresses the dynamics of prices and quantities, but is largely an "institution-free" perspective in which only functions "matter." It thus has nothing to say directly about the institutions that perform these functions and how they change over time.[14]

At the other extreme, there is a *static* institutional perspective, which assumes not only that institutions matter but also takes them as the conceptual "anchor." It views the objective of public policy to be to help the institutions currently in place to survive and flourish. Framed in terms of *the* banks or *the* insurance companies, managerial objectives are similarly defined in terms of what can be done to make those institutions perform their particular financial services more efficiently and profitably.

Because this institutional perspective is static in focus, it cannot explain the dynamics of institutional change. Moreover, from this perspective, financial innovation sometimes appears to threaten the stability of the system, by providing the means to circumvent institutionally based regulations at low cost.

Drawing on both the neoclassical and institutional perspectives, the functional perspective adopted here takes as a *given* the economic functions performed by financial institutions and then seeks to discover the best institutional structure for performing those functions at a given time and a given place. It does not assume that existing institutions, whether private sector or governmental, operating, or regulatory, will be preserved. Thus functions rather than institutions serve as the conceptual anchor. Because institutions "matter" but are not the anchors, institutional changes can be explained within this perspective.[15]

To illustrate the differences among the neoclassical economics perspective, the static institutional perspective, and the functional perspective, consider how many ways there are today to take a levered position in the Standard & Poor's 500 stocks:[16]

1. You can buy each stock individually on margin in the cash stock market.
2. You can invest in an S&P 500 Index fund and borrow from a bank to finance it.
3. You can go long a futures contract on the S&P 500.

---

14. This feature of the neoclassical perspective has been stressed by North (1994).
15. The functional perspective on the financial system falls within the research tradition of what Williamson (1985, p. 16) calls the New Institutional Economics.
16. This example is taken from Merton (1995).

4. You can go long an OTC forward contract on the S&P 500.

5. You can enter into a swap contract to receive the total return on the S&P 500 and pay LIBOR or some other standard interest rate.

6. You can go long exchange-traded calls and short puts on the S&P 500.

7. You can go long OTC calls and short puts.

8. You can purchase an equity-linked note that pays based on the S&P 500 and finance it by a repurchase agreement.

9. You can purchase from a bank a certificate of deposit with its payments linked to the return on the S&P 500.

10. You can either buy on margin or purchase the capital appreciation component of a unit investment trust (examples are Super Shares or SPDRs) that holds the S&P 500.

11. You can borrow to buy a variable-rate annuity contract that has its return linked to the S&P 500.

From a neoclassical economics perspective, all 11 of these are equivalent ways of achieving a desired exposure to the S&P 500. Indeed, the modern theory of asset pricing (based on the law of one price) relies on this equivalence to infer information from the market prices of these products. But these 11 different forms for investing in the S&P 500 are not simply cosmetic product differentiations among competing issuer institutions. They make it possible for investors facing different tax and regulatory structures and other institutional rigidities to take positions more efficiently. The neoclassical perspective offers little guidance in understanding the managerial or regulatory implications of the differences.

The static institutional perspective, on the other hand, tends to lead one to view the 11 different ways of taking a levered position in the S&P 500 with alarm. If regulators want to maintain the safety and soundness of financial institutions currently in place, the development of alternative ways of achieving an economically equivalent result poses a danger. A natural regulatory response is to try to slow down financial innovation or ban it altogether. The important question from a public policy perspective, however, is whether the institutions in place *ought* to be preserved.

The functional perspective offers an alternative view with very different policy implications. It is precisely the development of a multiplicity of institutional forms illustrated in our example that has facilitated the globalization of the financial system in the 1980s and 1990s. Given the diversity of the national currency, financial-cultural, and regulatory regimes that have become linked together, it seems remarkable in retrospect that the process of globalization has been so smooth. Financial innovation has made it possible to hook up these diverse national financial systems to a single global network.

Indeed, one can think of today's financial system as a global network (similar to the Internet) that can be freely accessed by any government or firm that has the standardized hardware, software, and trained personnel necessary to "hook up" to it. An important implication is that governments in countries with less well-developed domestic financial systems may not have to follow the same historical path as the United States or Germany and develop a complete set of organized financial markets and intermediaries. Instead of establishing local securities exchanges and the regulatory apparatus to oversee them, they can concentrate their limited resources on developing the financial and technological expertise needed to access the global financial network.[17]

Functions of the Financial System

As stated at the outset, the *primary* function of any financial system is to facilitate the allocation and deployment of economic resources, both across borders and across time, in an uncertain environment. From the most aggregated level of the single primary function of resource allocation, we can further distinguish six basic functions performed by the financial system:[18]

Function 1: Clearing and Settling Payments

- *A financial system provides ways of clearing and settling payments to facilitate the exchange of goods, services, and assets.*

There are alternative ways of clearing and settling payments. Collectively, the set of institutional arrangements for accomplishing this task is called the payments system. Depository financial intermediaries such as banks serve this function with wire transfers, checking accounts, and credit/cash cards. Other intermediaries such as money market mutual funds offer transaction-draft accounts, and firms whose principal business is not financial, such as AT&T, General Electric, and General Motors, offer general credit cards.

---

17. The World Bank (1990) reports that in 1989 it launched the Financial Technical Assistance on Asset and Liability Management Project to help selected groups in the public and private sectors gain expertise in the use of modern techniques of financial risk management.
18. Other functional classification schemes have been suggested in the finance literature. An appendix to this chapter briefly discusses several of them.

Mechanisms for clearing and settling securities transactions are designed to deal with the costs and the risks associated with the process. Costs arise in the form of processing fees, transfer taxes, and the maintenance of collateral. Risk arises because one of the parties to a transaction may not fulfill its terms. For example, the buyer may not be able to arrange financing, or the seller fails to deliver. The key elements for managing these costs and risks include netting arrangements, efficient use of collateral, delivery-versus-payment, immobilization of securities, and extension of credit.

Chapter 2 examines these basic mechanisms. It takes a broad view of the payment system, to include not just systems for clearing and settlement, but also derivative instruments, traditionally *not* viewed as integral to the payment system, except with respect to their own clearing and settlement. The chapter establishes that derivative instruments serve as an important extension of the payment system because they substitute in a variety of ways for trading in cash market instruments.

The chapter compares the payment system demands of cash market security trading strategies with those of derivatives-based strategies. It shows how the derivatives-based strategies typically transform a small number of large payments into a large number of small payments spread over time. By reducing the occurrence of relatively large funds transfers, the use of the derivatives alternative can significantly reduce the risk of a major disruption caused by a single default.

Chapter 2 concludes by focusing on the foreign exchange market and examining alternatives for dealing with credit risk induced by different time zones ("Herstatt risk"). It illustrates how these alternative approaches to the reduction of this risk, including netting and the use of derivatives, can serve as functional substitutes with very different implications for institutional change.

Function 2: Pooling Resources and Subdividing Shares

- *A financial system provides a mechanism for the pooling of funds to undertake large-scale indivisible enterprise or for the subdividing of shares in enterprises to facilitate diversification.*

In modern economies, the minimum investment required to run a business is often beyond the means of an individual or even several individuals. From the perspective of firms raising capital, the financial system provides a variety of mechanisms (such as security markets and financial intermediaries) through which individual households can pool (or aggregate) their wealth into larger amounts of capital for use by business firms. From the perspective of individual savers, the financial system provides opportunities for households to participate in large indivisible investments.

Mutual funds that hold stocks and bonds are examples of financial intermediaries that provide virtually full divisibility in subdividing the individual unit size of the traded securities they hold. Chapter 3 explores the role of mutual funds in detail. It also identifies the process of securitization as one key to future gains in the efficiency of pooling. *Securitization* is essentially the removal of (nontraded) assets from a financial intermediary's balance sheet by packaging them in a convenient form for outside investors and selling the packaged securities in a financial market.

Function 3: Transferring Resources Across Time and Space

- *A financial system provides ways to transfer economic resources through time, across geographic regions, and among industries.*

A well-developed, smooth-functioning financial system facilitates the efficient life-cycle allocations of household consumption and the efficient allocation of physical capital to its most productive use in the business sector. A well-developed, smooth-functioning capital market also makes possible the efficient separation of ownership from management of the firm. This in turn makes feasible efficient specialization in production according to the principle of comparative advantage.

Intermediaries that serve this function include banks and thrifts in financing corporate investments and housing, insurance companies and pension funds in financing corporate investments and paying retirement annuities, and mutual funds that invest in virtually all sectors.

Chapter 4 explores this function in depth. In particular, it identifies the incentive problems of adverse selection and moral hazard as the main barriers to greater efficiency in the transfer of capital resources around the world. As in the chapter on the pooling function, *collateralization, credit enhancement,* and *securitization* are seen as the key to future improvements in the performance of the resource transfer function.

Function 4: Managing Risk

- *A financial system provides ways to manage uncertainty and control risk.*

A well-functioning financial system facilitates the efficient allocation of risk-bearing. Through often elaborate financial securities and through private sector and government intermediaries (including the system of social insurance), the financial system provides risk-pooling and risk-sharing opportunities for both households and business firms. It facilitates efficient life-cycle risk-bearing by households, and it allows for the separation of the providers of working capital for *real* investments (i.e., in personnel, plant, and equipment) from the providers of risk capital who bear the *financial* risk of those investments.

In both an international and a domestic context, this separation of real investment and risk-bearing permits specialization in production activities according to the principle of comparative advantage. Insurance companies are the classic example of a financial intermediary offering risk protection. They sell protection against loss in value of human capital (e.g., death and disability), physical property (e.g., fire and theft), and financial assets (e.g., contract guarantees including bond-default insurance). Mutual funds help control risk by providing diversification.

Chapter 5 explores the risk management function in detail, including the three basic ways to manage risk: *hedging, diversifying,* and *insuring.* Chapter 5 identifies the emergence of derivative securities as an important innovation, because like the purchase of insurance contracts, derivatives allow for the separation of risk management from the transfer of resources. The chapter also discusses the impact of these developments on the stability of the financial system and the possible need for regulation of derivatives trading.

Function 5: Providing Information

- *A financial system provides price information that helps coordinate decentralized decision-making in various sectors of the economy.*

The manifest function of financial markets is to allow individuals and businesses to trade financial assets. An additional latent function of the capital market is to provide information useful for decision-making. Interest rates and security prices, for example, are information that households or their agents use in making their consumption–saving decisions and in choosing the portfolio allocations of their wealth. These same prices provide important signals to managers of firms in their selection of investment projects and financings.

As the diversity of financial markets has increased during the past two decades, so too have the opportunities to extract useful information from the prices of financial instruments. Chapter 6 illustrates how information about the future volatility of changes in security, currency, and commodity prices can be extracted from options and option-like securities. Volatility is a critical input for virtually all decisions relating to risk management and strategic financial planning.

The introduction of exchange-traded options in 1973 and the concurrent development of the theory of contingent claims pricing have made it possible to infer beliefs about future volatility of an asset directly from the prices of options and other derivatives whose payoffs depend in a nonlinear way on the asset's price. The estimate extracted in this way is called *implied volatility.* An important, if unintended, consequence of the proliferation of derivatives will be a richer information set that can facilitate more efficient resource allocation decisions.

Function 6: Dealing with Incentive Problems

- *A financial system provides ways to deal with the incentive problems when one party to a financial transaction has information that the other party does not, or when one party is an agent for another.*

A well-functioning financial system reduces the incentive problems that make financial contracting difficult and costly. These problems arise because parties to contracts cannot easily observe or control one another, and because contractual enforcement mechanisms are not costless to invoke. These contractual "frictions" take a variety of forms: moral hazard, adverse selection, and information asymmetries.[19]

Chapter 7 focuses on the impact of incentive problems on the contractual relationships between a firm's managers and its capital providers. In short, incentive problems make it more costly for companies to raise external capital than to use internal capital. The nature and size of these additional costs affect, and are affected by, three major aspects of corporate behavior: financing policies; investment and capital budgeting policies; and risk management policies.

Chapter 7 shows how the financial system can respond to overcome those incentive problems. It discusses recent security innovation and the use of derivatives within corporate risk management programs as examples of how innovation can reduce the scope and the costs of incentive problems.

The Functional Perspective at Four Levels of Analysis

The functional perspective is applicable at several levels of analysis: system-level, institution-level, activity-level, and product-level.

Level of the System

The functional perspective offers a useful frame of reference for analyzing a country's entire financial system. In the former Communist countries of

---

19. For detailed development and a review of the literature of asymmetric information and agency theory in a financial market context, see Strong and Walker (1987). See also Ross (1973), Jensen and Meckling (1976), Fama (1980), Grossman and Hart (1982), Barnea, Haugen, and Senbet (1985), Fama and Jensen (1985), Jensen (1986), Townsend (1990), and Milgrom and Roberts (1992).

Eastern Europe, changing the financial system is a major part of a general restructuring of the entire economic system, from one based on central planning and government ownership of business to one based on free markets and private ownership. A number of other countries with well-developed free markets for nonfinancial goods and services still have centralized government control of their financial systems.

With total control over both the banking and pension systems and restrictions on cross-border capital flows, these governments collect almost all the savings of the household sector and allocate most of the capital to the business sector. In at least some of these countries, reforms to privatize large parts of the financial system are under consideration. And even in countries like the United States, with highly developed private financial markets and institutions, important changes in the way government regulates the system are actively being debated. An example is the system of financing retirement income.[20]

In general, such analyses begin with a description of the functions served by the pension system and a determination of how they are currently accomplished. From this base, the analysis then continues by examining alternative institutional arrangements used at other times and in other countries.

It is unlikely that solutions developed in one country or group of countries cannot be improved upon. Functional analysis seeks new institutional arrangements or new combinations of existing ones that might improve the performance of the functions, given the specific local economic, political, and cultural circumstances.

Level of an Institution

Application of the functional perspective is not limited to analyses at the level of the financial system. A functional perspective is also useful in the study of a particular institutional form. Examples are the savings and loans (S&Ls) in the United States during the 1970s and 1980s, or U.S. commercial banks during the 1990s.[21]

Evolving as specialized institutions in the United States during the first half of this century, S&Ls or "thrifts" came to have two core economic functions: to provide long-term financing for residential homeowners at fixed interest rates and to provide a riskless, liquid, short-term savings vehicle for large numbers of small savers. These are separable functions that need not be performed by the same intermediary.

---

20. See, for example, Bodie and Merton (1992, 1993).
21. See Merton and Bodie (1992b) for a discussion of S&Ls and Merton and Bodie (1993) for a discussion of commercial banks.

Nevertheless, the U.S. public policy response to the difficulties faced by thrifts during the 1970s and 1980s was to try to find ways of making them healthy again. The S&L problem was thus framed in terms of taking the existing institutions as a given (i.e., maintaining the institutional structure) and asking what changes could be made to improve the thrifts' competitive position. It is difficult to rationalize this public policy toward the thrifts during the 1980s unless preservation of existing financial institutions was a *primary* objective of that policy.

Ironically, while the government was struggling at great cost to save the thrifts during the 1980s, both of the thrifts' principal economic functions were being taken over by other institutional mechanisms. The creation of securitized mortgage instruments, ostensibly to help the thrifts, led to the creation of a national mortgage market that then allowed mutual funds and pension funds to become major funding alternatives to the thrifts. These funding markets also allowed entry by agent-like institutions such as investment banks and mortgage brokers to compete with the traditional principal-like thrifts for the origination and servicing fees on loans and mortgages.

Level of an Activity

To illustrate application of the functional perspective to a financial activity, consider *lending*. Lending is often treated as a homogeneous activity in both private sector and public sector decision-making. But from a functional perspective, lending in general is multi-functional, involving two of the six basic functions of the financial system.

Lending in its "purest" form is free of default risk, so it falls under a single basic functional category: *the intertemporal transfer of resources.* But, of course, with few exceptions, payments promised in loan agreements are subject to some degree of default risk. Lending therefore also involves a second basic functional category: *risk management.* When a loan is made, an implicit guarantee of that loan (a form of insurance) is involved.

To see this, consider the fundamental identity, which holds in both a functional and a valuation sense:

$$\text{Risky Loan} + \text{Loan Guarantee} \equiv \text{Default-Free Loan}$$
$$\text{Risky Loan} \equiv \text{Default-Free Loan} - \text{Loan Guarantee}$$

Thus, whenever lenders make dollar-denominated loans to anyone other than the U.S. government, they are implicitly also selling loan guarantees. The lending activity therefore consists of two functionally distinct activities: pure default-free lending (the intertemporal transfer function), and the sale of default risk insurance by the lender to the borrower (an example of the risk management function).[22]

The relative weighting of these two functions varies considerably across the various debt instruments. A high-grade bond (rated AAA) is almost all default-free loan with a very small guarantee component. A below-investment-grade or "junk" bond, on the other hand, typically has a large guarantee component.

Level of a Product

To see an application of the functional perspective at the level of an individual financial product, consider municipal-bond insurance.[23] In the United States, there are specialized insurance companies that sell insurance contracts that guarantee interest and principal payments on municipal bonds against default by the issuer. The policies are typically sold to the issuer, which "attaches" them to the bonds to give them an AAA credit rating. To succeed as a guarantor, the insurance company itself must be seen as a very strong credit.

In evaluating the firm's competitive standing, a manager with an *institutional* perspective would focus on other insurance companies as competitors. A manager with a *functional* perspective would instead focus on the best institutional structure to perform the function, which may *not* be an insurance company.

Consider as one alternative an option exchange that creates a market for put options on municipal bonds. In such a market investors could achieve the same protection against loss by buying an uninsured municipal bond and a put option on that bond.[24] Note that both structures serve the same function for investors—protection against loss from default— but the institutions are entirely different: An options exchange is not an insurance company. Furthermore, the put option traded on the exchange is a different product from the insurance guarantee. Although the products and institutions that provide them are both quite different, the *economic function* they serve is the same.

In certain environments, it is surely possible that an options exchange with mark-to-market collateral and a clearing corporation could be a

---

22. For analysis of the default-insurance guarantee business, see Merton and Bodie (1992b).
23. This example is taken from Merton (1993, pp. 28–29).
24. With a standard fixed exercise price, the put would actually provide more protection because it covers losses in the value of the bond for any reason, not just issuer default. The coverage could effectively be "narrowed" to only default risk by making the exercise price "float" to equal the current price of an AAA bond with comparable terms to those of the covered bond.

better credit than an insurance company and also thereby be a superior institutional structure to serve the guarantee function. In such environments, *the institutionally oriented manager may miss recognizing the firm's prime competitor.* Regulatory bodies for financial services are almost exclusively organized along institutional lines, so they face similar problems. Because options are not insurance products, and exchanges are not insurance companies, insurance regulators would have no control over the option exchange even though its product is a perfect substitute for an insurance product.

The Financial Innovation Spiral

The evolution of the financial system can be viewed as an *innovation spiral*, in which organized markets and intermediaries compete with each other in a *static* sense and complement each other in a *dynamic* sense. That intermediaries and markets compete to be the providers of financial products is widely recognized. Improving technology and a decline in transactions costs have added to the intensity of that competition. Inspection of Finnerty's (1988, 1992) extensive histories of innovative financial products suggests a pattern in which products offered initially by intermediaries ultimately move to markets. For example:

- The development of liquid markets for money instruments such as commercial paper allowed money market mutual funds to compete with banks and thrifts for household savings.

- The creation of "junk"-bond and medium-term note markets made it possible for mutual funds, pension funds, and individual investors to service those corporate issuers that had historically depended on banks as their source of debt financing.

- The creation of a national mortgage market allowed mutual funds and pension funds to become major funding alternatives to thrift institutions for residential mortgages. Creation of these funding markets also made it possible for investment banks and mortgage brokers to compete with the thrift institutions for the origination and servicing fees on loans and mortgages.

- Securitization of auto loans, credit card receivables, and leases on consumer and producer durables has intensified the competition between banks and finance companies as sources of funds for these purposes.[25]

---

25. For a comprehensive discussion of the implementation of asset securitization, see Zweig (1989), Norton and Spellman (1991), and the entire Fall 1988 issue of the *Journal of Applied Corporate Finance.*

This pattern may seem to imply that successful new products will migrate from intermediaries to markets. That is, once they become familiar, and perhaps after some incentive problems are resolved, those products will trade in a market. Exclusive focus on the time path of individual products can be misleading, however, not only with respect to the apparent secular decline in the importance of intermediation, but also with respect to the general relations between financial markets and intermediaries. Just as venture capital firms that provide financing for start-up businesses expect to lose their successful customers to capital market sources of funding, so do the intermediaries that create new financial products.

Financial markets tend to be efficient institutional alternatives to intermediaries when the products have standardized terms, can serve a large number of customers, and are well-enough understood for transactors to be comfortable in assessing their prices. Intermediaries are better suited for low-volume customized products. As products such as futures, options, swaps, and securitized loans become standardized, and move from intermediaries to markets, the proliferation of new trading markets in those instruments makes feasible the creation of new custom-designed financial products that improve "market completeness"; to hedge their exposures on those products, the producers (typically, financial intermediaries) trade in these new markets and volume expands; increased volume reduces marginal transactions costs and thereby makes possible further implementation of more new products and trading strategies by intermediaries, which in turn leads to still more volume. Success of these trading markets and custom products encourages investment in creating additional markets and products, and so on it goes, spiraling toward the theoretically limiting case of zero marginal transactions costs and dynamically complete markets.

Consider, for example, the Eurodollar futures market that provides organized trading in standardized LIBOR (London Interbank Offered Rate) deposits at various dates in the future.[26] The opportunity to trade in this futures market provides financial intermediaries with a way to hedge more efficiently custom-contracted interest rate swaps based on a floating rate linked to LIBOR. A LIBOR rather than a U.S. Treasury rate-based swap is better suited to the needs of many intermediaries' customers because their cash market borrowing rate is typically linked to LIBOR and not to Treasury rates.

At the same time, the huge volume generated by intermediaries hedging their swaps has helped make the Eurodollar futures market a great

---

26. This example is taken from Merton (1993).

financial success for its organizers.[27] Furthermore, swaps with relatively standardized terms have recently begun to move from being custom contracts to ones traded in markets. The trading of these so-called plain vanilla swaps in a market further expands the opportunity structure for intermediaries to hedge and thereby enables them to create more-customized swaps and related financial products more efficiently.

Eurodollar futures appear to be a nearly perfect substitute for LIBOR-based fixed- to floating-rate swaps. One might therefore think that non-financial firms would simply transact directly in the LIBOR futures market and bypass the financial intermediary altogether. Yet the futures require a mark-to-market collateralization of positions, and OTC swaps need not. Thus, intermediaries that issue such swaps to corporations and hedge them in the futures market in effect perform the service of managing the collateralization process for these nonfinancial business customers.

As this example shows, intermediaries help markets grow by creating the products that form the basis for new markets and by adding to trading volume in existing ones. In turn, markets help intermediaries to innovate new more-customized products by lowering the cost of producing them. Thus, although markets and intermediaries are competitors, they also are complementary to one another.[28]

The Future of the Global Financial System

Consider now a small sampling of the implications of the functional perspective for the future evolution of the global financial system. In our most likely scenario, aggregate trading volume expands secularly, and trading is increasingly dominated by institutions such as mutual funds and pension funds. As more financial institutions employ dynamic strategies to hedge their product liabilities, incentives rise for further expansion in round-the-clock trading to allow for more effective implementation of these strategies. Supported by powerful trading technologies for creating financial products, financial services firms will increasingly focus on providing individually tailored solutions to their clients' investment and financing problems. Sophisticated hedging and risk management will become an integrated part of the corporate capital budgeting and financial management process.

The Household Sector

Retail customers ("households") will continue to move away from direct, individual financial market participation such as trading in individual

---

27. See, for example, Antilla (1992) on the Chicago Mercantile Exchange.
28. A general development of this observation is presented in Merton (1993).

stocks or bonds where they have the greatest (and growing) comparative disadvantage. Better diversification, lower trading costs, and less informational disadvantage will continue to move their trading and investing activities toward aggregate bundles of securities, such as mutual funds, basket-type and index securities, and custom-designed products issued by intermediaries.

This secular shift, together with informational effects as described in Gammill and Perold (1989), will enhance liquidity in the basket/index securities, while individual stocks become relatively less liquid. With ever greater institutional ownership of individual securities, there is less need for the traditional regulatory protections and other subsidies of the costs of retail investors trading in stocks and bonds. The emphasis on disclosure and regulations to protect those investors will tend to shift up the "security aggregation chain" to the interface between investors and investment companies, asset allocators, and insurance and pension products.

The Nonfinancial Business Sector

Just as there will be changes in the financial products and services offered to households, so too nonfinancial firms will face a very different set of opportunities.[29] As shown in Chapter 7, the development of low-cost financial tools that enable firms to hedge particular risks has profound implications for their investment, financing, and risk management strategies.

The management of risk has traditionally focused on capital. Equity capital is the "cushion" for absorbing risks of the firm. Management does not have to predict the source of loss, because equity protects the firm against all forms of risk. But the very characteristic of the equity cushion that makes it attractive to managers is the characteristic that creates a moral hazard for the shareholders who provide that equity cushion. The resulting agency and tax costs are the main reasons equity financing can be expensive.[30]

The other fundamental means for controlling risk is through hedging. In contrast to equity capital, which is all-purpose, hedging is a form of risk control that is targeted. Hedging can be very efficient, but it carries with it the requirement that its users have a deep quantitative understanding of their business. They must understand much more about their structures than in the case of all-purpose equity capital. Developing this deeper understanding of their business is going to require some retraining of the ways managers think about their businesses if they are to use hedging effectively.

---

29. This section is based on Merton (1995).
30. See, for example, Grossman and Hart (1982), Jensen (1986), Scholes and Wolfson (1992), and Merton (1993).

Consider, for instance, the example of a "synthetic refinery." Imagine a firm with extensive crude oil reserves and a chain of gasoline stations. Suppose that strategic analysis concludes that there are serious risk concerns about ensuring the firm's access to the production process that links those two activities together. The need to eliminate that risk in the past would have been satisfied perhaps by acquiring a refinery.

The alternative today, especially if the firm has no expertise in refining or managing a refinery, would be to enter into contracts in which the firm agrees to deliver so many barrels of crude oil and, perhaps with some time delay, receives in return a certain amount of high-grade gasoline. That contract functionally creates a synthetic refinery. It may not be appropriate for every such firm, but entering into a simple contract may be a lot safer and a lot more efficient than acquiring the refinery itself. Thus, while creating a synthetic refinery may require the firm's management to increase its knowledge in one area (use of financial tools), not having to build and manage an actual refinery also reduces the managers' need for expertise in another area (building and managing a refinery).

As the skills needed to apply these kinds of risk management are acquired by institutions and their customers, one of the outcomes may be changes in the industrial organization and governance systems in parts of the nonfinancial sector of the economy. In particular, there is the choice between being a private firm (by that we mean a firm with a relatively small number of owners) or being a public firm with ownership held by public shareholders.[31]

Consider some of the trade-offs that owner–managers weigh when making the choice between the firm being private and public. The advantages of being private are headed by reduced agency costs, lower costs of transferring information including external reporting, protection of key information from competitors, and greater flexibility to optimize with respect to taxes and regulation.

What are the benefits of going public? Most important are the risk-sharing benefits. If a small group of owners is bearing the full risks of the firm, then at some point if this risk becomes large enough, the shadow price placed by them on the firm is lower than the public market price would be because they cannot achieve the diversification that public shareholders have. Hence, private owners internalize parts of the firm's risks that are diversifiable with widespread ownership. The other key

---

31. This discussion ties into the work by Jensen (1986) on the corporate form of organization and Williamson (1985) on the boundaries of the firm. Williamson (1988) compares and contrasts his transaction-cost approach with Jensen's agency approach to the study of economic organization.

benefit has to do with capital expansion. The private firm runs into limits on debt as a function of the absolute variability of the business.

Consider such a firm with needs for funding and risk-sharing that believes it must move to the public ownership domain with all its costs (that reflect what the firm gives up by going public). If the firm were instead able to use efficient hedging to strip away the risks of the business that are not adding to value (e.g., commodity price risks, interest rate risks, or currency risks), it could reduce the total volatility or riskiness of the business, without lowering its profitability. In so doing, it reduces the risk exposure to its private owners. The reduced risk will also allow the firm to expand its capacity to raise capital in the debt market without going public.

To the extent that hedging becomes widespread, a macro shift back toward greater private ownership of firms could appear as these hedging tools are developed. This shift in institutional structure for firms marks one type of influence that financial innovation can have beyond the financial sector.

The Financial Sector

Whether the financial services industry becomes more concentrated or more diffuse in this scenario is ambiguous. The central functions of information and transactions processing would seem to favor economies of scale. Similarly, the greater opportunities for netting and diversifying risk exposures by an intermediary with a diverse set of products suggest both fewer required hedging transactions and less risk capital per dollar of product liability as size increases.[32]

Increased demand for custom products and private contracting services would seem to forecast that more of the financial service business will be conducted as principal instead of agent, which again favors size. On the other hand, expansion in the types of organized trading markets, reductions in transactions costs, and continued improvements in information processing and telecommunications technologies will all make it easier for a greater variety of firms to serve the financial service functions.

These same factors also improve the prospects for expanding asset-based financing, and such expanded opportunities for securitization permit smaller, agent-type firms to compete with larger firms in traditionally principal-type activities. Continuing the scenario, locational and regulatory advantages currently available to some financial institutions will be

---

32. For a detailed discussion of the allocation of risk capital in financial firms, see Merton and Perold (1993).

reduced, because more firms will be capable of offering a broader range of financial products and servicing a wider geographic area. Traditional institutional identifications with specific types of products will continue to become increasingly blurred.

As in other innovating industries, competition to create new products and services, and to find new ways to produce established ones at lower costs could make the research and development activity the lifeblood of the financial services firm. Along this hypothetical path, the need to distribute a higher volume and more diverse set of products promises continued relative growth of the firm's sales activity.

Controlling actual and perceived default risk for its customer-held liabilities has always been a key requirement for success of any financial intermediary. Higher customer expectations for service and greater complexity of products will intensify the attention given to this issue in the future. The finance function of financial services firms will be significantly expanded to cover not only increased working capital needs of the firm, but also the management of its credit risk exposure to counterparties.

As technological advances continue to drive down trading and custodial costs, the posting and careful monitoring of collateral is likely to be more widely adopted as the primary means for ensuring counterparty performance, especially among financial institutions. Implementation of this practice will in turn require enhanced trading skills for the firm. The trading activity is also likely to expand to meet the execution requirements for implementing more complex product technologies.

This framework for analysis underlies the next six chapters, which offer in-depth analyses and illustrations of each of the core functions of the financial system.

Appendix: Other Functional Classification Schemes

The essence of the functional perspective is its reliance on functions instead of institutional forms as the conceptual anchors for analyzing the financial system. Which functional classification scheme to use depends on its effectiveness in analysis. Table A shows how various authors view the functions that we have described.

As is evident from columns 2 through 4 of Table A, *providing liquidity* and *lending* are sometimes listed as core functions of the financial system. We note in the body of the chapter that lending can be analyzed as a combination of the resource transfer and risk management functions. Here we analyze liquidity in terms of two of our core functions: clearing and settling (function 1), and dealing with the incentive problems arising from asymmetric information (function 6).

Table A Functional Classification Schemes

Function (1)	Hubbard (2)	Kohn (3)	Rose (4)	Sanford (5)
Clearing and settling	Providing liquidity	Providing liquidity	Providing liquidity	Transaction processing
Pooling	No	Yes	No	No
Transferring resources	Lending	Lending	Lending	Financing
Risk management	Yes	Yes	Yes	Yes
Information	Yes	No	No	Advising
Incentives	No	Yes	No	No

Sources: Sanford (1993), Hubbard (1994), Kohn (1994), and Rose (1994).
Note: Sanford also has a functional category called "trading and positioning." In the scheme here, it would be included in the category of risk management.

Liquidity is defined as the relative ease and speed with which an asset can be converted into the medium of exchange, money. In our view, the quantitative measure of an asset's liquidity is its bid–ask spread.[33] A perfectly liquid asset trades with a zero bid–ask spread.[34] Illiquidity can arise because of the costs and risks of trading an asset or because of incomplete and asymmetric information about the value of an asset.

Liquidity is sometimes confused with *certainty of payment*. But liquidity and price certainty are logically distinct properties of assets. Thus, shares of stock traded on securities exchanges can be highly liquid yet subject to considerable uncertainty about temporal changes in the transaction price. The converse is that an individual's claim to a government pension may be completely riskless, with no price uncertainty, yet totally illiquid.

It is sometimes claimed that a core function of commercial banks is to create liquidity.[35] In the traditional bank arrangement, there is a mismatch between the liquidity of the deposits issued by the bank and the loans backing those deposits. Indeed, it is this mismatch in liquidity that is often cited as the root cause for banking panics.

The current environment of low and secularly declining transactions

---

33. See Hooker and Kohn (1994) for an alternative measure of liquidity in terms of search cost.
34. In addition, the size of a transaction can affect the bid–ask spread. One should therefore measure an asset's liquidity by the bid–ask spread for a transaction of a given size.
35. Diamond and Dybvig (1986), for example, identify liquidity creation as one of the core functions performed by banks. Indeed, they oppose policy moves toward 100% reserve banking because it "would prevent banks from fulfilling their primary function of creating liquidity" (p. 57).

costs for securitization supports a *hierarchical* or *incremental* chaining approach as an efficient means for providing liquidity. Liquidity is enhanced whenever a collection of assets is "repackaged," and the resulting liabilities created have a smaller bid–ask spread than the original assets. Thus highly illiquid and opaque assets can be financed with instruments of different degrees of liquidity—stocks, bonds, and short-term debt instruments.[36] Portfolios of the more liquid of those securities, in turn, can be used as assets to back other securities that will have even greater liquidity, and so on.

Thus, at each link in the chain, the differential in liquidity is relatively small. Cumulatively, it is possible to create virtually perfectly liquid securities while minimizing the danger to the system of ever experiencing a "crisis" because of a mismatch between the liquidity of an intermediary's assets and liabilities.

References

Allen, F., and D. Gale (1988), "Optimal Security Design," *Review of Financial Studies*, 1 (Fall): 229–263.

———— (1990), "Incomplete Markets and Incentives to Set Up an Options Exchange," *Geneva Papers on Risk and Insurance Theory*, 15 (March): 17–46.

———— (1994), *Financial Innovation and Risk Sharing*, Cambridge, MA: MIT Press.

Antilla, S. (1992), "Wall Street: Boom and Bluster at the Merc," *New York Times*, September 6, D:15.

Barnea, A., R.A. Haugen, and L.W. Senbet (1985), *Agency Problems and Financial Contracting*, Englewood Cliffs, NJ: Prentice-Hall.

Bateman, H., and J. Piggott (1993), "Australia's Mandated Private Retirement Income Scheme: An Economic Perspective," University of New South Wales Centre for Applied Economic Research, Superannuation Economics Research Group, Research Paper Series, Number 10 (March).

Benston, G.J., and C. Smith (1976), "A Transaction Cost Approach to the Theory of Financial Intermediation," *Journal of Finance*, 31 (May): 215–231.

Black, F., (1985), "The Future for Financial Services," Chapter 8 in *Managing the Service Economy*, R.P. Inman, ed., Cambridge: Cambridge University Press.

Black, F., M.H. Miller, and R.A. Posner (1978), "An Approach to the Regulation of Bank Holding Companies," *Journal of Business*, 51 (July): 379–412.

Black, F., and M.S. Scholes (1974), "From Theory to New Financial Product," *Journal of Finance*, 29 (May): 399–412.

Bodie, Z., and R.C. Merton (1992), "Pension Reform and Privatization in International Perspective: The Case of Israel," Harvard Business School Working Paper

---

36. Ultimately, the economic uncertainties associated with illiquid assets are borne collectively by participants in the financial system. But the form in which they are borne can influence the degree of liquidity available.

No. 92–082, Boston (May). (Published in Hebrew, The Economics Quarterly, August 1992, 152.)

———— (1993), "Pension Benefit Guarantees in the United States: A Functional Analysis," in *The Future of Pensions in the United States,* R. Schmitt, ed., Philadelphia: University of Pennsylvania Press.

Borch, K.H. (1990), *Economics of Insurance,* Amsterdam: North-Holland.

Brennan, M.J. (1993), "Aspects of Insurance, Intermediation, and Finance," *Geneva Papers on Risk and Insurance Theory,* 18 (June): 7–30.

Davis, E.P. (1995), "An International Comparison of the Financing of Occupational Pensions," Chapter 8 in *Securing Employer-Based Pensions: An International Perspective,* Z. Bodie and O.S. Mitchell, eds., Philadelphia: University of Pennsylvania Press.

de la Vega, J. (1688), *Confusion de Confusiones.* English translation by H. Kallenbenz, no. 13, The Kress Library Series of Publications (Harvard University, 1957).

Diamond, D.W. (1984), "Financial Intermediation and Delegated Monitoring," *Review of Economic Studies,* 51 (July): 393–414.

Diamond, D.W., and P. Dybvig (1986), "Banking Theory, Deposit Insurance, and Bank Regulation," *Journal of Business,* 59 (January): 55–68.

Diamond, D.W., and R.E. Verrecchia (1982), "Optimal Managerial Contracts and Equilibrium Security Prices," *Journal of Finance,* 37 (May): 275–287.

Duffie, D., and M. Jackson (1989), "Optimal Innovation of Futures Contracts," *Review of Financial Studies,* 2: 275–296.

Fama, E. (1980), "Agency Problems and the Theory of the Firm," *Journal of Political Economy,* 88 (April): 288–307.

Fama, E., and M.C. Jensen (1985), "Organizational Forms and Investment Decisions," *Journal of Financial Economics,* 14 (March): 101–118.

Financial Derivatives: Actions Needed to Protect the Financial System (1994), Washington, D.C.: United States General Accounting Office Report GAO/GGD-94-133 (May).

Finnerty, J.D. (1988), "Financial Engineering in Corporate Finance: An Overview," *Financial Management,* 17 (Winter): 14–33.

———— (1992), "An Overview of Corporate Securities Innovation," *Journal of Applied Corporate Finance,* 4 (Winter): 23–39.

Gammill, J., and A.F. Perold (1989), "The Changing Character of Stock Market Liquidity," *Journal of Portfolio Management,* 13 (Spring): 13–17.

Gorton, G., and G. Pennacchi (1992), "Money Market Funds and Finance Companies: Are They the Banks of the Future?" in *Structural Change in Banking,* M. Klausner and L. White, eds., Homewood, IL: Irwin.

Grossman, S.J., and O.D. Hart (1982), "Corporate Financial Structure and Managerial Incentives," in *The Economics of Information and Uncertainty,* J.J. McCall, ed., Chicago: University of Chicago Press.

Hayes, S.L. III (1993), Chapter 9 in *Financial Services: Perspectives and Challenges,* S.L. Hayes III, ed., Boston: Harvard Business School Press, 247–258.

Homer, S. (1977), *A History of Interest Rates,* second edition, New Brunswick, NJ: Rutgers University Press.

Hooker, M.A., and M. Kohn (1994), "An Empirical Measure of Asset Liquidity," Dartmouth College Department of Economics Working Paper.

Hubbard, R.G. (1994), *Money, the Financial System, and the Economy,* Reading, MA: Addison-Wesley.

Jensen, M.C. (1986), "Agency Costs of Free Cash Flow, Corporate Finance, and Takeovers," *American Economic Review,* 76 (May): 323–329.

Jensen, M.C., and W. Meckling (1976), "Theory of the Firm: Managerial Behavior, Agency Costs and Ownership Structure," *Journal of Financial Economics,* 3 (October): 305–360.

Kohn, M. (1994), *Financial Institutions and Markets,* New York: McGraw-Hill.

Merton, R.C. (1989), "On the Application of the Continuous-Time Theory of Finance to Financial Intermediation and Insurance," *Geneva Papers on Risk and Insurance,* 14 (July): 225–262.

—— (1990), "The Financial System and Economic Performance," *Journal of Financial Services Research,* 4 (December): 263–300.

—— (1992a), "Financial Innovation and Economic Performance," *Journal of Applied Corporate Finance,* 4 (Winter): 12–22.

—— (1992b), *Continuous-Time Finance,* revised edition, Oxford: Basil Blackwell.

—— (1993), "Operation and Regulation in Financial Intermediation: A Functional Perspective," in *Operation and Regulation of Financial Markets,* P. Englund, ed., Stockholm: The Economic Council.

—— (1994), "Influence of Mathematical Models in Finance on Practice: Past, Present and Future," *Philosophical Transactions of the Royal Society of London,* 347 (June): 451–463.

—— (1995), "Financial Innovation and the Management and Regulation of Financial Institutions," *Journal of Banking and Finance,* 19 (July): 461–482.

Merton, R.C., and Z. Bodie (1992a), "A Framework for Analyzing the Financial System," Harvard Business School Working Paper, Boston (May).

—— (1992b), "On the Management of Financial Guarantees," *Financial Management,* 22 (Winter): 87–109.

—— (1993), "Deposit Insurance Reform: A Functional Approach," in *Carnegie-Rochester Conference Series on Public Policy,* A. Meltzer and C. Plosser, eds., 38 (June).

Merton, R.C., and A.F. Perold (1993), "Theory of Risk Capital in Financial Firms," *Journal of Applied Corporate Finance,* 5 (Fall): 16–32.

Merton, R.K. (1957), *Social Theory and Social Structure,* revised and enlarged edition, Glencoe, IL: The Free Press.

Milgrom, P., and J. Roberts (1992), *Economics, Organization and Management,* Englewood Cliffs, NJ: Prentice-Hall.

Miller, M. (1992), "Financial Innovation: Achievements and Prospects," *Journal of Applied Corporate Finance,* 4 (Winter): 4–11.

North, D.C. (1994), "Economic Performance Through Time," *American Economic Review,* 84 (June): 359–368.

Norton, J., and P. Spellman, eds. (1991), *Asset Securitization: International Financial and Legal Perspectives,* Oxford: Basil Blackwell.

Pierce, J.L. (1991), *The Future of Banking*, New Haven, CT: Yale University Press.

——— (1993), "The Functional Approach to Deposit Insurance and Regulation," in *Safeguarding the Banking System in an Environment of Financial Cycles*, R.E. Randall, ed., Proceedings of a Symposium of the Federal Reserve Bank of Boston (November): 111–130.

Porter, M. (1994), *Capital Choices*, Washington, D.C.: Council on Competitiveness.

Remolona, E.M. (1992), "The Recent Growth of Financial Derivative Markets," *Federal Reserve Bank of New York Quarterly Review* (Winter): 28–43.

Rose, P.S. (1994), *Money and Capital Markets*, fifth edition, Burr Ridge, IL: Irwin.

Ross, S.A. (1973), "The Economic Theory of Agency: The Principal's Problem," *American Economic Review*, 63 (May): 134–139.

——— (1976), "Options and Efficiency," *Quarterly Journal of Economics*, 90 (February): 75–89.

——— (1989), "Institutional Markets, Financial Marketing, and Financial Innovation," *Journal of Finance*, 44 (July): 541–556.

Sanford, C.S., Jr. (1993), "Financial Markets in 2020," Federal Reserve Bank of Kansas City Economic Symposium (August).

Scholes, M.S. (1994), "Financial Infrastructure and Economic Growth," Conference on Growth and Development: The Economics of the 21st Century, Center for Economic Policy Research, Stanford University (June).

Scholes, M.S., and M.A. Wolfson (1992), *Taxes and Business Strategy: A Planning Approach*, Englewood Cliffs, NJ: Prentice-Hall.

Schumpeter, J.A. (1911), *The Theory of Economic Development* (translated by Redvers Opie), Cambridge, MA: Harvard University Press, 1934.

Strong, N., and M. Walker (1987), *Information and Capital Markets*, Oxford: Basil Blackwell.

Townsend, R.M. (1990), *Financial Structure and Economic Organization*, Oxford: Basil Blackwell.

Williamson, O.E. (1985), *The Economic Institutions of Capitalism*, New York: The Free Press.

——— (1988), "Corporate Finance and Corporate Governance," *Journal of Finance*, 43 (July): 567–591.

World Bank (1990), *Annual Report*, Washington, D.C.

——— (1994), "Averting the Old Age Crisis: Policies to Protect the Old and Promote Growth," Policy Research Report (June).

Zweig, P.L., ed. (1989), *The Asset Securitization Handbook*, Homewood, IL: Dow Jones-Irwin.

CHAPTER TWO

The Payment System and Derivative Instruments

ANDRÉ F. PEROLD

Securities transactions are generally both risky and costly. Transactions *risk* arises because of failure to consummate a trade, perhaps because the buyer could not arrange financing or because the seller failed to deliver. Transactions risk, in other words, arises in the process of clearing and settlement, where *clearing* refers to the processing of payment instructions, and *settlement* refers to the actual discharge of the obligations of buyer and seller through the transfer of funds and securities.

Transactions *costs* also arise in clearing and settlement in the form of processing fees and the costs of financing or maintaining collateral. In addition, transactions costs arise at the time of trade execution in the form of brokerage commissions and the bid–ask spread, and various forms of taxation.[1]

Transactions risks and costs are strong influences on markets. When Sweden enacted transactions taxes, over 50% of the volume in Swedish shares moved to London, and bond market volume declined by 85%. The

I thank Eileen Bedel, Fischer Black, Frank DeMarco, Jacques Marson, John McPartland, Jim Moser, Jacques Perold, Albert Petersen, Todd Petzel, Verne Sedlacek, Gene Snyder, Bruce Summers, Andrew Threadgold, Dung Vukhac, and Jim Walsh for instructive conversations and for information they provided on particular aspects of the payment system.

1. Taxation includes transfer taxes and capital gains taxes. Other forms of transactions cost might include search costs and reporting expenses.

market for Swedish interest rate derivatives essentially evaporated. Swedish stock prices declined by 2.2% when imposition of these taxes was first announced.[2]

Events as dramatic have occurred in the area of clearing and settlement. For example, in the United States in 1968 and 1969, stock market trading was curtailed when brokerage firm back offices could not keep up with the paperwork associated with the newly increased volume of trading.[3] The paperwork crisis directly or indirectly caused the demise of over 100 member firms. In the early 1970s in the Eurobond market, multifold increases in trading and new-issue volume were enabled by the creation of new clearing and settlement systems, Euroclear and Cedel, which today settle trades in greater volume than the major organized stock exchanges (Table 2-1).[4] During the stock market collapse in October 1987, intervention of the U.S. Federal Reserve to alleviate liquidity strains in the payment system is widely credited with having "averted a meltdown."[5] And in Bombay in 1992, the stock market fell by 40% following settlement failures in government securities transactions worth $1.2 billion.[6]

These cases illustrate how important the need to manage transactions risks and costs is to the financial system. Indeed, many of the financial innovations of the past several decades can be seen as either aimed at the direct reduction of transactions risks or costs per se, or as responses to changed transactions risks or costs. Witness the mushrooming of the volume of payments and of the volume of security transactions, as well as the many new instruments whose viability directly or indirectly depends on low transactions risks and costs. At the time of this writing, it

---

2. See Campbell and Froot (1993), and Umlauf (1993). An initial 1% tax on share transactions was imposed in 1984, and raised to 2% in 1986. Transactions taxes on fixed-income instruments and interest rate derivatives were levied in 1989. The tax on fixed-income instruments was up to 3 basis points, while the tax on interest rate derivatives ranged as high as 15 basis points of underlying notional value. During 1990–1991, all transactions taxes were removed.

3. In early 1968 and 1969, trading hours were shortened by 90 minutes each day. For a 30-week period ending in January 1969, the market was closed on Wednesdays but operated full hours on other days. In addition, a system of restrictions and significant penalties was put in place that effectively forced brokerage firms to moderate their client trading. The value of "fails" during this period ran in the billions of dollars per month, peaking at $4.1 billion in December 1968. See *The New York Stock Exchange, The First 200 Years* (1992), and *The Wall Street Journal*, January 16, August 16, and November 22.

4. See Walmsley (1991).

5. Bernanke (1990).

6. In the interbank government securities market in India, transactions are "settled" five days after the trade date with the issuance of bank receipts (to the buyer, in return for cash). The receipt issuer has up to 85 days to make final settlement in actual securities. Receipts were embezzled or issued fraudulently and sold for cash used to speculate in the booming Bombay stock market. *Business India*, Bombay May 11–24, 1992, 57–60.

Table 2-1 Turnover in International Securities Markets ($billions)

	1988	1992
Cedel		
U.S. Dollar Securities	$ 575	$1,269
Other Securities	1,161	3,475
Total	1,736	4,745
Euroclear		
U.S. Dollar Securities	1,498	2,178
Other Securities	1,423	7,570
Total	2,921	9,748
New York Stock Exchange		
Equities	1,356	1,745
Federation of German Securities Exchanges		
Equities	183	440
Bonds	518	1,026
	701	1,466
Tokyo Stock Exchange		
Equities	2,234	477
Bonds	713	118
	$2,947	$ 595

Source: Bank for International Settlements (1993).

takes only three days for the volume of funds transfers flowing through the U.S. payment system to equal all of annual gross national product. The large majority of these flows (by value) stem from financial transactions, with foreign exchange-related payments alone accounting for about 45%.[7]

The volume of payments has changed dramatically over time. Figure 2-1 graphs U.S. payments volume relative to GNP since 1854.[8] There

---

7. Foreign exchange-related payments account for about 80% [Goldstein et al. (1993)] of the value of CHIPS funds transfers, which in 1993 totaled $265.7 trillion. FedWire transfers totaled $207.6 trillion. Foreign exchange-related payments thus account for $212.6 trillion out of $473.3 trillion (FedWire plus CHIPS), or 44.9%. See later discussion of CHIPS and the FedWire.
8. Payments volume is measured as follows: from 1854 to 1912 as the value of payments cleared through the New York Clearing House (NYCH); from 1913 (when the FedWire began operations) to 1986 as NYCH volume plus FedWire volume, where NYCH volume includes CHIPS volume from the latter's inception in 1970; and from 1987 to 1993 as only CHIPS volume (which accounts for over 96% of NYCH volume) and FedWire volume. NYCH and CHIPS volumes were provided by the New York Clearing House, private

Figure 2-1 U.S. Payments Volume/GNP: 1854–1993 (log scale)

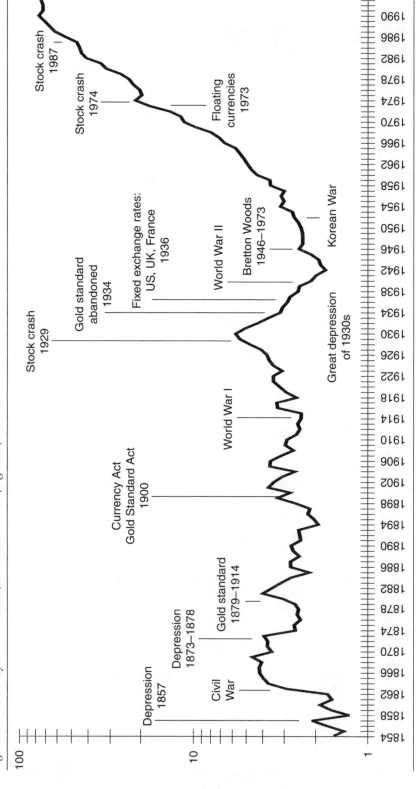

appear to have been two regimes. For more than a century—the period 1854 to about 1965—payments volume remained relatively constant, in the range of one-and-a-half times annual GNP to five times annual GNP. Beginning in the 1960s, however, payments volume began to accelerate, reaching over 70 times annual GNP by 1993. A cursory analysis of the series indicates that the variation in payments volume until the 1960s is more or less coincident with macroeconomic events such as economic depressions and large market declines, but not obviously related to wars, changes in the monetary standard, and eras of fixed or floating exchange rates. Since then, the orders-of-magnitude growth of payments volume seems entirely attributable to a *structural change:* lower transactions risks and costs stemming from technological and financial innovation.[9]

While increased volume and lower transactions risks and costs are strongly contemporaneously correlated, the causal relation between them is more complex. In certain instances, lower transactions risks and costs seem to have accommodated latent demand for trading, while in others lower transactions risks and costs seem actually to have impelled increased trading volume and the proliferation of instruments.

A case in point is the Eurobond market. Its initial growth stemmed directly from imposition of the Interest Equalization Tax in the United States in the 1960s.[10] Imposition of the tax led to demand for the issuance and trading of fixed-rate Eurobonds, which were then greatly facilitated by the creation of Euroclear and Cedel.[11] Subsequent Euro-market inno-

---

communication; FedWire volume from 1969 to 1993 was obtained from the Board of Governors of the Federal Reserve System, private communication.

FedWire volume for 1968 and prior is not publicly available. An estimate for the period 1924 to 1968 is calculated from the annual reports of the Board of Governors of the Federal Reserve as follows: the item "transfers of funds" is multiplied by 0.6 to eliminate double-counting. The 60% factor was suggested in private communication by an official at the Federal Reserve as being "very reasonable." As a check, over the period 1969 to 1977, the ratio of actual FedWire payments to reported "transfers of funds" was 0.61 with a standard deviation of 0.04; there was no time trend in this ratio. I estimate FedWire volume for 1913 (when the FedWire first began operating) to 1923 by linearly interpolating the FedWire share of payments volume from zero in 1912 to its known value of 20% in 1924. GNP data are taken from Mitchell (1993).

9. Of course, variation in payments volume around the trend since the 1960s might also be explained by macroeconomic factors and events. The implication of the structural change for the importance of the velocity of money and its measurement falls outside the scope of this chapter but is an interesting question.

10. See Allen and Mason (1986) for background on the Eurobond market. The Interest Equalization Tax was levied on U.S. investors when they purchased foreign securities issued domestically (so-called Yankee securities). This had the effect of increasing the cost of dollar borrowings in the United States by foreign corporations, creating an incentive for these borrowers to turn to the Eurodollar market.

11. Through the creation of depositories to allow for transfers to be effected through electronic book entry, and by establishing associated credit facilities, Euroclear and Cedel

vations such as floating-rate notes—of both the "vanilla" and the complex variety with imbedded options such as caps and floors—and bond warrants were induced by trading demand that occurred in already existing liquid and low-transactions-cost debt markets.

This chapter examines the basic mechanisms in the financial system that function to manage the risks and costs of securities transactions. I take a broad view of the payment system, to include not just systems for clearing and settlement, but also derivative instruments, traditionally *not* viewed as integral to the payment system, except with respect to their own clearing and settlement. I establish that derivative instruments serve as an important extension of the payment system because they substitute in a variety of ways for trading in cash market instruments. Thus, derivatives transactions and positions represent "virtual" cash market transactions and hence effectively constitute an alternative payment mechanism.

Moreover, the demand for derivative instruments is often driven by the same considerations that underlie the design and organization of modern-day systems for clearing and settlement, considerations integral to the management of transactions risks and costs. Examples include netting arrangements, the efficient use of collateral, and the immobilization of securities. I explicitly compare the payment system demands of cash market trading strategies with those of derivatives-based strategies, showing how the latter typically transform payments demands from a small number of large payments to a large number of small payments spread over time. As forward agreements, derivatives uniquely permit the netting of payments over time, compared to formal netting approaches that offset payments among participants at an instant in time. By reducing the occurrence of large funds transfers, derivatives usage can substantially lower the risk of payments failures.

The chapter concludes by considering alternative approaches to mitigating the problem of "Herstatt risk" (time zone-induced credit risk) in foreign exchange payments. This includes a discussion of an innovative new foreign exchange derivative instrument designed specifically to reduce transaction and payment system demands. The comparison of alternatives usefully illustrates some of the core mechanisms underlying the payments system, and how different methods can serve as functional substitutes with very different implications for institutional change.

---

reduced the credit risks and high financing costs associated with the clearing and settlement of securities held in the form of paper certificates. These developments occurred in parallel with resolution of the paperwork crisis in the United States. See the discussion of immobilization.

Sketch of the Payment System

The present payment system can be viewed as broadly organized around the funds transfer systems operated by central banks (each in its own currency) often in conjunction with private sector financial market participants. Figure 2-2 identifies the so-called large-value transfer systems of various countries, and the hours in which they operate.

Connected to these funds transfer systems are the systems for clearing and settlement of transactions in particular instruments, each typically including a clearinghouse as well as an associated depository in the case of "physical" securities. The clearinghouses in turn are linked to financial institutions—principally banks and large securities firms—that serve customers, both institutional and retail.[12] The services financial institutions provide include financing of positions, keeping custody of client securities, acting as paying agent, and performing other back-office tasks. To varying degrees, large banks and securities firms also provide services of clearing and settlement.[13]

In the United States, the cornerstone funds transfer system comprises the FedWire and CHIPS (the Clearing House Interbank Payments System),[14] which together account for around 85% of the value of all noncash U.S. dollar payments, as shown in Table 2-2. These flows stem mostly from securities and foreign exchange transactions. Check and credit card payments account for only about 13% and 0.1%, respectively, of the value of noncash payments, although they account for the vast majority of pay-

---

12. This is a functional simplification. In the United States, for example, actual connections between the clearinghouses and the FedWire occur through depository institutions.

13. The markets for U.S. government and agency securities provide an interesting example. Almost all government and agency securities, including FNMA ("Fannie Mae") and FHLMC ("Freddie Mac") mortgage-backed securities, are held in electronic book-entry form at the Federal Reserve and are cleared and settled over the FedWire. Because of this, only members of the Federal Reserve System—insured depository institutions—can offer clearing and settlement services to customers for these securities. The Bank of New York and Chemical Bank are the two predominant custodian banks offering these services; their major clients are securities firms. GNMA ("Ginnie Mae") and certain other mortgage-backed securities, on the other hand, are held by the Participants Trust Company (PTC) depository, a private cooperative of banks as well as broker/dealers [see Table 2-3 and Stehm (1992)]. Securities firms thus can offer clearing and settlement services with respect to Ginnie Mae securities directly to customers.

14. Specifically, this is the FedWire for Funds Transfer Service, as distinct from the FedWire Securities Transfer Service, which is used for "wiring" Treasury and other securities held at the Federal Reserve in book-entry form. The FedWire links insured depository institutions and the various Federal Reserve Banks. CHIPS is a cooperative of mostly large New York money center banks and New York branches of foreign banks.

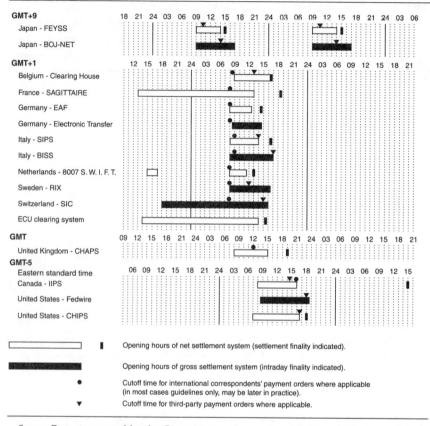

Source: Report prepared by the Committee on Payment and Settlement Systems of the Central Banks of the Group of Ten countries, 1993.

Note: The diagram shows the opening hours, as of August 1993, of selected interbank funds transfer systems as they relate to the same value day: some systems, including SAGITTAIRE and the ECU clearing system, may accept payment orders for a number of value days. As indicated, some systems open the day before the value day. For Canada, settlement finality for IIPS occurs on the next business day, with retroactive value dating.

ments measured by number of transfers. Cash payments are estimated to account for 1% by value of total U.S. payments volume.[15]

The major systems for clearing and settlement of securities transactions in the United States are shown in Table 2-3. In all, there are 15 clearing-houses with 5 depositories serving 30 markets. Some of the large and

---

15. See "Managing Payments Risk" (1993).

Table 2-2   Breakdown of U.S. Payments Volume in 1992

	Volume of Transactions		Value of Transactions	
	($ millions)	(%)	($ trillions)	(%)
Checks issued[a]	58,400	80.5	67,000	13.0
Payments by Card				
Debit Cards	505	0.7	22	0.0
Credit Cards	11,700	16.1	529	0.1
Paperless credit transfers				
CHIPS	39	0.0	238,300	46.4
FedWire	68	0.0	199,200	38.8
Federal Reserve ACH	1,190	1.6	2,691	0.5
Direct Debits				
Federal Reserve ACH	654	.9	5,767	1.1
Total Payment Transactions	72,555	100.0	513,509	100.0
Securities Transactions				
Government Securities[b]	12		139,700	
Corporate and Municipal Securities[c]	83		19,400	

Source: Bank for International Settlements (1993).

a. Includes personal checks, commercial and government checks, commercial and postal money orders, and travelers' checks.

b. U.S. Treasury and agency securities transfers processed through the Federal Reserve's book-entry securities settlement system.

c. Book-entry securities deliveries processed by the Depository Trust Company's next-day funds settlement system.

well-established financial markets have no centrally organized clearing system. These are the markets for over-the-counter (OTC) derivatives and the foreign exchange interbank market, both of which now clear and settle on a bilateral basis. For example, when a corporate issuer enters into an interest rate swap with a dealer, the swap is cleared and payments transmitted on an ongoing basis through direct contact between the back offices of the two parties.[16] (Parties to trades on organized exchanges rarely have any direct connection with one another, communicating and settling instead through a clearinghouse.)

16. Corporations will often outsource this back-office function. Bankers Trust's C-TRAC+ product is an example.

Table 2-3 U.S. Securities Markets and Systems for Clearing and Settlement

Futures Markets (13)	Clearinghouses (9)
Chicago Board of Trade (CBOT)	Board of Trade Clearing Corp. (BOTCC)
Chicago Mercantile Exchange (CME)	CME Clearing House Division (CME)[a]
New York Mercantile Exchange (NYMEX)	NYMEX Clearing House Division (NYMEX)[a]
Commodity Exchange, Inc. (COMEX)	Comex Clearing Association (CCA)
Coffee, Sugar & Cocoa Exchange (CSCE)	CSC Clearing Corp. (CSCCC)
New York Cotton Exchange (NYCE)	Commodity Clearing Corp. (CCC)
New York Futures Exchange (NYFE)	Intermarket Clearing Corp. (ICC)
MidAmerica Commodities Exchange (MidAm)	BOTCC
Kansas City Board of Trade (KCBOT)	KCBOT Clearing Corp. (KCBOTCC)
Minneapolis Grain Exchange (MGE)	MGE Clearing House Division (MGE)[a]
Chicago Rice & Cotton Exchange (CRCE)	BOTCC
Amex Commodities Corp. (AmexCC)	ICC
Philadelphia Board of Trade (PHBOT)	ICC

Options Markets (6)	Clearinghouses (1)
Chicago Board Options Exchange (CBOE)	Options Clearing Corp. (OCC)
American Stock Exchange (Amex)	OCC
Philadelphia Stock Exchange (PHLX)	OCC
New York Stock Exchange (NYSE)	OCC
Pacific Stock Exchange (PSE)	OCC

Table 2-3 (continued)

National Association of Securities Dealers (NASD)	OCC

Stock Markets (8)[b]	**Clearinghouses (3)/Depositories (3)**[c]
New York Stock Exchange	National Securities Clearing Corp. (NSCC)/Depository Trust Co. (DTC)
American Stock Exchange (Amex)	NSCC/DTC
National Association of Securities Dealers (NASD)	NSCC/DTC
Pacific Stock Exchange (PSE)	NSCC/DTC
Boston Stock Exchange (BSE)	NSCC/DTC
Philadelphia Stock Exchange (PHLX)	Stock Clearing Corp. of Philadelphia (SCCP)/Philadelphia Depository Trust Co. (PDTC)
Midwest Stock Exchange (MSE)	Midwest Clearing Corp. (MCC)/Midwest Securities Trust Co. (MSTC)
Cincinnati Stock Exchange (CSE)	NSCC/DTC

U.S. Government and Agency Securities (3)	**Clearinghouses (2)/Depositories (2)**
U.S. Treasury securities	Government Securities Clearing Corp (GSCC)/FedWire book entry
FNMA and FHLMC	Mortgage-Backed Securities Clearing Corp (MBSCC)/FedWire book entry
GNMA	MBSCC/Participants Trust Company (PTC)

Sources: Rutz (1988) and Parkinson et al. (1992).

a. Clearinghouse is a department within the exchange; all other clearinghouses are separately incorporated.

b. There are numerous additional securities clearing agencies involved in securities markets other than the stock market.

c. A clearing member may designate any clearinghouse to clear and settle stock traded on any exchange.

Core Functions of Systems for Clearing and Settlement

The organization and management of systems for clearing and settlement is largely dictated by the type of security being settled, by the structure of the banking system, and by laws governing transfers of funds and securities.[17] At the same time, there are a number of important operational and structural features common to most modern-day systems for clearing and settlement: performance of the purely operational aspects of clearing; immobilization of physical securities; netting; delivery-versus-payment; finality of settlement; provision of performance guarantees; and the extension of credit.

Operational Aspects of Clearing

Transactions are typically executed on the basis of oral or other "soft" commitments among traders. The function of clearing is to formalize these commitments to resolve discrepancies and to allow counterparties to track their settlement obligations and exposures. Clearing thus involves the operational tasks of trade-matching, trade confirmation, and determination of settlement commitments. This includes, for example, confirming that the buyer and seller both agree to the terms of the transaction, and ascertaining that the buyer and seller have the means to deliver the funds and securities. Such steps are necessary and crucial to reduce the risk of settlement failure.[18] (Other payments functions often ascribed to "clearing"—such as netting and the provision of guarantees—are properly discussed separately.)

The efficiency and reliability of clearing depend heavily on communications and computing technology,[19] as well as on standardization of communications protocols. Most communications with respect to international payments are transmitted today over the SWIFT (Society for Worldwide Interbank Financial Telecommunication) network using highly standardized message formats. SWIFT provides financial guarantees against performance failure in its network.[20]

---

17. Juncker and Summers (1991) and Parkinson et al. (1992) provide excellent overview treatments of clearing and settlement in the U.S. securities markets.
18. See Stehm (1991).
19. See Sendrovic (1994) for a discussion of computer technology and operational risk.
20. Founded in 1977, SWIFT is a cooperative of member banks. In 1992, SWIFT provided services to 3,582 users in 88 countries. Users included 2,074 member banks and also certain non-bank financial institutions. The network handled over 1.8 million messages per day. According to SWIFT, it "assumes financial liability for the accuracy, completeness and timely delivery of all validated messages between the moment they enter and the moment they leave the network." The guarantee covers lost interest on settlements

Significant technological failures in clearing systems are not uncommon. A notable instance occurred on October 20, 1987, when the link between the Chicago Fed and the New York Fed suddenly shut down between 11:00 A.M. and 1:30 P.M. EST, when billions of dollars were being moved from New York to Chicago to meet futures and options margin calls. The cause reportedly was a bug in the software at the Chicago Fed. This communications shutdown is believed to have contributed to the financial "gridlock" that day.[21]

Another dramatic example occurred on November 21, 1985, when a computer malfunction prevented the Bank of New York, one of the two large clearers of government securities, from settling trades. The Federal Reserve ended up extending the Bank of New York $30 billion in daylight credit and $23.6 billion in the form of an overnight loan to pay for securities received—the largest ever discount window borrowing. The loan was collateralized by the securities in question, and the Federal Reserve charged interest at the rate of $7\frac{1}{2}\%$ per year, or $5 million. This represented a direct out-of-pocket expense to Bank of New York, as buyers of the securities received a windfall in the form of free overnight financing of their positions.[22] The resulting surplus of funds caused the federal funds rate to fall to $5\frac{1}{2}\%$ from $8\frac{3}{8}\%$.[23]

The malfunction also had systemwide operational effects. Back-office systems around the country were kept open until the Federal Reserve finally closed the securities wire at 1:30 A.M. and the funds wire at 2:15 A.M. on November 22; even then, market participants were unable to complete their end-of-day processing.

Immobilization

A basic mechanism to enhance the efficiency and safety of a clearing and settlement system is the use of a depository to immobilize securities. Depositories "dematerialize" securities through storage in a fixed location, and by recording their ownership in electronic book-entry form. This avoids having to move stock certificates physically between counterparties. Immobilization of certificates was a key element in solving the late 1960s paperwork crisis in the United States—by creation of the Central Certificate Service (later succeeded by Depository Trust Corp.). More

---

delayed by operational errors up to 50 million Belgian francs per year and losses due to "errors, omissions and fraud" of up to 6 billion Belgian francs per year. See SWIFT Annual Report, 1992, and SWIFT's Product Portfolio marketing literature.

21. *The Wall Street Journal,* 1/14/88.
22. See Corrigan (1986).
23. *The Wall Street Journal,* 11/25/85.

recently, the 1992 Bombay crisis had its roots in *lack* of immobilization of securities, as certain traders could exploit the long settlement lags required with the need to deliver physical certificates.

Immobilization of securities has become the norm in most major markets, with the notable exception of the U.K. share market. Immobilization occurs implicitly with exchange-traded options and futures contracts because these bilateral contracts are written between the client and the clearinghouse, and are effectively canceled (netted out) when closed out by the client.[24]

Netting

Netting is a basic device used to reduce transactions costs and risks. The decision to employ (or not to employ) netting schemes is a key design feature of systems for clearing and settlement. Moreover, as I will develop more fully, netting of exposures is the economic essence of many derivative instruments. Netting is therefore a powerful tool for risk management and risk assessment. Netting procedures also can create dysfunctional externalities.

Netting is a prime function that clearinghouses were originally created to formalize. In London, for example, prior to the formation of the London Clearing House in 1773, banks found it considerably more efficient to send messengers to a central location—the bank district coffeehouses—where debits and credits could be offset against each other than for each bank to send a messenger to every other bank to collect balances due.[25] This is an instance of *multilateral* netting, which can be illustrated by considering an example in which Party A needs to pay $200 to Party B, and Party B needs to pay $100 to each of parties A and C. The three payments total $400. Under multilateral netting, Party B's pending receipt of $200 is exactly netted out against its need to pay two sums totaling $200, leaving Party A paying $100 to Party C. This method of settlement—called "ringing"[26]—assumes Party C is as comfortable receiving payment from Party A as it is receiving payment from Party B.

The example illustrates the way netting can significantly reduce both the dollar flow of payments (here, from $400 to $100) and the number of transactions (here, from three to one). Clearinghouses formalize the netting process. In certain instances, they also guarantee the net payments.

---

24. Exceptions include exchange-traded warrants, which are examples of options that are typically immobilized, cleared, and settled in the same fashion as traditional equity securities.
25. Moser (1994).
26. *Ibid.*

For example, in the so-called centralized model, they do this by acting as receiver of all net debits and payer of all net credits. In this arrangement, each party makes to or receives from the clearinghouse a single payment. Spahr (1926) describes such clearinghouse netting as "beyond all question, the simplest, the most economical, and when applicable, the most efficient of all modes of paying debts."

Bilateral netting, in which commitments are offset between two parties at a time, is less effective in reducing the number and size of transfers. In the example, it would reduce only the settlement obligations between Party A and Party B (to $100 from Party A to Party B, leaving Party B still to pay $100 to Party C). Bilateral netting between a clearinghouse and its individual participants is equivalent to multilateral netting as discussed above.

Multilateral netting is used in certain funds transfer systems, like CHIPS, and also in most systems for the clearing and settlement of securities transactions. For example, shares traded on the organized U.S. exchanges are generally cleared and settled through the National Securities Clearing Corporation (NSCC), which uses netting in determining both share transfers and payments. The FedWire does not use netting (each payment is settled on a gross basis), in part because transfers are settled with finality continuously throughout the day, leaving no window of time over which a sufficient accumulation of payments can occur for netting to be effective. (See later discussion under efficiency of payment systems.) Multilateral netting is not yet widely used in cross-border transactions such as foreign exchange for a variety of reasons, including the complexity and uncertainty created by jurisdictional differences across countries, as well as opposition from local regulatory authorities on the grounds that this form of netting leaves less of an "audit trail" to track payments flows.[27]

Table 2-4 illustrates the reduction in payments and/or securities transfers that netting makes possible for certain instruments and settlement procedures. The reduction can be considerable. For CHIPS it averaged 99% from the beginning of 1993 through August 1994. The gross volume of payments through CHIPS averages in excess of $1 trillion per day, while the net payments flow averages around only $10 billion per day.[28]

In the case of securities transfers, the benefits of netting [measured as a ratio in terms of avoided transfers/total transfers (absent netting)] are largest when there are lengthy settlement periods. The Paris Bourse, for

27. This example illustrates how institutional arrangements usually serve multiple functions, one of them here being that of maintaining an audit trail. These functions must be clearly rationalized if institutional change is to take place efficiently.
28. CHIPS, private communication.

Table 2-4   Netting Ratios for Different Types of Securities Settlement[a]

Settlement System	Instrument	Settlement Period	Netting Ratio[b]
CHIPS	Payments	End of Day	99%
Paris Bourse	Shares	Monthly	70
Paris Bourse	Shares	T + 3	13
MBS Clearing Corporation	Mortgage-Backed Securities	T + 60 (average)	90
National Securities Clearing Corporation	Shares	T + 5	75
National Securities Clearing Corporation	Payments	T + 5	94
National Securities Clearing Corporation	# Transfers of Shares	T + 5	92

a. See the text under "netting" for comments on and explanation of individual entries.

b. The netting ratio is the percentage of the dollar value of transfers or the percentage of the number of share transfers or the percentage of the number of transfers that were removed through multilateral netting.

example, offers both fixed monthly and rolling T + 3 settlement.[29] The latter was offered first in March 1992, and in 1993 accounted for 6% of total settlements. In 1993, an average of 12% of share deliveries were avoided through netting in the case of rolling T + 3 settlement, and 70% in the case of monthly settlement.[30] In the United States, mortgage-backed securities too are settled [through the MBS Clearing Corporation (MBSCC)] principally on fixed periodic dates over intervals as long as five months, with a median settlement length of around two months. Netting reduces deliveries between participants (mostly dealers) by about 90%.[31] Finally, for shares traded on the U.S. organized exchanges (cleared and settled on a rolling T + 5 basis through NSCC), netting ratios in

29. In the case of a fixed settlement period, all trades that take place within the period settle on a given day after the end of the period. In the case of rolling settlement periods, for example, T + 3, all trades that take place on day T settle on day T + 3.

30. Paris Bourse, private communication. The netting is among brokers who each process transfers for their own clients. The netting ratio for rolling settlement during 1993 ranged from a low of 3.5% to a high of 43.1%, and for monthly settlement from a low of 69.3% to a high of 72.1%, a much narrower range.

31. MBSCC, private communication.

individual shares are of the order of 75%, while netting ratios for the associated payments are in excess of 90%.[32]

Netting can be extended to contractual agreements such as derivative instruments, where it serves a variety of purposes: in clearing and settlement, where the rights and obligations of counterparties are accumulated by various forms of bilateral netting into a single contract that is dynamically updated as new positions are added;[33] in risk assessment, such as determining collateral and capital requirements;[34] and in reducing funds transfers associated with changes in collateral requirements (or variation margin, as will be discussed later).

Some potential problems that can arise under netting are discussed below in the context of delivery-versus-payment and finality of payment.

Delivery-versus-Payment

Delivery-versus-payment (DVP) is a method of settlement in which funds and securities are transferred simultaneously, or, more generally, where funds transfer is considered final only once securities have been transferred, and vice versa. DVP eliminates the most significant of settlement risks, where the seller delivers securities (or foreign currency) without receiving payment, or the buyer makes payment without taking delivery

---

32. NSCC, private communication. On the peak volume day in 1993, NSCC cleared trades valued at $76 billion, which resulted in net payments of $4 billion, a reduction of 94%. NSCC believes this ratio is typical of average volume days. During the month of May 1993, NSCC cleared a total of 42.6 billion shares (purchases plus sales) of which 10.7 billion were actually transferred, for a netting ratio of 74.9%. The market value of gross shares traded (purchases + sales) was $1,209 billion, and that of net shares transferred was $265.7 billion, for a netting ratio of 78.0%. Netting reduced the number of net share transfers from 13,159,183 to 1,140,379 for purchases, for a netting ratio of 91.3%, and from 13,159,183 to 1,107,070 for purchases, for a netting ratio of 91.6%.

33. The two standard forms involve "netting by novation," where a new position is substituted for cumulative prior positions in a single contract, and "master agreements," which are used to combine a number of potentially heterogeneous contracts into a single agreement. Netting by novation is commonly used by clearinghouses; master agreements are used for OTC derivatives contracts. The enforceability of netting agreements in general and master agreements in particular is jurisdiction-dependent and not fully resolved even in the United States. See Moser (1994) for a historical account of the early netting methods used in the clearing and settlement of futures positions. Duffie and Hwang (1994) model the spreads on swap contracts under varying netting arrangements and assumptions regarding their resolution in the event of default.

34. For example, a long position in September S&P 500 futures coupled with a short position in December S&P 500 futures is less risky than either of these positions alone, and hence needs less collateral for protection against counterparty credit risk. "Cross-margining," a form of collateral management, is another example. See The Chicago Mercantile Exchange (1993a). For a discussion of the use of collateral in the management of credit risk, see Merton and Bodie (1992).

of the securities (or foreign currency). This form of settlement risk is often called "Herstatt risk."

In 1974, the German bank *Bankhaus Herstatt* failed while settlement of a mark–dollar transaction was still in process. The failure occurred at the end of the German business day after the marks had been paid, but before the end of the U.S. business day, with the dollar leg of the transaction yet to be completed. Parties to the transaction that had paid the marks but were owed dollars had to file for claims along with other Herstatt general creditors, and ended up suffering significant losses.[35]

Herstatt risk can exist in any settlement procedure that treats the payment and delivery legs asymmetrically. In the case of foreign exchange transactions, the asymmetry arises out of the different operating hours of the funds transfer systems of different countries, as well as differences in correspondent banking arrangements.[36] Even within a single currency, asymmetric settlement practices can arise as a result of netting differences. Securities transfers may take place on a gross basis with no netting, for instance, while funds transfers may take place on a net basis.[37] There is thus a minimum symmetry required in settlement of the different legs of a transaction for DVP to be feasible and effective.

Finality of Settlement

The finality of transfer of funds and securities is a defining feature of any payment system. Delivery-versus-payment mechanisms are one such example where, as just described, the transfer of securities is not final until the transfer of funds has occurred, and vice versa. In general, finality of settlement depends on several factors: the legal validity and enforceability of the transfers and any associated contractual obligations; the performance guarantees offered by the operator of the settlement system together with the creditworthiness of the operator; and the settlement mechanism itself.[38]

A comparison of the FedWire and CHIPS provides an instructive example. The FedWire is operated by the Federal Reserve, which extends daylight credit for intraday transfers, all occurring with finality. Because of this credit extension, the safety and finality of FedWire transfers depend critically on the central bank's essentially unlimited access to liquidity.[39] CHIPS, on the other hand, is a privately operated cooperative that per-

---

35. See Bank for International Settlements (1993).
36. See Summers (1994).
37. See Bank for International Settlements (1992a).
38. See Bhala (1994) for a discussion of the U.S. legal system as it pertains to transfers.
39. See Spindler and Summers (1994).

forms end-of-day settlement by transmitting net payments over the Fed-Wire. These *net* payments are of course final by virtue of the finality of any FedWire payment. Individual gross payments settled on CHIPS, however, even though they are considered "final" by CHIPS rules, until recently were potentially contestable in the event an institution failed after "sending" a payment but before completion of settlement at the end of the day. That is, the failed institution (or its bankruptcy trustee/liquidator) might have been able to demand immediate settlement of the (gross) payments it was due to receive, while defaulting on the (gross) payments it was obligated to make.[40] This risk was eliminated, in the case of CHIPS, with passage of the Federal Deposit Insurance Corporation Improvement Act (FDICIA) in 1991, which includes a provision establishing the legal integrity of netting among U.S. depository institutions.

The contestability of a netting arrangement is a potential dysfunctional externality for any system that relies on netting to reduce the size and volume of transfers.[41] The problem can be mitigated by performance bonds and loss-sharing arrangements among members, as will be discussed.

A second example to illustrate the potential difficulty of achieving finality of settlement arises in the case of share settlements, where there may be different netting amounts for share transfers and for funds transfers, as the latter can be netted across the many different share issues traded.[42] Consider the case of U.S. equity transactions, which clear and settle through NSCC continuously throughout the five-day settlement period. NSCC does considerably more payments netting than share netting (as is shown in Table 2-4). Because of this, the continuous settlement of share transactions takes place only *provisionally*. That is, settlement becomes final only when the net payments are made at the end of the five-day interval. Securities that have been cleared but not yet settled with finality nevertheless may be pledged by the receiving parties to others,

---

40. No settlement failures on CHIPS have occurred. See "The Clearing House Interbank Payments System" (1991), for elaboration of CHIPS settlement procedures.
41. See Bank for International Settlements (1989) ("The Angell Report") and Bank for International Settlements (1990) (The "Lamfalussy Report") for a detailed discussion.
42. For example, the transactions on a given day in IBM and GM shares by the customers of the various "wirehouses" whose shares are held in "street name" are netted multilaterally over the course of the settlement period. The result might be that, by the end of the period, Broker A needs to deliver net shares of IBM to Broker B in return for $100,000, and Broker B needs to deliver net shares of GM to Broker A in return for $100,000. The payments associated with the share transfers of both IBM and GM shares will be netted against each other. In this example, therefore, only shares are transferred because the payments net out to zero.

giving rise to potentially complex unwinding problems in the event of a payments failure or a contesting of the validity of the netting process.[43]

Provision of Performance Guarantees

A key role of the clearinghouse is to guarantee the performance of the settlement mechanism. Such a guarantee makes all payments or contracts homogeneous with respect to credit risk, adding an important dimension of standardization and fungibility.[44] A common type of guarantee is that the clearinghouse substitutes itself as the buyer to the seller and as the seller to the buyer, and discharges any obligations between parties to the original transaction. To back the guarantee, clearinghouses typically require their members to post collateral (usually in the form of government securities) and to agree to loss-sharing arrangements. Clearinghouse safeguards include selectivity with respect to membership, imposition of exposure limits, and marking exposures and collateral to market.[45]

In the case of CHIPS, there is no centralized guarantee mechanism, but rather a system of exposure limits and cross-guarantees. Each member sets a "credit limit" on the maximum net daily payment it is willing to receive from any other member.[46] These limits also determine the amount of collateral posted as well as the loss-sharing rule. The collateral posted by a member is 5% of the maximum net payment that that member is willing to accept from any other member. In 1994, the collateral posted by CHIPS' 119 members collectively ranged from $250 to $300 million.[47]

If a member defaults at settlement time on a $20 million debit, say, that member's collateral can be used to cover the payment. Any amount owed in excess of the defaulting member's collateral is covered by other members in proportion to the credit limits they had set for the defaulting member. If they do not fund this residual amount, their collateral can be used. In the event defaults on loss-sharing cannot be covered by the collateral pool, and surviving members cannot agree to fund the shortfall, the settlement fails and is unwound.

The clearinghouse operated by the Chicago Mercantile Exchange operates on the basis of a centralized system of guarantees. The CME estimated that, as of September 30, 1993, its clearinghouse could draw on all

43. See Parkinson et al. (1992).
44. See Bernanke (1990). See also Merton (1992a, Ch. 14; 1993) for a discussion of credit sensitivity and the notion that market participants can be "customers" rather than "investors."
45. See Parkinson et al. (1992).
46. See "The Clearing House Interbank Payments System" (1991) for elaboration.
47. CHIPS, Private communication.

or a portion of specified assets to satisfy obligations it could incur as a result of member defaults:[48]

Aggregate Performance Bond Deposits ($ millions)[49]	$6,511
Market Value of Memberships Pledged for Clearing[50]	293
Surplus CME Funds	36
Security Deposits	56
Common Bond of Clearing Members[51]	19,500
Total	$26,396

The CME also has a Trust Fund of $50.7 million (as of June 30, 1993) to protect *customers* of CME clearing members.

The loss-sharing arrangements at the CME involve assessments against clearing members for amounts in excess of the surplus funds of the exchange and the security deposits of members. The assessment is a function of both the capital and the activity of individual clearing members, as follows: 50% in proportion to clearing members' capital; 25% in proportion to clearing members' shares of the total number of contracts cleared during the preceding six months; and 25% in proportion to clearing members' shares of the total open commitment as of the close of the tenth business day preceding the day of loss.[52]

Performance guarantees by clearinghouses are a dimension of competition between the organized derivatives exchanges and the over-the-counter derivatives markets. This is exemplified in a recent set of exchange-offered products, "FLEX options," which are privately negotiated options written on cash market instruments but supported by the Chicago Board Options Exchange clearing system and its associated performance guarantees.[53] In the over-the-counter market, on the other hand, a number of the largest securities firms—typically with single-A parent ratings—have established AAA-rated subsidiaries for the sole purpose of credit enhancement of derivatives.[54]

---

48. The Chicago Mercantile Exchange (1993a).
49. *Ibid.* Only the performance bond deposits of the defaulting firm are available to the CME.
50. *Ibid.* Only the exchange memberships pledged by the defaulting firm are available to the CME.
51. *Ibid.* Common Bond represents the total shareholder and partnership equity plus subordinated debt of CME clearing members as determined by an analysis of each clearing member's most current financial statement as of September 30, 1993.
52. The Chicago Mercantile Exchange (1994). Capital is defined under Common Bond in the previous footnote.
53. See Barclay (1994).
54. See Mason and Singh (1994) for discussion of the design features of these AAA vehicles.

Extension of Credit

Payment systems, as well as financial market participants making payments or settling trades, tend to rely heavily on the extension of credit. The extension of credit occurs in essentially four contexts:

1. Credit is extended for both buyer and seller from the time a trade is agreed upon to either final settlement or resolution with a clearinghouse.[55] This type of credit is inherent in any system that operates on the basis of lagged settlement, as the seller is giving the buyer time to pay and the buyer is giving the seller time to deliver.

2. Credit is extended similarly when direct commitments between buyer and seller are replaced by commitments with a clearinghouse. The clearinghouse side of this credit provision stems typically from "mutualized" performance guarantees (members guarantee one another) or guarantees from a central bank as in the case of some central bank-operated systems like the FedWire.

3. Even in a system where trades settle instantly, demands to borrow funds or securities occur for reasons of liquidity. Demand for intraday liquidity can arise in the simple case where Party A sells 100 bonds to Party B, who soon after sells them to Party C. With Party A in possession of the securities and Party C having funding, but with Party B having neither full funding nor credit, these trades may fail to settle in systems that do not perform multilateral netting.[56] More generally, and independent of the settlement system, buyers may prefer borrowing funds over hastily selling assets (and incurring higher than necessary transactions costs). Sellers too may be unable to access their securities, perhaps because they have lent them out on a term basis.[57]

4. Demand for credit can arise to meet liquidity needs of a system-wide nature, for example, as when the Federal Reserve provided credit during the stock market collapse in October 1987,[58] or to

---

55. Credit is extended not just for a specific amount of cash (by the seller), but also for a specific quantity of securities (by the buyer).

56. A system like Euroclear, which does only limited netting, would be able to settle these trades without Party B having funding or credit. Euroclear would not be able to settle more complex "chains" such as Party A sells to Party B who sells to Party C who sells to Party D, in the event that neither Party B nor Party C has funding or credit. *Source:* Euroclear, private communication.

57. Bodurtha and Quinn (1990) examine the benefits of "patient" trading. See also the later discussion of exchange-for-physical (EFP) transactions. For a discussion of securities lending, see Perold and Singh (1993).

58. Bernanke (1990).

counter an operational malfunctioning in the clearing and settlement system such as faced by the Bank of New York in 1985 (discussed earlier under clearing). In the latter instance, the clearing *agent* (Bank of New York) had given no formal financial guarantees of its performance, yet had to borrow and advance the $23.6 billion in funds to satisfy the liquidity needs of its dealer customers and others who had sold Treasury securities and were expecting payment.

For operational efficiency, the provision of credit for liquidity purposes is sometimes bundled along with clearing and settlement services or custody services. For example, as the two large custodians of U.S. government securities, the Bank of New York and Chemical Bank also perform clearing and settlement for dealers (who cannot be members of the Federal Reserve because they are not depository institutions), provide lines of credit, and facilitate securities lending and borrowing through the repurchase agreement (repo) market. The sheer size of the U.S. government securities repo market, estimated at $700 billion per day, illustrates the scale of short-term financing employed to effect securities transactions and positioning.[59]

Euroclear and Cedel each also offer a similar bundle of services. In these systems, an additional demand for credit arises from the fact that both systems facilitate settlement of trades in any of a variety of currencies. In the case of Euroclear, participants obtain both intraday and overnight credit by establishing facilities with Morgan Guaranty Bank. Securities loans among participants are not collateralized with cash or other securities (as is standard practice in the repo and other securities lending markets) but rather with letters of credit purchased from Morgan Guaranty.[60] In contrast, Cedel itself provides intraday credit to its participants.[61] Overnight credit is provided through tripartite agreements among participants, Cedel, and certain associated banks. Securities loans too are collateralized with letters of credit, here provided by a bank syndicate.[62]

In none of these examples is credit extended by a clearinghouse itself. The reason is that the settlement systems employed are "true" delivery-versus-payment. That is, funds and securities are exchanged simultaneously and with finality, without multilateral netting, obviating much of the need for a clearinghouse guarantee.

---

59. See MacRae (1993).
60. See Perold and Singh (1993).
61. Cedel has estimated capital of $120 million.
62. Walmsley (1991), Ch. 17; and Euroclear, private communication.

Payment System Design and Efficiency

The various payment system design features discussed above generally depend on particular aspects of the system to influence efficiency. The FedWire is a good example. Because it offers continuous intraday transfers with finality, the gains from netting are likely to be small. That is, netting derives its efficiency from a sufficient *accumulation* of positions, which necessarily can occur only episodically or at discrete points in time. Moreover, FedWire transfers can clear and settle with virtually no delay because of the Fed's willingness and ability to extend credit (within limits) to its highly select group of members (insured depository institutions).[63]

The Swiss Interbank Clearing System (SIC) provides an interesting contrast. Operated by the Swiss central bank, it too offers continuous intraday transfers with finality, but without the extension of intraday credit. Accordingly, transfers must be queued until they can be fully funded, and sending banks must manage the queue by prioritizing which payments are to be sent, given a level of funding. The SIC system is more prone to "gridlock" resulting from delays in unwinding the queues (which may indirectly induce credit risk). The FedWire system, which facilitates much faster payment, is in principle more directly prone to deteriorating credit, which may in turn induce gridlock.[64]

Payment Systems and Derivative Instruments: Delayed Settlements as Forward Agreements

One way to look at derivative instruments and their relation to the payment system is to start with the lag that generally exists between trade execution and final settlement. Relatively few markets operate on the basis of same-day settlement, notable exceptions being the U.S. commercial paper and repo markets. The U.S. stock markets are organized on the basis of a rolling five-day settlement period. Other markets require settlement at fixed calendar dates, such as monthly in the French and Italian stock markets. The U.K. stock market settled on a fixed-date, biweekly basis until recently when it moved to rolling T + 10.[65]

When there are settlement lags, securities transactions are effectively forward market transactions. This has several implications of note. First,

---

63. A particularly notable example is the $30 billion of intraday credit and $23.6 billion of overnight credit extended to the Bank of New York discussed earlier.
64. See Horii and Summers (1994) for more detail and discussion of large-value transfer systems.
65. The United States and other markets are in the process of moving to T + 3 in compliance with the Global Derivatives Study Group (1993) "Group of Thirty" recommendations.

Table 2-5 Illustration of Lagged Settlement with Fixed and Rolling
Settlement Dates

Date	Event	Action
0	Purchase of Shares	
12	Sale of Shares	
	Rolling T + 20 Settlement	
20	Settle Purchase Transaction	Pay for Purchase Receive Shares
32	Settle Sale Transaction	Receive Proceeds Deliver Shares
	Fixed Settlement	
20	Settle Both Transactions	Pay/Receive Net Monetary Value

transactions prices should reflect the carrying costs associated with delayed payment and delivery. This is verified empirically in Solnik (1990), who finds a significant month-end effect in the French stock market. In France, all transactions that take place during the month ending on day T settle on day T + 7.[66] The prices of stocks traded on day T—the end of the current settlement month—should thus reflect a seven-day carrying cost,[67] while the prices of stocks traded on date T + 1—the beginning of the next settlement month—should reflect a 37- or 38-day carrying cost. Solnik finds the change in prices between days T and T + 1 to be significantly higher than the price changes on other days, consistent with the hypothesized carrying cost relation.

Second, investors with short holding periods may find it more efficient to close out a transaction before it formally settles. Table 2-5 illustrates the case of Party A who purchases shares of stock on day 0 for settlement 20 days later. Suppose Party A decides to sell those shares 12 days from the date of purchase. In terms of payment system usage, it matters how and when this sale transaction settles.

If settlement occurs with the same 20-day lag as the purchase transaction (so that the sale transaction settles on day 32), Party A will need to take delivery of the purchased shares on day 20, only then to deliver the same shares in settlement of the sale transaction on day 32. In addition, Party A has to finance the position for the 12 days between the two settlement dates. This is what ordinarily occurs under rolling settlement.

If, instead, the sale transaction is settled with a shorter lag of 8 days,

---

66. As I mention in the discussion of netting, France introduced rolling T + 3 in 1992, and about 6% of French share settlements currently take place in this manner.
67. Seven days of interest minus dividends expected to be paid during the seven days.

also on day 20, Party A can effectively be removed from the settlement process by (1) netting the obligation to deliver shares on day 20 against the right to receive shares on day 20, and (2) netting the purchase price of the shares against the sale price of the shares. When the settlements are executed in this manner, therefore, Party A receives or makes a *net* cash payment equal to the difference between the purchase and sale transaction prices, without having to take delivery of, or deliver, the underlying shares. This approach to transacting can be less risky, and require much less financing. It is generally less costly for investors who wish only to benefit from short-term movements in the market price of a security.

This form of netting, which is obtained when a position is closed out without taking delivery of the underlying instrument, is inherently different from the type of payment system netting discussed earlier. The former offsets transfers across participants at an *instant in time;* the latter offsets payments (bilaterally) over *intervals of time.*

Netting over time is inherent in almost any forward market, as seen in the commodity and financial futures markets. Figure 2-3 shows how the open interest in cattle futures and S&P 500 index futures declines dramatically as the expiration dates of the contracts approach, meaning that most contracts are in fact closed out prior to expiration, and very few actually settle at expiration. During the year ended September 30, 1993, only 0.64% of total U.S. futures volume (all commodities) actually settled, either in cash or physical delivery.[68]

Physical markets with long settlement lags operate very similarly. Settlement lags in the U.S. mortgage-backed securities market range out to five months. These settlement lags are so long that traders are sometimes required to post margin as they do with forward and futures contracts. Moreover, trades are made on a TBA (to be announced) basis so that the seller has delivery options much like futures contracts on nonhomogeneous commodities (such as cattle and bond futures).[69] Finally, there can be significant within-settlement period "round-tripping" behavior, suggesting that many market participants use long-dated settlements in the physical markets as they would forward agreements in the derivatives markets. A major dealer in mortgage-backed securities reports that, during 1992 and 1993, trades in mortgage-backed securities closed out by its

---

68. Commodity Futures Trading Commission, 1993 Annual Report.
69. Under Public Securities Association guidelines, sellers of mortgage-backed securities can deliver any of three pools (agreed upon at the time of sale). See Fabozzi and Modigliani (1992). Live-cattle futures can be settled by delivering cattle in a range of weights, averaging 1,050 to 1,200 pounds; U.S. Treasury bond futures can be settled by delivering any bond with maturity of the first call date in excess of 15 years. See Kolb (1991).

Figure 2-3 Average Open Interest of S&P 500 and Cattle Futures
(for contracts maturing between 2/91 and 9/92

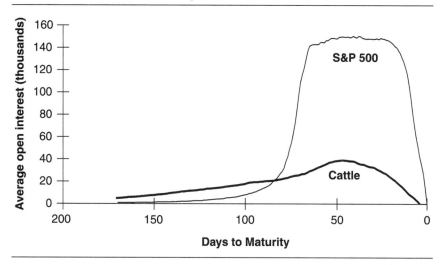

customers prior to settlement ranged between 14% and 20% of its total volume.

Finally, settlement lags create counterparty credit risk for market participants similar to the risk borne by parties to a forward contract. That is, one party may default on its obligation to consummate the trade, giving rise to an important element of transactions risk. This is no different from a party to a forward contract failing in its obligations to pay for or deliver the underlying instrument or commodity.[70]

The point is that lagged settlement creates a blurring of transactions in physical securities and transactions in forward contracts. Lagged settlement is economically nothing other than a simple forward contract. It is priced in the same manner as a forward contract, it has the same type of credit risk, and investors use it the same way they use forward contracts to obtain netting over time—that is, to obtain short-run exposure to fluctuations in the market price of a physical instrument without having to deliver or take delivery of the actual instrument.

The equivalence between lagged settlement and forward agreements raises accounting, management, and regulatory issues for financial institutions. For example, the current standard accounting treatment views forward agreements and other derivative instruments as off-balance sheet

---

70. In the case of forward contracts that settle in cash rather than in kind, counterparty exposure is limited only to the market value of the contract. The same is the case of forward contracts that settle in kind with "true DVP" settlement.

items and physical instruments as on-balance sheet items. Physical instruments bought or sold for lagged settlement can be recorded either on- or off-balance sheet, potentially affecting the calculation of reported capital and/or required regulatory capital. This illustrates the arbitrariness of methods that distinguish between physical assets and forward agreements in accounting for the balance sheet of the financial institution.[71]

Similar issues can arise in accounting for gains and losses. A good illustration is the case of false profits generated by a Kidder, Peabody & Co. trader who exploited the miscalculation of profits by the firm's accounting system for certain trades settled with long lags.[72]

Derivative Instruments as Substitutes for Trading in Physical Securities

Two features of simple forward contracts are common to most traded derivatives: lagged settlement, and the permitting of exposure to an instrument without directly transacting in that instrument. These features are of crucial significance for the payments system because derivative instruments can make it possible for investors to avoid (or reduce) the costs and risks of using the payment system. The virtual transactions embedded in the use of derivative instruments might therefore *greatly reduce* demand for direct payments services, *ceteris paribus*. Some examples will illustrate the point.

Interest Rate Swaps

Interest rate swaps are agreements in which parties commit to exchange fixed-rate for floating-rate interest payments. A standard use of such contracts allows debt issuers to alter their interest rate exposures from fixed rate to floating rate or vice versa. The all-in fee for engaging in such a swap is typically a few basis points per year, and the cash flows that result are simply the periodic flows of the *net* of the fixed and floating amounts. The alternative is for the issuer to manage its interest rate risk exposure by transacting in its own debt, perhaps by issuing floating-rate debt and using the proceeds to redeem or defease its fixed-rate debt. If the issuer later wants to return to a fixed-rate exposure, it can in principle reverse these transactions.

The costs of such an approach would include underwriting spreads and registration fees associated with the corporate issuance of securities, and would be several orders of magnitude larger than the costs of using

---

71. Chapter 8 discusses the need for "risk accounting" for financial institutions.
72. The accounting system did not take into account the cost-of-carry differential between forward and spot prices in its calculation of short-term profits. See Lynch (1994).

Table 2-6   Average Gross Payments on Interest Rate Swap Contracts (3 month
LIBOR for fixed, on a $100 notional amount, paid quarterly)

Swap Maturity	Average Gross Payments	Number of Payments
2 Years	$ 6.50	8
5 Years	17.50	20
10 Years	30.00	40

Note: The swap payments are based on quarterly historical interest rates from December
31, 1975, to June 30, 1994. The two-, five-, and ten-year swap rates are assumed to equal
the rates on two-, five-, and ten-year Treasury notes, respectively, plus 40 basis points.
The 40 basis point spread is typical of the current swap market.* The 79 quarters of data
permit calculation of gross payments for 68 two-year swaps, 56 five-year swaps, and 36
ten-year swaps. For any given swap, the gross payments are the sum over the life of the
swap of the absolute differences between LIBOR and the swap rate divided by four.
    *See Alworth (1993).

swaps.[73] Interest rate swaps can also be used by lenders and investors to
alter their risk exposures more cheaply than they can by trading in the
underlying fixed- and floating-rate debt instruments.

The incremental demand for payment system services caused by swap
transactions is relatively minimal when compared to transacting in the
underlying debt. There are no principal flows, only differential interest
payments. Even over long holding horizons such as five to ten years, the
aggregate of these differential payments (sum of the absolute values) is
unlikely to be large.

Table 2-6 gives historical averages of swap payments over various
maturities. Total payments for two-, five-, and ten-year swaps average
$6.50, $17.50 and $30.00, respectively, on a $100 notional amount with
quarterly payments. On the other hand, if demand for payment system
services is measured in terms of the *number* of transactions, the use of
swaps results in *increased* use: 8, 20, and 40 payments for the swaps
described.[74] This trade off—between making a few large payments versus
a large number of small payments—is common to the use of many
derivative instruments.

Futures Contracts

Futures contracts are similar to forward contracts whose credit risk is
managed with the posting of collateral (initial margin) plus periodic

---

73. A precursor to the interest rate swap is the "parallel loan," which involved the exchange
    of both interest and principal. See Smith and Taggart (1989).
74. Collateral payments (sometimes applicable) are excluded in this analysis.

settling up (variation margin) based on marking the position to market, usually daily. The net sum of the variation margin payments over a holding period equals the total return on the underlying instrument over the period, adjusted for carrying costs such as interest and dividends. Except for the timing of payments, this net flow is identical to the payoff on a forward contract that settles only at maturity.[75] In this sense, futures contracts can have much the same benefit as forward contracts (or delayed settlement): lower payment system demands than spot market transactions in the underlying instrument.

The periodic settling up does impose additional payment system demands, however, both because it involves a large number of (small) payments and because the gross sum of payments of variation margin will always exceed the net sum. The amount depends on several factors. It is proportional to the length of the holding period and the volatility of the underlying instrument during the holding period, and is nonlinear in the frequency of settling up.

As Table 2-7 illustrates, the gross flows of variation margin can range widely. They are considerably larger at higher frequencies of settling up, in principle becoming indefinitely large as the period between settlements becomes very short (although, as the settlement period becomes shorter, the size of any one payment of variation margin declines). Futures contracts thus divide up the net flow over the holding period into finer payments, but because these payments occur incrementally over time, they aggregate to the gross fluctuations or "total variation" over the holding interval.[76] Total variation can be likened to the actual distance traveled along a zigzagging path in contrast to net linear distance measured "as the crow flies."

Stock Index Futures

Index futures are futures contracts on particular baskets of securities such as the stocks making up the S&P 500 index. They have several special features. First, index futures contracts typically settle in cash, so that even at expiration, they involve minimal use of the payment system.[77]

---

75. The differences in timing result in almost negligible differences between futures and forward prices. See Cox, Ingersoll, and Ross (1981).
76. In the extreme of "continuous" settling up, the total variation is infinite, although the expected *net* variation is small or even zero. See Merton (1992a) for a discussion of the mathematical properties of Wiener processes used to model speculative prices.
77. With cash settlement, only the net difference between the market price of the physical securities at maturity of the contract and the contract price is paid or received. See Miller (1986) for a discussion of the expiration effects of cash versus physical settlement.

Table 2-7 Expected Gross Variation Margin Payments on Futures Contracts
(Initial futures price is $100; volatility is 15% per year)

Holding Period	Frequency of Settling Up					
	Daily	Weekly	Monthly	Quarterly	Half-Yearly	Yearly
Day	$ 0.6					
Week	4.4	$ 1.7				
Month	19.1	7.2	$ 3.5			
Quarter	57.2	21.6	10.4	$ 6.0		
Half-Year	114.3	43.2	20.7	12.0	$ 8.5	
Year	228.7	86.3	41.5	23.9	16.9	$12.0

Note: The periodic dollar return on the futures contract is assumed normally
distributed with constant annualized variance σ^2 and mean zero. Specifically, let there
be T settling-up periods in the year of length $\Delta = 1/T$. Let F_t be the futures price at the
end of period t and let r_t be the fractional change in F_t. Then $F_t = F_{t-1}(1+r_t)$ where r_t
has mean zero and variance $\sigma^2\Delta$. The assumption of a mean return of zero for a futures
contract is equivalent to assuming a zero risk premium for the underlying instrument.
The effect of a nonzero risk premium is negligible for our purposes here.

The expected variation margin payment for one period (conditional on F_{t-1}) is equal
to $E\{|F_{t-1}\cdot r_t|\} = 0.8\sigma\sqrt{\Delta}F_{t-1}$.* Over a holding period of h settling-up periods, the
expected gross variation margin payments are $0.8\sigma\sqrt{\Delta}hF_0$, which is tabulated above for
$F_0 = \$100$, $\sigma = 15\%$, and various values of h and Δ.

The diagonal elements in the table show the expected payment when the settling-up
period and the holding period coincide. These are the expected payments associated
with simple forward contracts of that maturity. The below-diagonal elements are the
expected gross variation margin payments for holding periods longer than the
settling-up period.

*The "0.8" in this formula is an approximation to $\sqrt{2/\pi} = 0.79788$.

Second, by eliminating the need to transact in the underlying stocks,
index futures avoid the risks and costs of clearing, settling, and holding
custody of a large number of different securities. Round-trip charges to
cover clearing, settlement, and custody fees alone are in the range of $36
per issue for U.S. stocks, amounting to $18,000 per S&P 500 basket, which
on a million dollar position is 1.8%.[78]

78. In fact, a $1 million position in the S&P 500 index is even more costly because it is too
small to be accomplished in minimum 100-share lots. In September 1994, the minimum
value of an S&P 500 basket containing at least 100 shares of each of the 500 companies
was $38 million. With odd-lot holdings in at most 50 companies, the minimum value
of an S&P 500 basket was $10 million. The weight of these 50 companies in the index
was 1.16%. A $1 million basket would have involved odd-lot positions in 446 companies
constituting 56.7% of the value of the index. From a private communication with a

Third, an even more significant savings occurs through the bid–ask spread, which can be as much as two orders of magnitude lower when stocks are traded in packaged forms such as index futures than as individual securities. A key explanation for this large spread difference is that it is much more likely that traders possess information material to the pricing of an individual company's shares (such as knowledge of sales and earnings prior to their announcement) than possess information material to the pricing of the entire stock market (such as the future direction of interest rates). Accordingly, market makers in stock index futures and other forms of packaged trading require less spread protection from "information traders" than market makers in individual company shares. Competition thus lowers the spreads on instruments like index futures.[79]

Although most forms of packaged trading offer lower bid–ask spreads than stocks traded individually, the degree to which they use the payment system can vary significantly. For example, SPDRs, a popular form of S&P 500 unit trust traded on the American Stock Exchange, have low bid–ask spreads (for the reasons cited above), but involve settlement in the full amount of the transaction value. Another frequently used mechanism is to "cross" buyers and sellers of S&P 500 packages at closing prices or in between the bid and the ask.[80] This eliminates the spread cost on the amount traded but not the need to clear and settle in 500 individual issues.

Options and Other Contingent Claim Securities

Option contracts and other contingent claim securities provide holders with nonlinear payoffs on the value of an underlying instrument.[81] The demands for nonlinear payoffs stem from particular portfolio management and risk management needs of market participants, such as to obtain downside protection but maintain upside exposure.[82] An alternative approach to obtaining nonlinear payoffs is through a strategy of

---

mutual fund manager. See Perold (1992) for discussion of the generic costs associated with holding the underlying equities. In addition to these charges, the costs can include withholding taxes, rebalancing expenses associated with changes to the index (resulting, for example, from mergers or bankruptcies), and high bid–ask spreads. These costs can be offset somewhat by fees charged for securities lending.

79. See Gammill and Perold (1989).
80. See Perold (1991).
81. For example, the payoffs on European call and put options are $\max(S - K, 0)$ and $\max(K - S, 0)$, respectively, where S is the value of the underlying instrument at maturity of the option, and K is the strike price.
82. See, e.g., Chapter 5.

Table 2-8 Turnover in Option Replication

Option Maturity	Revision Frequency		
	Daily	Weekly	Monthly
Month	0.9 x	0.3 x	0.2 x
Quarter	1.5	0.6	0.3
Half-Year	2.2	0.8	0.4
Year	3.1	1.2	0.6
2 Years	4.3	1.6	0.8
5 Years	6.8	2.6	1.2

Note: The table shows the expected turnover in the underlying instrument that would result from an option replication strategy for payout-protected European call options. Turnover is defined as marginal round-trip transactions (purchases plus sales ÷ 2) to maintain the exposure of the position to the underlying instrument equal to that of the option. These estimates *exclude* the transactions to initiate and close out the position.

For convenience, the strike price here is chosen to equal the initial price of the underlying instrument plus interest that accrues at the riskless rate. These are thus at-the-money options in a zero interest rate environment.

The turnover estimates use the formula derived in Leland (1985) for option replication with trading at discrete intervals: Turnover = $\exp(-d^2/2)\sqrt{f/(2\pi)}$ where f is the number of equally spaced revision periods during the life of the option and $d=\ln(Se^{rT}/K)/(\sigma\sqrt{T})+\sigma\sqrt{T}/2$ with S, K, r, T, and σ being the initial value of the underlying instrument, the strike price, the riskless rate, the option life, and the volatility of the underlying instrument. In our case, $K = Se^{rT}$ so that $d = \sigma\sqrt{T}/2$. The expected turnover is insensitive to volatility for typical values of σ, and can be closely approximated as $0.16\sqrt{f}$, which is the tabulated statistic.

dynamic hedging in the underlying instrument. Indeed, the insight of Black and Scholes (1973) that the contractual and dynamic hedging approaches to obtaining nonlinear payoffs are equivalent under certain circumstances underlies the derivation of their celebrated option pricing formula. The dynamic hedging approach also lies at the heart of the production technology used by institutions that issue nonlinear contract liabilities.[83]

Table 2-8 shows the expected turnover from *marginal* transactions that would be required in the underlying instrument to replicate the payoffs on common types of option contracts. Turnover increases with the life of the option and also with the frequency of trading *(revision frequency)*. The

83. See Leland (1980), Cox and Huang (1989), Merton (1989, 1992a), Black and Perold (1992), and Tufano (1993a, 1993b) in the vast literature on the subject of nonlinear payoffs and their replication through dynamic trading.

higher the revision frequency, the more accurate the replication of the option payoff. Thus, for example, to replicate a one-year call option with daily trading in the underlying instrument will on average involve 3.1 times turnover (purchases plus sales ÷ 2) in that instrument. This implies expected gross flows through the payment system of 12.4 times the initial value of the underlying instrument: 6.2 times for the purchases and sales in the instrument, and 6.2 times for the purchase and sale of Treasury bills. This illustrates the trading and payment system demands *avoided* by an investor who buys and holds the option to maturity. (The potential spillover effects of such a decision on the trading demands of others are discussed separately below.)

The analysis in Table 2-8 ignores any initiating or closing transactions that might accompany the decision to purchase and hold an option. For example, someone purchasing an option may simultaneously be liquidating a position in the underlying instrument and investing the proceeds (after purchase of the option) in Treasury bills. These additional transactions add to the payment system demands of the decision to purchase the option.

On the other hand, the strategy of replicating the option would involve the liquidation of only a portion of the incoming position in the underlying instrument (and the proceeds used to purchase Treasury bills).[84] In this case, the payments demands for replicating the option position are overstated in Table 2-8. Conversely, however, if the purchase of the option merely involves payment of the premium, the dynamic hedging strategy requires putting on an initial position in the underlying instrument funded mostly with borrowing. These payment system demands must be added to those shown in Table 2-8.

Similar considerations must be taken into account at expiration. As with futures and forward contracts, options can settle in kind or in cash when they do not expire worthless.[85] Selling the option prior to expiration has relatively small expected payment system implications, comparable to cash settlement, but taking delivery of the underlying instrument through exercise of the option results in additional payments demands.

---

84. The option replication strategy involves maintaining the number of shares held in the underlying instrument equal to the "delta" of the option. Deltas for near-term at-the-money options are around 0.5, for example. The replication strategy for such contracts written on $100 worth of the underlying instrument would have an initial position of about $50 in this instrument. See Rubinstein and Leland (1981) for an explanation of option replication strategies.

85. For example, traditional stock options settle in kind. Interest rate caps and floors and stock index options use cash settlement. Options on futures settle in both cash and delivery of the underlying futures contract to reduce the risk of inefficient pricing of the futures contract at exercise of the option.

Currency Hedging of International Investments

Currency hedging is a fairly common strategy employed by institutions and other investors in international equities and bonds.[86] For example, a U.S. investor might wish to be exposed to movements in the Japanese stock market without also having to bear the associated currency risk. One approach to implementing such a strategy is to purchase the shares of the companies that make up the Nikkei 225 stock index, and to effect the currency hedge by selling forward yen into U.S. dollars using standard currency forward contracts. The associated payments demands for a $100 investment hedged at face value are as follows:

- Exchange $100 for yen, settling the different legs at different times of day.
- Purchase the shares of the 225 companies making up the Nikkei index (or an approximating basket).
- Sell forward $100 worth of yen.
- In response to fluctuations in the Nikkei index, increase or decrease the currency forward position proportionately.
- At liquidation of the position, sell the stocks for yen currency, and either convert to U.S. dollars in the spot market, settling the forward positions in cash for the difference between the forward price and the spot price, or deliver the yen in direct settlement of the forward currency obligation.

An alternative is to invest the $100 principal domestically in U.S. Treasury bills and purchase Nikkei 225 index futures contracts through the Chicago Mercantile Exchange. The variation margin on these contracts is calculated in domestic currency (here, U.S. dollars), so that the return on these index futures is equivalent to what would be obtained with a position in the Nikkei 225 hedged against yen/U.S. dollar currency risk.[87]

The payments demands of this strategy are significantly different. They involve the purchase and sale of U.S. Treasury bills initially, at liquidation, and in the interim for the ebb and flow of variation margin. The strategy avoids both cross-border settlements of currency as well as transactions in multiple instruments: the shares of individual companies and currency forward contracts.

---

86. See, for example, Perold and Schulman (1988).
87. That is, the returns are equivalent up to implementation costs. Nikkei futures purchased in Tokyo would also work, provided that the variation margin, which settles in yen, is concurrently converted to or from U.S. dollars.

Exchange-for-Physicals (EFP)

Exchange-for-physicals is a method of settlement involving the simultaneous exchange of futures and physical instruments. For example, Party A who is long the S&P 500 index might find it cheaper to sell an equivalent number of S&P 500 index futures and, through an EFP, exchange this long–short position for cash, than to sell the stocks in the index directly. The other side of this transaction might be Party B, who wishes to purchase the S&P 500 index, and does so by first going long S&P 500 index futures, and then entering into the EFP. The long futures position of Party B is canceled by its assumption of the short futures position of Party A.[88]

EFPs are used for many types of commodities, and can be effective in reducing transactions costs. In our example, the EFP permits Parties A and B to adjust their risk exposures to the S&P 500 separately from the actual purchase or sale of the shares of the underlying companies. The desired exposures are effected using low-cost index futures, and the parties can then bide their time until an opportunity arises to transact at low cost. The EFP is thus an example of derivatives use not to bypass the payment system per se, but rather to buy time to settle some transactions more cost-effectively.

The Relationship Between Cash Market Volume and Derivatives Volume

So far, we have focused on the effects on payment system demands created by the use of derivatives as seen from the perspective of a single user, holding all else fixed. In principle, though, the cash market transactions avoided or altered by one party's use of derivatives may simply be shifted to the counterparty to that transaction. For example, issuers of options may have to engage in dynamic hedging to offset the riskiness of these liabilities, resulting in the same overall transactions demands; sellers of stock index futures may be engaging in index arbitrage, which involves the additional hedging transaction of purchasing the underlying stocks.

The spillover cash market trading that results from the need to hedge positions taken in derivative instruments usually will be less than one-for-one, however, and might even be minimal. For example, issuers of

---

88. The closing out of futures positions with EFPs takes place away from the floor of the futures exchange. Being privately negotiated, the EFP is the single exception to the requirement that all futures trades take in the pit. See Kolb (1991). See Zurack (1991) for a description of the use of EFPs in equity portfolio transactions.

Figure 2-4   Index Futures and Stock Market Volume

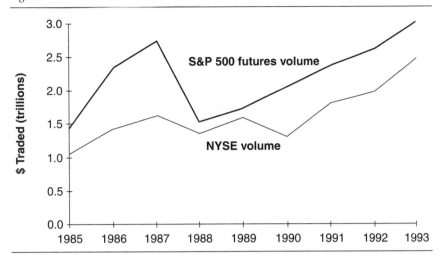

options can hedge their risk by purchasing offsetting options.[89] Or they can lower their transactions costs by engaging in dynamic hedging with smaller trades and relatively long revision intervals (such as weekly), bearing more risk in return for these savings. Or they can do some of each.[90]

The availability of derivative instruments also can lead to *increased* demands for cash market trading. Derivatives can be used in conjunction with cash market positions to alter payoffs, and thus enhance the attractiveness of the overall portfolio. For example, stocks are safer to own when "insured" with put options. Put options thus can increase the demand for stock ownership, leading possibly to *increased* cash market trading volume.

Whatever the relationship between the existence of derivative instruments and the volume of cash market trading, there is evidence that a considerable amount of derivatives trading in fact occurs without direct spillover to the cash markets. S&P 500 stock index futures are a good example. As shown in Figure 2-4, the volume of these futures contracts routinely exceeds the volume of shares traded on the New York Stock Exchange, implying that a considerable fraction of stock index futures volume occurs without directly offsetting transactions in individual stocks.

89. Issuers of options often act as market makers, crossing sellers with buyers but inserting themselves between the two (like a clearinghouse) to enhance and/or "homogenize" the credit risk of the contract. See the discussion of performance guarantees.
90. For two interesting examples, see Tufano (1989; 1994a and 1994b). See Constantinides (1986) and Dumas and Luciano (1991) for the effect of transactions costs on optimal portfolio rebalancing strategies.

Table 2-9 Relationship Between Bond Futures Volume and Bond
Market Volume

Country	1987	1988	1989	1990	1991
France	2.7	2.5	2.4	4.6	5.4
Germany	NA	1.3	1.5	3.0	3.5
Italy	NA	NA	NA	NA	0.1
Japan	0.9	1.3	1.5	1.5	1.6
Netherlands	NA	0.2	0.1	0.2	0.1
United Kingdom	0.2	0.2	0.1	0.2	0.2
United States[a]	0.4	0.4	0.4	0.4	0.4

Source: Bank for International Settlements (1992b).

Note: Transactions in futures cover contracts on government securities traded on exchanges worldwide.

[a]Cash market transactions include Treasury bills.

In a particular instance, October 19, 1987 ("Black Monday"), about $20 billion face value of index futures were sold (and, of course, purchased) of which only $1.2 billion worth was attributed to index arbitrage.[91]

In the case of bond futures, the relation between cash and futures market volume is quite varied. Table 2-9 shows the ratio of the volume of futures to cash market transactions in the government debt securities of various countries. In 1991, for example, the volume of French government bond futures was 5.4 times that of French sovereign debt; the comparable ratio was 3.5 times in Germany, and 1.6 times in Japan. In contrast, the volume of U.S. Treasury bond futures—one of the most active and liquid futures markets ever—was only 40% of the volume of U.S. Treasury securities.

The low ratio of U.S. bond futures volume to cash market volume can be explained at least partly by the relatively low comparative advantage offered by bond futures. That is, the cash market offers unprecedented liquidity, and positions are easily financed through the well-established repo market (estimated at $700 billion a day). These features of liquidity and low-cost convenient financing stem in large part from the fact that the clearing and settlement of U.S. government securities takes place in the most efficient and riskless manner possible: through book entry and true DVP over the FedWire.

In general, the comparative advantage of—and hence demand for us-

---

91. "Report of the Presidential Task Force on Market Mechanisms" (1988) ("The Brady Report").

ing—any particular trading mechanism, including the choice between actual trading in cash market instruments and "virtual trading" through means of contractual agreements, depends on transaction efficiencies as well as factors such as regulation and taxes. For example, risk-based capital requirements can make it cheaper for insurance companies to hold equities in the form of structured notes rather than through direct ownership; and differential tax treatment such as nonrecoverable withholding taxes on dividends for foreign investors can make it significantly less costly to make cross-border equity investments through derivatives than through ownership of the underlying shares. Factors such as these induce buy-and-hold behavior in the cash markets, shift equity trading to the derivative markets, and in effect "immobilize" cash instruments in much the same way depository use reduces the risks and costs of settling cash market transactions. Withholding taxes on dividends, for example, create incentives for local investors to hold shares and enter into equity swaps with foreign investors.[92]

It should be noted that while derivative instruments serve as alternatives to trading in cash market securities, they also perform the function of "completing markets."[93] That is, they permit investors to manage exposures to risks not easily accomplished in *any* other way. Some derivatives' trading volume, therefore, will arise for reasons unrelated to transactions costs. For example, contractual agreements are the only "pure" way to obtain exposure to, or hedge against, future price movements in nonstorable commodities like cattle, or seldom-traded assets such as real estate.

Options on traded securities represent perhaps the clearest example of contractual agreements that perform several disparate functions. Since they are priced on the basis of expected volatility, options not only offer an alternative to creating nonlinear payoffs on the underlying instrument through dynamic trading, but also provide the holder with exposure to changes in expected volatility.[94]

The Settlement Problem in Foreign Exchange

The settlement problem in foreign exchange is considered by many to be the single most important issue facing the global payment system today.

---

92. For example, there is at present a nonrecoverable 30% withholding tax on dividends paid by U.S. companies to investors residing in "tax havens" like Luxembourg. With roughly a 3% annual dividend yield on the S&P 500, this represents a deadweight loss of 1% per year that can be avoided through the use of derivatives. See Perold (1992). Merton (1992b) makes a similar proposal in the case of emerging markets equities.
93. See Chapter 5 for a full discussion of the role and importance of so-called Arrow-Debreu securities for completing markets.
94. See Chapter 6.

Table 2-10 Breakdown of U.S. Foreign-Exchange Volume in 1992

Spot Currency Transactions	51%
Currency Swap Transactions	32%
Forward Currency Transactions	5%
Options Transactions	8%
Exchange-Traded Currency Futures and Options	4%
Total	100%

Source: Chicago Mercantile Exchange (1993b).

Note: Volume is measured as the U.S. dollar value of transactions. Options and futures volume is measured in terms of the notional amounts of the contracts traded.

The problem, I noted earlier, arises because of the different operating hours of the large-value funds transfer systems of various countries, meaning that the legs of many foreign exchange transactions must settle at different times of day. The problem is most acute with respect to U.S. dollar/yen transactions, which, as can be seen in Figure 2-2, are subject to a 15-hour gap between final payment in yen and final payment in U.S. dollars (or a 9-hour gap if the U.S. dollar leg is settled first).

Table 2-10 breaks down the volume of U.S. foreign exchange-related payments. Eighty-eight percent of the volume takes place through the interbank spot, swap, and forward markets, which involve the exchange of currency with T + 2 or longer settlement lags; 8% of the volume stems from interbank currency options, of which probably 50% are actually exercised; and only 4% of the volume takes place in the form of exchange-traded options or futures contracts—which settle in cash (for the net movement in the currency) in a single location and thus are not subject to the settlement differential introduced by time zones. With U.S. foreign exchange-related payments alone approaching $1 trillion a day, the result is the extension of large amounts of "time zone" credit, and consequently the assumption of significant exposures to the "Herstatt risk" discussed earlier.

There are a number of potential solutions to this problem of Herstatt exposure, all of which have the same functional goal, yet involve significantly different institutional arrangements. A comparison of these alternatives is useful to illustrate some of the core mechanisms underlying the payments system, as well as the extent to which various mechanisms serve as functional substitutes.

The first and conceptually simplest approach is to extend the hours of operation of the world's large-value transfer systems (and appropriately modify correspondent banking practices) to enable simultaneous funds transfer with finality in all major currencies. All else equal, this approach will leave the flow of payments unchanged, but eliminate Herstatt risk.[95]

A second, related approach could take the form of a noncentral bank-operated payment system, similar to the Globeset product recently introduced by Bankers Trust.[96] In this system, each party to a foreign exchange transaction purchases shares of a money market fund that holds short-term paper denominated in the currency in which payment is to be made. (There is one money market fund for each currency.) At a mutually agreed-upon time, the parties exchange their *shares* in these respective funds, which they then can redeem at their convenience or use in a subsequent currency exchange.

The initial purchase and the later redemption of the respective money market fund shares occur at different times of day—each during the operating hours of the local payment system.[97] This need not involve any settlement risk, however, as each local transfer can be accomplished through simultaneous delivery-versus-payment. The exchange of shares in the respective money market funds is also straightforward, through simultaneous delivery-versus-payment, thus effectively eliminating settlement risk.

The system succeeds by creating new currencies—shares of money market funds—whose transfer is not constrained by existing institutional barriers. By requiring the advance purchase of money market fund shares, however, this design suffers from the same drawback as any payment system that operates without extension of credit: the creation of settlement queues and the delays that result as they take time to unwind. (Recall my comparison of the FedWire and the Swiss large-value transfer system.)

A third, wholly different alternative is to exploit the fact that the *net* interbank foreign exchange-related payments flow—when calculated multilaterally—is small in comparison to the *gross* flow. Multilateral netting through a global clearinghouse, some have estimated, would reduce foreign exchange-related settlement volume by 80%, compared to 25% if

---

95. The simplest approach of all is to operate a multi-currency payment system in a single location and jurisdiction, such as in New York City. The unwillingness of local authorities to surrender control over their own payment systems makes this a remote possibility.
96. See Globeset marketing literature and fund prospectuses.
97. For example, suppose Party A needs to pay Party B $1,000 in exchange for 100,000 yen. Party A would purchase $1,000 worth of units in the U.S. dollar money market fund during U.S. payment system operating hours, while Party B would purchase 100,000 yen worth of units in the yen money market fund during Japanese payment system operating hours. Once both sets of purchases have been accomplished, Parties A and B can exchange shares of these funds at any time of their choosing.

netted bilaterally.[98] For multilateral cross-border netting to be effective, however, jurisdictional and other obstacles now in the way will need to be overcome. (Recall the earlier discussion of these obstacles under netting.) This approach does not alter the basic settlement mechanism. It simply represents a way, through netting, to make less use of the mechanism.

The fourth approach involves netting over time through the use of derivatives. It is perhaps best exemplified by the Rolling Spot currency futures contract introduced in 1993 by the Chicago Mercantile Exchange. The contract is unusual in that it is *explicitly* designed to offer an alternative to spot market foreign exchange positioning by traders. When a trader purchases foreign exchange, say, British pounds for U.S. dollars, the dollars are borrowed, and the pounds purchased with these dollars are lent out, usually on a rolling overnight basis until the position is closed out by selling the pounds and repaying the dollars. Each overnight rolling of the position involves pounds flowing in as a return from the previous night's loan, and then being relent, and dollars flowing out to pay off the previous borrowings, and then being reborrowed. Thus, maintaining a foreign exchange position involves four cash flows per day, representing a pair of in- and outflows for each currency.[99] The net gain or loss from rolling such a position is the amount by which the value of the currency moves in excess of the lending/borrowing interest rate differential.

The Rolling Spot currency futures contract is designed to result in precisely the same net gain or loss as would be obtained through overnight rolling of a spot currency position. It does this by requiring the parties to the contract to settle up explicitly on the overnight interest rate differential. That is, if the overnight rate on pounds is 8% annually, and the overnight rate on dollars is 5%, the seller of a pounds Rolling Spot contract pays the buyer net interest at the rate of 3% per year. Since this cost-of-carry is calculated separately and on an overnight basis, the actual contract price will vary only with currency movements.[100] Because variations in the contract price are also settled on a daily basis, the net daily flow is the sum of the interest rate differential and the change in the spot currency price, which is precisely the net gain or loss on an overnight spot currency position. The key difference is that there are no gross payments to settle, and therefore there is no exposure to Herstatt risk.

The alternative approaches to reducing Herstatt risk clearly result in

---

98. See Smith (1991).
99. These flows are accomplished through means of a so-called spot/next currency swap. See the Chicago Mercantile Exchange (1993) for a detailed explanation.
100. Deviations from spot market currency prices provide arbitrage opportunities.

very different institutional arrangements. Moreover, they can result in vastly different payments flows. Approaches that find a common time of day to effect simultaneous settlement do not manifestly affect the volume of transfers; multilateral (cross-sectional) netting reduces actual funds transfers, but does not expressly affect the number and aggregate value of individual payment obligations; and derivatives approaches like Rolling Spot, through contractual netting over time, vastly reduce the actual underlying payments flows.

A Concluding Comment: Derivative Instruments and Payment System Risk

In my examination of the core functions of systems for clearing and settlement, I argue that derivative instruments should be considered an integral part of the payment system because they substitute in a variety of ways for trading in cash market instruments, typically transforming payments demands from a small number of large payments to a large number of small payments spread over time. This is perhaps best exemplified by the Rolling Spot currency futures contract, which is explicitly designed to eliminate foreign exchange payments flows and the associated Herstatt risk.

A key implication of this general thesis is that, all else equal, if the latent cash market transactions embedded in the use of derivatives transactions actually were executed in the cash markets, the volume of large payments would rise significantly. In many cases volume would more than double, given the generally high ratios of futures volume to cash market volume. This perspective suggests that derivatives serve the function of cushioning rather than exacerbating—as is often argued—pressures on the payment system.

References

Allen, W.B., and S.P. Mason (1986), "Note on the Eurodollar Debt Market," Harvard Business School Case No. 286-063, Boston.

Alworth, J.S. (1993), "The Valuation of U.S. Dollar Interest Rate Swaps," Bank for International Settlements Economic Paper, No. 35.

Bank for International Settlements (1989), *Report on Netting Schemes*, Basle.

——— (1990), *Report of the Committee on Interbank Netting Schemes of the Central Banks of The Group of Ten Countries*, Basle.

——— (1992a), *Delivery Versus Payment in Securities Settlement Systems*, Basle.

——— (1992b), *Derivative Financial Instruments and Banks' Involvement in Selected Off-Balance-Sheet Business*, Basle.

———— (1993), *Payment Systems in The Group of Ten Countries*, Basle.

Barclay, W. (1994), "FLEX Options: A New Generation of Derivatives," Chapter 2 in R.A. Klein and J. Lederman, eds., *The Handbook of Derivatives and Synthetics*, Chicago: Probus.

Bernanke, B.S. (1990), "Clearing and Settlement During the Crash," *Review of Financial Studies*, 3, No. 1: 133–151.

Bhala, R. (1994), "Legal Foundations of Large-Value Transfer Systems," in *The Payment System*, B.J. Summers, ed., Washington, D.C.: International Monetary Fund, 53–72.

Black, F., and A.F. Perold (1992), "Theory of Constant Proportion Portfolio Insurance," *Journal of Economic Dynamics and Control* 16: 403–426.

Black, F., and M. Scholes (1973), "The Pricing of Options and Corporate Liabilities," *Journal of Political Economy*, 81: 637–654.

Bodurtha, S.G., and T.E. Quinn (1990), "Does Patient Program Trading Really Pay?" *Financial Analysts Journal*, 46 (3): 35–42.

Campbell, J.Y., and K.A. Froot (1993), "Securities Transaction Taxes: What About International Experiences and Migrating Markets?" Chicago: Midamerica Institute.

The Chicago Mercantile Exchange (1993a), "The Financial Safeguard System of the Chicago Mercantile Exchange."

———— (1993b), "An Introduction to Interbank Foreign Exchange and Rolling Spot."

———— (1994), "Rules of the Chicago Mercantile Exchange."

"The Clearing House Interbank Payments System" (1991), Federal Reserve Bank of New York.

Commodity Futures Trading Commission (1993), Annual Report.

Constantinides, G.M. (1986), "Capital Market Equilibrium With Transactions Costs," *Journal of Political Economy*, 94: 842–862.

Corrigan, E.G. (1986), Statements to Congress, *Federal Reserve Bulletin* (February): 117–125.

Cox, J.C., and C. Huang (1989), "Optimum Consumption and Portfolio Policies When Asset Prices Follow a Diffusion Process," *Journal of Economic Theory*, 49: 33–83.

Cox, J.C., J.E. Ingersoll, and S.A. Ross (1981), "The Relation Between Forward Prices and Futures Prices," *Journal of Financial Economics*, 9 (4): 321–346.

Duffie, D., and M. Hwang (1994), "Swap Rates and Credit Quality," Stanford University Working Paper, Stanford, CA.

Duffy, John J. (1985), "Prices End Lower in Response to Weak 30-Year Bond Auction," *The Bond Buyer*, 25 November: 3.

Dumas, B., and E. Luciano (1991), "An Exact Solution to a Dynamic Portfolio Choice Problem Under Transactions Costs," *Journal of Finance*, 46 (2): 577–595.

"Exchanges Vote Four Major Steps in Bid to Cut Paper Glut; Penalties are Included" (1968), *Wall Street Journal*, 16 August: 6.

Fabozzi, F.J., and F. Modigliani (1992), *Mortgage and Mortgage-Backed Securities Markets*, Boston: Harvard Business School Press.

Gammill, J.F., and A.F. Perold (1989), "The Changing Character of Stock Market Liquidity," *Journal of Portfolio Management*, 15 (3): 13–18.

Garsson, Robert M. (1988), "Payment-System Glitch Complicated Stock Crash: Brady Report Cites Wire Transfer Shutdown as One Factor in Market Turmoil," *The American Banker,* 14 January: 1.

Global Derivatives Study Group (1993), *Derivatives: Practices and Principles,* Group of Thirty, Washington, D.C.

Goldstein, M., D. Folkerts-Landau, P. Garber, L. Rojas-Suarez, and M. Spencer (1993), *International Capital Markets Part I: Exchange Rate Management and International Capital Flows,* Washington, D.C.: International Monetary Fund.

Horii, A., and B.J. Summers (1994), "Large-Value Transfer Systems," in *The Payment System,* B.J. Summers, ed., Washington, D.C.: International Monetary Fund, 73–88.

Juncker, G.R., and B.J. Summers (1991), "A Primer on the Settlement of Payments in the United States," *Federal Reserve Bulletin* (November): 847–858.

Kolb, R.W. (1991), *Understanding Futures Markets,* Third edition, Miami: Kolb.

Leland, H.E. (1980), "Who Should Buy Portfolio Insurance?" *Journal of Finance,* 35 (2): 581–594.

——— (1985), "Option Pricing and Replication With Transactions Costs," *Journal of Finance,* 40 (5): 1283–1301.

Lynch, G. (1994), *Report of Inquiring into False Trading Profit at Kidder, Peabody & Company Incorporated,* New York: Davis Polk & Wardwell.

MacRae, D. (1993), "How Big Will Global Repo Markets Become?" *International Securities Lending* (September): 57–60.

"Managing Payments Risk" (1993), Supplement to iCB Magazine, September/October, The Friary Press Ltd, London.

Mason, S.P., and K. Singh (1994), "Banque Paribas: Paribas Derives Garantis," Harvard Business School Case No. 295-008, Boston.

Merton, R.C. (1989), "On the Application of the Continuous-Time Theory of Finance to Financial Intermediation and Insurance," *GENEVA,* 14 (52): 225–261.

Merton, R.C. (1992a), *Continuous-Time Finance,* revised edition, Oxford: Basil Blackwell.

——— (1992b), "Financial Innovation and Economic Performance," *Journal of Applied Corporate Finance,* 4 (4): 12–22.

——— (1993), "Operation and Regulation in Financial Intermediation: A Functional Perspective," in *Operation and Regulation of Financial Markets,* P. Englund, ed., Stockholm: The Economic Council.

Merton, R.C., and Z. Bodie (1992), "On the Management of Financial Guarantees," *Financial Management,* 21 (4): 87–109.

Miller, M.H. (1986), "Financial Innovation: The Last Twenty Years and the Next," *Journal of Financial and Quantitative Analysis,* 21 (4): 459–471.

Mitchell, B.R. (1993), *International Historical Statistics: The Americas 1750–1988,* Second edition, New York: Stockton Press.

Moser, J.T. (1994), "Origins of the Modern Exchange Clearinghouse: A History of Early Clearing and Settlement Methods at Futures Exchanges," Working Paper 94–3, Federal Reserve Bank of Chicago.

"New York, American Exchanges Again Cut Trading Times Due to Crush of Paperwork" (1968), *Wall Street Journal,* 19 January: 2.

The New York Stock Exchange: The First 200 Years (1992), Essex, CT: Greenwich Publishing Group.

Parkinson, P., A. Gilbert, E. Gollob, L. Hargraves, R. Mead, J. Stehm, and M.A. Taylor (1992), "Clearance and Settlement in U.S. Securities Markets," Staff Study, Board of Governors of the Federal Reserve System.

Perold, A.F. (1991), "The Nikko Securities Co., Ltd.," Harvard Business School Case No. 292-002, Boston.

——— (1992), "BEA Associates: Enhanced Equity Index Funds," Harvard Business School Case No. 293-024, Boston.

Perold, A.F., and E.C. Schulman (1988), "The Free Lunch in Currency Hedging: Implications for Investment Policy and Performance Standards," *Financial Analysts Journal,* 44 (3): 45–52.

Perold, A.F., and K. Singh (1993), "The Boston Company: Securities Lending," Harvard Business School Case No. 294-024, Boston.

"Report of the Presidential Task Force on Market Mechanisms" (1988), Washington, D.C.: U.S. Government Printing Office.

Rubinstein, M., and H.E. Leland (1981), "Replicating Options with Positions in Stock and Cash," *Financial Analysts Journal,* 37 (4): 63–72.

Rutz, R.D. (1988), "Clearance, Payment, and Settlements Systems in the Futures, Options, and Stock Markets," *Review of Futures Markets,* 7 (3): 346–370.

"Stock Exchanges Set 5 Day Trading Beginning Jan. 6" (1968), *Wall Street Journal,* 22 November: 2.

Sendrovic, I. (1994), "Technology and the Payment System," in *The Payment System,* B.J. Summers, ed., Washington, D.C.: International Monetary Fund, 178–196.

Smith, D.J., and R.A. Taggart (1989), "Bond Market Innovations and Financial Intermediation," *Business Horizons* (November-December): 24–33.

Smith, P.B. (1991), "Foreign-Exchange Netting Needed to Reduce Enormous Exposures," *The Journal of Private Sector Policy* (January): 22–24.

Solnik, B. (1990), "The Distribution of Daily Stock Returns and Settlement Procedures: The Paris Bourse," *Journal of Finance,* 45 (5): 1601–1609.

Spahr, W.E. (1926), *The Clearing and Collection of Checks,* New York: The Bankers Publishing Co.

Spindler, J.A., and B.J. Summers (1994), "The Central Bank and the Payment System," in *The Payment System,* B.J. Summers, ed., Washington, D.C.: International Monetary Fund, 164–177.

Stehm, J. (1991), "Credit and Liquidity Risks and Risk Management in the Securities Clearing and Settlement Process," Thesis, University of Delaware.

——— (1992), "Clearance and Settlement of Mortgage-Backed Securities through the Participants Trust Company," Finance and Economics Discussion Series, Division of Research and Statistics, Division of Monetary Affairs, November, Federal Reserve Board, Washington, D.C.

Summers, B.J. (1994), "Introductory Remarks for a Panel Discussion on Expanded Fedwire Operating Hours," Paper prepared for the Money Transfer Conference, New York, November 14.

Tufano, P. (1989), "Goldman Sachs, Co.: Nikkei Put Warrants," Harvard Business School Case No. 292-113, Boston.

——— (1993a), "Leland O'Brien Rubinstein Associates, Inc.: Portfolio Insurance," Harvard Business School Case No. 294-061, Boston.

——— (1993b), "Leland O'Brien Rubinstein Associates, Inc.: Super Trust," Harvard Business School Case No. 294-050, Boston.

——— (1994a), "Shearson Lehman Hutton, Inc. (A): Entry into the Covered Warrant Business," Harvard Business School Case No. 291-016, Boston.

——— (1994b), "Shearson Lehman Hutton, Inc. (B): Euromarket Covered Warrant Execution," Harvard Business School Case No. 291-017, Boston.

Umlauf, S.R. (1993), "Transaction Taxes and the Behavior of the Swedish Stock Market," *Journal of Financial Economics*, 33 (2): 227–240.

Walmsley, J. (1991), *Global Investing: Eurobonds and Alternatives*, New York: St. Martin's Press.

Zurack, M.A. (1991), "Portfolio Trading in the United States," *Stock Index Research*, Goldman Sachs.

CHAPTER THREE

The Economics of Pooling

ERIK R. SIRRI AND PETER TUFANO

Financial systems facilitate *pooling,* or the aggregation of household wealth to fund indivisible or efficient-scale enterprises. Pooling is such an integral part of the financial system that it is difficult to imagine a world without it. In that counterfactual world, households could not jointly invest in projects. Firms could acquire no more external financing than a single household could provide, and businesses the size of Exxon, British Telecom, or Mitsubishi could not exist. Meaningful diversification would be beyond the reach of all but the wealthiest households, and significant portions of households' liquidity needs would remain unsatisfied. The economy would suffer large deadweight costs, with insufficiently capitalized firms operating at suboptimal scales and individuals holding inferior portfolios.

This chapter sets out the two subtly different levels at which pooling arrangements are structured. We document how the demands for pooling arise, both from producers who seek capital to run their firms, and from investors who seek liquidity and superior risk-bearing opportunities. Whenever pools are created, the potential exists for unintentional side effects that impose economic and social costs on investors and producers. The financing of projects with multiple outside investors, for example, creates problems arising from differences in information and incentives among the parties. Outside investors may worry about managers' effort and competence, and the decisions that managers and investors make may be distorted by these concerns. If these distortions are large enough, their costs can dwarf the benefits of pooling.

Pooling can be carried out either through well-developed financial markets or through financial intermediaries. These two mechanisms allow different ways of dealing with difficulties that arise from pooling, such as informational asymmetries, agency costs, and liquidity costs. We illustrate this contrast by comparing delegated investment management, where pooling is accomplished through financial intermediaries, to asset securitization, where financial markets are used to pool investment wealth.

Although pooling is a stable function, changing laws, transactions costs, and information processing costs have altered the technology and structure used to form pools. We speculate on continuing evolution in pooling by considering limits to pooling as information, pricing, and contracting technologies continue to improve.

The Levels of Pooling Complexity

A world with absolutely no pooling would be characterized by autarky, in which each firm is independent or self-sufficient with a single owner. Every project or firm could have only a single supplier of capital, with a single bilateral contract between the firm and the sole investor specifying the rights and responsibilities of each party. In the extreme, the sole supplier of capital also runs the firm, thus forming a sole proprietorship. In autarky, firm size is thus limited by an individual's personal wealth and resources.

Adding a level of complexity allows the capital supplier to be distinct from the firm, with the arrangement governed by a single bilateral contract. If the capital supplier is a family member, the owner's contract may be implicit, governed by social norms or customs. More generally, the bilateral contract is explicit, prescribing the precise economic relationship between the owner and the capital provider. All these arrangements are forms of autarky in that the enterprise exists in a world of self-sufficiency.

To reach the simplest level of pooling requires the aggregation of household wealth to fund enterprise, accomplished by *multiple* bilateral contracts between households and a firm. For any one firm, the multiple bilateral contracts with investors could be the same, in which case all would be equity holders of the firm. Alternately, the investors could differ, and the firms might issue distinct debt and equity claims. Perhaps the most critical early advances in pooling through multiple bilateral contracts were the development of contract theory and the conception of a firm or corporation as a legal entity. In the Western world, for example, the earliest firm resembling what we call a corporation was the joint stock company founded in 1553 as the "Russian Company."[1] In that endeavor, 28 persons each invested £6,000 in the common stock of the company to open up trade routes to Russia and China. What distinguished this entity is that it was defined as "one bodie and perpetuall fellowship and communaltie," and that it held legal rights of an individual: It could hold title, sue, and be sued under its own seal.

The creation of a legal entity that could serve as a vehicle for pooling was a critical development in facilitating the evolution of more complex pools. Without a legally defined "firm" or "corporation," investors would need a nexus of contracts binding one to each of the others, instead of linking each investor to a central legal entity or hub. Costs of commerce would be high, as if a telephone system were to connect each house to every other, instead of routing all calls into a central exchange.

A second level at which pooling takes place is through the creation of *multilateral contracts* between a set of investors and a set of firms. For example, thousands of investors can jointly entrust their wealth to a single mutual fund, which can then invest in hundreds of firms. The fund management company constructs bilateral contracts between mutual fund investor and fund, and between the fund and the firms in which it purchases equity or debt. Each mutual fund investor does not have a *direct* contract with each of the hundreds of firms he or she ultimately finances. This multilateral or multi-level contract conception of pooling produces entities that intercede between households and firms—financial intermediaries that take the form of banks, pension funds, mutual funds, and diversified conglomerates.

Pooling as multilateral contracting has a long history. In the United States alone, the first land banks were established in the early 1700s, the Bank of North America was established in 1781, the first insurance company in 1792, the first thrift in 1831, the first trust company in 1818, the first pension plan in 1875, and the first investment company in 1890.[2] Although all these financial institutions accomplish pooling, they differ with respect to the mix of other financial functions delivered, as well as the delivery mechanism. More recently, developments in multilateral contracting have produced pooling in the form of specific capital market instruments: mortgage- and asset-backed securities along with vehicles that repackage these pools to create instruments such as collateralized

---

1. See Scott (1912) for a historical study of the early development of the corporation. There are five earlier types of quasi-commercial organizations that Dewing (1934) identifies as prototypes of the corporation: the borough, the merchant guild, the fair, the chartered alien merchants, and the university. Even earlier firms resembling joint stock firms have been identified in Genoa, Italy, in the fourteenth century.
2. See Thygerson (1992), Chapter 8.

mortgage obligations. A mortgage-backed security allows many investors to finance hundreds of mortgages through a single conduit. Advances in pooling through multilateral contracting are enabled by developments that have removed legal impediments, but more importantly by systems and technologies that allow for low-cost and highly reliable collection, analysis, and processing of information.

The distinction between pooling as multiple bilateral contracts and as multilateral contracts is mirrored in the demand for pooling by enterprises and by households, as discussed below. Pooling benefits enterprises as they move from autarky to multiple bilateral contracts: With many investors, the firm can operate at an efficient scale. Pooling benefits households as they move from multiple bilateral to multilateral contracts: By joining with others, households can enjoy efficient diversification, monitoring, and liquidity.

The Demand for Pooling by Enterprises: Scale Economies

To maximize profits through economies of scale, firms must be free to select the size at which they will operate. Without pooling, autarky would prevail, and household wealth would impose binding capital constraints on firms and severely limit entrepreneurs' decisions. Absent pools created through bilateral contracting, most of the world's largest firms could not operate at their current scales. In a no-pooling world, as firms fail to enjoy scale economies, entrepreneurs and consumers would likely be less well-off.

Optimal Firm Size

Elementary microeconomic theory demonstrates that, in a competitive economy, profits are maximized by minimizing costs. In the face of increasing marginal costs, a profit-maximizing entity would choose to produce at the lowest cost, or minimum efficient scale (MES) point, as shown in Figure 3-1. Absent capital constraints, technological considerations dictate optimal firm size in this stylized model of firms.

The notion that firm size is dictated by the production function of firms underlies an important strand of traditional industrial organization theory.[3] Plant-level scale economies are known to result from the use of specialized production processes and from economies of massed reserves or backup production facilities. Firm-level efficiencies result from exploiting economies in research and development, sales promotion, or capital raising [Scherer (1980, Chapter 4)]. Industry studies establish that sig-

---

3. See Scherer (1980) or Tirole (1988) for a review of this literature.

Figure 3-1   Costs of Production and Minimum Efficient Scale

Given a production technology, firms will choose output levels so that they operate at their minimum average cost if the industry is competitive. The curve AC is the average cost curve for the industry; curve M is the marginal cost curve. By definition, the marginal cost curve crosses the average cost curve at Q′, which is the minimum average cost, or the minimum efficient scale (MES).

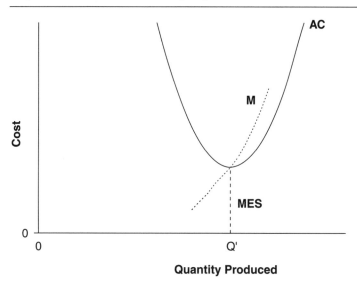

nificant scale economies exist. Table 3-1 reports a cross-industry study of minimum efficient scale that details the cost disadvantages small firms face. In the industries studied, if enterprise size shrinks by two-thirds, production costs rise an average of 6.8%, although they may increase by as much as 26%. These scale economies are not immaterial, given the thin profit margins in some industries, which confirms the important role of cost and scale considerations as determinants of firm size.

Were there no economies of scale, firm size would be indeterminate. Large firms would have no advantages over small firms, and we would be as likely to see large and small firms in every industry. Not surprisingly, this is not the case. Table 3-2 shows that large firms dominate capital-intensive industries, which presumably enjoy larger scale economies, e.g., industrial production, equipment manufacturing, and natural resources. Small firms dominate labor-intensive service industries that may enjoy lower economies of scale, such as repair services, legal services, and building contractors. Technological differences among industries lead to different optimal firm sizes, which in turn place varying demands upon the financial system to provide pooling.

Table 3-1 Industry, Scale, and Cost Advantages

For varied industries, the table lists the minimum efficient scale (MES) of operation in units of output produced. For each industry, the table also compares plant-level MES to total U.S. demand. The last column presents the rise in unit production cost if a given plant operating at MES shrinks to one-third its original size.

Industry	Minimum Efficient Scale (MES)	Percentage of U.S. Demand	Percentage by which Unit Cost Rises at One-Third MES
Beer Brewing	4.5 million (31 U.S. gallon) barrels per year capacity	3.4%	5.0%
Cigarettes	36 billion cigarettes per year; 2,275 employees	6.6	2.2
Cotton and Synthetic Broad-Woven Fabrics	37.5 million square yards per year; 600 employees in modern integrated plants	0.2	7.6
Paints	10 million U.S. gallons per year; 450 employees	1.4	4.4
Petroleum Refining	200,000 (42 U.S.-gallon) barrels per day crude oil processing capacity	1.9	4.8
Non-Rubber Shoes	1 million pairs per year; 250 employees on single-shift operation	0.2	1.5
Glass Bottles	133,000 tons per year; 1,000 employees	1.5	11.0
Portland Cement	7 million 376-pound barrels per year capacity	1.7	26.0
Integrated Steel	4 million tons per year capacity	2.6	11.0
Anti-Friction Bearings	800 employees	1.4	8.0
Refrigerators	800,000 units per year	14.1	6.5
Automobile Storage Batteries	1 million units per year; 300 employees	1.9	4.6

Source: F.M. Scherer, *Industrial Market Structure and Economic Performance,* Chicago: Rand McNally College Publishing, 1980, pp. 96–97.

Table 3-2   Large Business- and Small Business-Dominated Industries in 1987

The table lists industries dominated by large firms (column 1), as measured by their share of total industry employment (column 2), and industries dominated by small firms (column 3), as measured by their share of total industry employment (column 4).

Large Business-Dominated Industry	Large Firms' Share of Employment	Small Business-Dominated Industry	Small Firms' Share of Employment
Tobacco Manufacturers	98.3	Miscellaneous Repair Services	97.3
General Merchandise Stores	95.3	Special Trade Contractors	94.5
Petroleum and Coal Products	93.2	Automotive Dealers and Service Stations	92.6
Transportation Equipment	92.1	Legal Services	92.2
Instruments and Related Products	83.5	General Building Contractors	87.8
Chemicals and Allied Products	83.2	Wholesale Trade: Durable Goods	87.4
Paper and Allied Products	77.0	Automotive Repair, Services, and Parking	84.3
Metal Mining	76.6	Personal Services	80.3
Primary Metal Industries	74.9	Wholesale Trade: Nondurable Goods	80.2
Electrical and Electronic Equipment	73.9	Furniture and Home Furnishing Stores	80.1

Table 3-2   (continued)

Large Business-Dominated Industry	Large Firms' Share of Employment	Small Business-Dominated Industry	Small Firms' Share of Employment
Food and Kindred Products	72.4	Amusement and Recreation Services	77.4
Textile Mill Products	72.0	Building Materials and Garden Supplies	75.9
Coal Mining	62.0	Engineering and Architectural Services	72.9

Source: The State of Small Business: A Report of the President, Washington, D.C.: United States Government Printing Office, 1992, pp. 76 and 85.

The Mismatch Between Optimal Firm Size and Family Wealth

Without pooling to aggregate household wealth to fund enterprises, firm size would be constrained by the wealth under the control of a single household. Pooling relieves society of this limitation, bridging firms' capital needs and households' investing needs. To document the degree that pooling addresses the mismatch between household wealth and firm size, we examine the capacity of individual households to fund enterprises, both now and decades ago.

Table 3-3 compares the external funds required by the largest publicly owned U.S. enterprises in 1992 with the wealth of the nation's richest families.[4] If each firm had to rely on a single household for its external financial requirements, virtually none of the largest U.S. firms could exist. For example, America's wealthiest family, the Waltons of Wal-Mart fame, with wealth of approximately $25 billion, could not provide enough financing for any of the top 48 firms in the United States.[5] Of the top 200 publicly traded firms, only three (Minnesota Mining and Manufacturing,

---

4. See Appendix A for a discussion of these data.
5. Of course, were they not able to pool and obtain initial capital from others, many wealthy families would have been unable to amass their wealth.

Table 3-3 Firm Size and the Wealthiest U.S. Family Units in 1991

The table presents the identity and wealth of the richest American families in 1991, and the largest firm whose entire market capitalization (including long- and short-term debt and equity) they could fund completely. The column "Rank" gives the firm rank based on the market capitalization of U.S. firms in 1991, with smaller numbers representing larger firms.

Family Name	1991 Wealth ($ billions)	Largest Firm Family Could Finance Completely	
		Rank	Name
Walton	24.9	49	Minnesota Mining & Manufacturing Co.
Du Pont	8.6	161	Conagra Inc.
Mars	8.0	170	Amerada Hess Corp.
Gates	6.4	207	Corestates Financial Corp.
Kluge	5.9	221	American Stores Co.
Newhouse	5.6	229	Upjohn Co.
Bass	5.1	253	Marion Merrell Dow Inc.
Rockefeller	5.0	259	Blockbuster Entertainment Corp.
Cargill	5.0	260	Medco Containment Services Inc.
Pritzker	4.6	287	Borden Inc.
Buffett	4.4	300	Morton International Inc.
Hearst	4.4	301	United Healthcare Corp.
Mellon	4.3	311	Hercules Inc.
Allen	4.1	321	Galen Health Care Inc.
Cox	4.0	329	Louisiana-Pacific Corp.
Wexner	3.7	347	Fluor Corp.
Koch	3.6	358	USAir Group
Hillman	3.3	378	Wrigley (Wm.) Jr Co.
Arison	3.3	379	Deluxe Corp.
Redstone	3.2	386	Aflac Inc.
Tisch	2.9	409	Nordstrom Inc.
Phipps	2.5	447	Sigma-Aldrich
Packard	2.4	459	Burlington Industries
Perot	2.2	491	Harris Corp.
Crown	2.1	508	Maxus Energy Corp.
Haas	2.1	509	Avery Dennison Corp.
Murdoch	2.0	524	Multimedia Inc.
Dorrance	2.0	525	Kansas City Southern Industries
Turner	2.0	526	Hawaiian Electric Industries
Scripps	1.8	560	Giant Food Inc.
Wattis	1.8	561	Costco Wholesale Corporation
Lauder	1.8	562	Ecolab Inc.
Annenberg	1.7	584	Illinois Central Corp.
Hall	1.7	585	Minnesota Power & Light
Stephens	1.7	586	Goodrich (B.F.) Co.
Simplot	1.7	587	Trinity Industries

Table 3-3 (continued)

Family Name	1991 Wealth ($ billions)	Largest Firm Family Could Finance Completely	
		Rank	Name
Ford	1.7	588	Comsat Corp.
Knight	1.6	604	Asarco Inc.
Bancroft	1.6	605	St Joe Paper Co.
Hillenbrand	1.6	606	MGM Grand Inc.
Fisher	1.6	607	Synoptics Communications Inc.
Van Andel	1.5	632	King World Productions Inc.
Blaustein	1.5	633	Dreyfus Corp.
Perelman	1.5	634	Provident Life & Accident
DeVos	1.5	635	Heilig-Meyers Co.
Gund	1.5	636	American National Insurance
Milliken	1.5	637	Cracker Barrel Old Country Store
Chandler	1.4	653	Kaufman & Broad
LeFrak	1.4	654	Lafarge Corp.
McCaw	1.4	655	IES Industries Inc.
Kerkorian	1.4	656	Informix Corp.
DeBartolo	1.4	657	Mark IV Industries Inc.
Hewlett	1.4	658	Noble Affiliates Inc.
Taubman	1.3	680	Universal Corp-Va
Hunt	1.3	681	Thomas & Betts Corp.
Davis	1.3	682	IMC Fertilizer Group
Heyman	1.3	683	Penn Traffic Co.
Helmsley	1.3	684	Catellus Development Corp.
Smith	1.3	685	Reliance Electric Co.
Bechtel	1.3	686	Fingerhut Companies Inc.
Kroc	1.3	687	Tandem Computers Inc.
Ziff	1.3	688	Stryker Corp.
Busch	1.3	689	Ball Corp.
Getty	1.3	690	Kaiser Aluminum Corp.
Gallo	1.3	691	Cintas Corp.
Hoiles	1.2	710	Nerco Inc.
Disney	1.2	711	Triton Energy Corp.
Field	1.2	712	Dean Foods Co.
Johnson, S.	1.2	713	Trinova Corp.
Stern	1.2	714	Plum Creek Timber Co.
Ludwig	1.2	715	IP Timberlands
Icahn	1.2	716	Tidewater Inc.
Reynolds	1.1	743	Nacco Industries
Johnson, E.	1.1	744	Adobe Systems Inc.
Mandel	1.1	745	Commonwealth Energy System
Murdock	1.1	746	Warnaco Group Inc.
Gaylord	1.1	747	RPM Inc-Ohio

Table 3-3 (continued)

| Family Name | 1991 Wealth ($ billions) | Largest Firm Family Could Finance Completely | |
		Rank	Name
Bren	1.1	748	Orange & Rockland Utilities
Geffen	1.1	749	Central Hudson Gas and Electric
Fribourg	1.1	750	Carter-Wallace Inc.
Carlson	1.0	780	Clark Equipment Co.
Collier	1.0	781	Ferro Corp.
Cooke	1.0	782	Autodesk Inc.
Rudin	1.0	783	Scripps Howard Broadcasting
Malone	1.0	784	Family Dollar Stores
Brown	1.0	785	Wesco Financial Corp.
Dayton	1.0	786	Belo (A.H.) Corp.
Anschutz	1.0	787	First Brands Corp.
Lilly	1.0	788	Cilcorp Inc.
Reed	1.0	789	TNP Enterprises Inc.
Hill	1.0	790	Coors (Adolph)
Nordstrom	1.0	791	Hanna (M.A.) Co.
Kleberg	1.0	792	Pacificare Health Systems

Source: Losee (1992), and Seneker (1992).
Note: For details on the methods used to create this table, see Appendix A.

ConAgra, and Amerada Hess) could be funded completely by any single family.

Figure 3-2 shows the percentage of external funding requirements that could be provided by matching wealthy families to corporations one-to-one, broken down by the size of enterprise being funded. In the aggregate, without pooling, only 11.7% of U.S. firms with external capital needs exceeding $1 billion could be funded by single U.S. families.

The mismatch between household wealth and firm size is a long-standing feature of the U.S. economy. A comparison of U.S. family wealth and enterprise size in 1924, detailed in Appendix B and summarized in Table 3-4, reveals the robustness and importance of the pooling function. Of the largest 150 firms in the United States in 1924, only about one-third could have been funded by the wealth of individual families. The disparity between household wealth and firm size has widened; over seven decades, wealthy households have become less able to fund the nation's largest enterprises. Firms have grown faster than the wealth of even the richest families, as changes in technology, transportation, and labor have increased minimum efficient scales and the financial system has supported greater pooling.

Figure 3-2   The Relative Size of Largest U.S. Firms and the
Wealthiest U.S. Families

The chart depicts the percentage of the funding needs of U.S. firms with enterprise
value of $1 billion or more that could be provided by individual U.S. households with
wealth of $1 billion or more, as of 1991. For example, there were $239 billion of firms
with size $3–$4 billion, and of these, 9% of their financial needs could be met by families
with wealth greater than $1 billion.

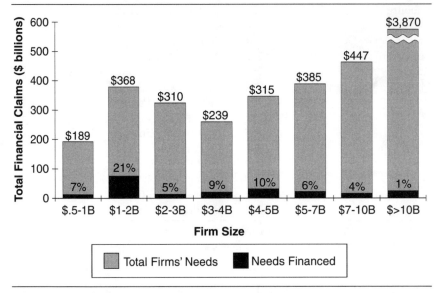

For details on the methods used to create this chart, see Appendix A.

The gap between household wealth and enterprise scale is a worldwide
phenomenon. Figure 3-3 summarizes information on the wealthiest families and largest enterprises in 22 countries. In virtually every country, single wealthy families can fund less than one-fourth of the capital needs of
firms with total external financial needs of $1 billion. In highly industri-
alized countries like Japan, wealthiest households can support less than 2%
of large firms' financial needs. These international imbalances of wealth
and enterprise size can be supported only by substantial pooling of funds,
both within and among countries.

The Effect of Pooling on Social and Private Welfare

Were firms not free to enter into multiple bilateral contracts, there would
be social losses due to lower output and higher unit production costs, as
well as substantial redistribution of wealth. Table 3-5 gives some indica-
tion of the magnitude of the social costs by examining the impact on a

Table 3-4 U.S. Family Wealth and U.S. Firm Size in 1924

The table lists the identities and wealth of the richest U.S. families in 1924, and the identity of the largest U.S. firm they could fund completely. Wealth figures are expressed in 1924 dollars. The column "Rank" gives the firm rank based on the market capitalization of U.S. firms in 1924, with smaller numbers representing larger firms.

Family Name	1924 Wealth ($ millions)	Largest Firm Family Could Finance Completely	
		Rank	Name
Rockefeller	$1,077	2	New York Central Railroad
Morgan Inner Group	728	4	AT&T
Ford	660	8	Chicago, Milwaukee & St. Paul Railway Co.
Harkness	451	13	Erie RR Co.
Mellon	450	14	Chicago & North Western Railway Co.
Vanderbilt	360	19	Illinois Central Railroad Co.
Standard Oil Group	356	20	Cities Service
Whitney	322	21	Chicago, Rock Isl. & Pacific Railway Co.
Du Pont	239	28	Denver & Rio Grande Railroad Co.
Mc Cormick	211	30	Wabash Railway Co.
Baker	210	31	Pennsylvania Co.
Fisher	194	35	Swift & Co.
Guggenheim	190	36	American Smelting & Refining
Field	180	38	Pacific Gas & Electric
Curtis-Bok	174	43	Cleveland, Cinncinati, Chicago & St. Louis Railway Co.
Duke	156	48	Chile Copper
Berwind	150	49	Minneapolis, St. Paul & Sault St. Marie Railway Co.
Lehman	129	58	Spokane, Portland & Seattle Ry Co.
Widener	119	62	Sears, Roebuck
Reynold	117	63	Standard Oil (California)
Astor	114	64	Ford Motor
Timken	111	66	American Can
Ryan	108	69	Pere Marquette Railway Co.
Foster	106	71	K.C. Southern Railway Co.
Winthrop	104	74	Colorado & Southern Railway Co.
Stillman	102	75	Singer Manufacturing
Pitcairn	100	77	Texas & Pacific Railway Co.
Warburg	97	81	Western Pacific Railroad Co.
Metcalf	91	87	Michigan Central Railroad Co.
Clark	90	88	International Harvester
Phipp	89	90	Chicago & Eastern Illinois Railroad

Table 3-4   (continued)

Family Name	1924 Wealth ($ millions)	Largest Firm Family Could Finance Completely	
		Rank	Name
Kahn	86	96	Gulf Oil
Johnson	75	104	National City Bank of N.Y.
Green	72	106	Mexican Petroleum
James	72	107	Atlantic Gulf & West Indies Steamship
Nash	66	116	Cuba Cane Sugar
Schiff	66	117	Deere & Co.
Patterson	61	119	Baldwin Locomotive Works
Hayden	60	121	Associated Oil
Patten	60	122	Union Oil of California
Blumenthal	54	126	National Lead
Tafts	54	127	Atlantic Refining
Weber	54	128	International Nickel
Deering	50	131	Vacuum Oil
Mills	48	134	General Chemical
Cochran	42	137	Inland Steel
Friedsam	42	138	Magnolia Petroleum
Higgins	42	139	Cudahy Packing
McLean	42	140	RJ Reynolds Tobacco
De Forest	41	141	Youngstown Sheet & Tube
Baruch	38	142	Procter & Gamble
Kirkwood	38	143	Chase National Bank
Tyson	36	144	Aluminum Company of America
Huntington	35	145	Great Northern Iron Ore
Storrow	35	146	WR Grace

Source: Ferdinand Lundberg, *America's 60 Families,* New York: The Vanguard Press, 1937, pp. 26–27.

Note: For details on the methods used to create this table, see Appendix B.

single industry, were pooling to be forbidden. We compare the current worldwide automobile industry with the wealth of the wealthiest families around the globe. Even if the wealthiest families funded the auto industry to the exclusion of all others, the largest auto producer that could be supported would be Fiat, with annual unit production of under two million cars and trucks. There would be no firms the size of General Motors, Ford, Toyota, or Nissan. According to one study of economies of scale in the auto industry, even the largest automaker in a no-pooling world would fail to achieve minimum efficient scale in either research

Figure 3-3 International Firm Size and International Family Wealth

The chart displays the percentage of the funding needs of firms with enterprise value of $1 billion or more that could be provided by individual domestic households with wealth of $1 billion or more in 1991.

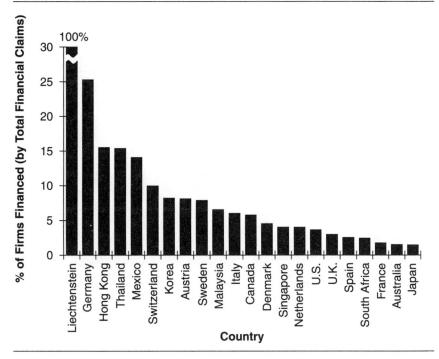

Note: For details on the methods used to create this chart, see Appendix A.

and development or financing.[6] Furthermore, a greater share of the world's autos would be produced by firms smaller than Fiat, which would fail to meet MES in production activities, causing consumers to pay more for the equivalent quality of car.[7]

Pooling also plays a critical role in the distribution of wealth. Without pooling, an initial skewed distribution of household wealth would create

6. Rhys (1989) uses statistical analyses to estimate minimum efficient scales (MES) for ten activities in the auto industry. MES ranges from 250,000 units for painting, to 1 million units for engine block casting, to 5 million units for research and development.
7. Compensating mechanisms would certainly evolve in a no-pooling auto industry. Smaller firms could specialize and vertically integrate by coordinating their activities to capture the appropriate economies at each step of the production process. Yet it is reasonable to speculate that auto consumers would be served more poorly by this fragmented industry structure that incurred higher transactions and coordination costs.

Table 3-5 The World Auto Industry and World Family Wealth

The table contrasts the size and output of the largest 15 passenger car manufacturers in the world with the assets of the world's wealthiest families in 1991. The table indicates that the largest four auto manufacturers could not be funded by any single family unit.

Company Name	1992 Units Produced (000s)	Country	Total Financial Claims ($ billion)	Hypothetical Funding Family	Wealth ($ bil.)	Country
General Motors	7,146	USA	$141.5	none		
Ford Motor	5,764	USA	126.9	none		
Toyota Motor	4,696	JPN	74.0	none		
Nissan	2,983	JPN	44.8	none		
Fiat	2,231	ITA	34.8	Sultan Waddaulah	$37.0	Brunei
Chrysler	2,159	USA	32.5	none		
Daimler-Benz	688	DEU	26.7	none		
Honda	1,828	JPN	21.7	Walton	24.9	United States
Volkswagen	3,499	DEU	19.7	none		
Mitsubishi Motors	1,832	JPN	13.4	none		
BMW	580	DEU	10.6	Mori	13.0	Japan
Mazda	1,460	JPN	10.4	Queen Elizabeth	11.7	U.K.
Isuzu Motors	473	JPN	9.6	Tsutsumi	10.0	Japan
Peugeot	2,050	FRA	9.2	King Fahd	10.0	Saudi Arabia
Volvo	123	SWE	8.3	Du Pont	8.6	United States

Source: Ward's Automotive Yearbook 1993, Ward's Automotive, Southfield, MI, 59, and *Automotive News,* May 26, 1993, p. 3, Compustat Global Vantage.
Note: See Appendix A for more details.

a similar distribution of enterprise size. Yet, if economies of scale existed, larger firms could earn supernormal profits in a system where prices are set by higher-cost smaller competitors. Over time, these higher profits might allow large firms to grow even larger and more profitable, exacerbating disparities in firm size or permitting large firms to drive small firms out of business. The richer firms would grow richer, as would the richer households. As poorer households could not join together to fund competitive firms, the initial uneven distribution of wealth would grow more pronounced.

Pooling, however, allows funds to flow from less wealthy households to large efficient businesses, permitting poorer citizens to benefit as part-owners of these profitable firms. Similarly, it permits funds to flow to capital-starved enterprises, allowing entrepreneurs with good projects but little cash to operate their firms at more efficient scales. As returns accrue to successful entrepreneurs, wealth imbalances are reduced through market forces. Through pooling, financial markets simultaneously affect both industry structure and income distribution.

The social benefits of pooling come at a cost. Multiple bilateral contracts produce a dispersed ownership base. The greater the degree of pooling or dispersion of ownership, the greater the problems of asymmetric information. As households own smaller fractions of a larger number of the productive enterprises, their incentives to monitor each firm fall and they prefer to free-ride in the costly monitoring of others. Managers can take actions unobservable to, and not in the best interests of, outside investors (the moral-hazard problem), or they may be able to disguise important information (adverse selection). Although these problems exist in a world without pooling, they are likely to be exacerbated by pooling and diffuse ownership.[8]

Alternative Forms of Pooling Capital

From a firm's perspective, the extent to which its capital is widely held—the degree of pooling—has important implications. Research shows that firms can increase their market value by increasing the number of investors knowledgeable about the firm. Merton (1987) demonstrates that, in a world of imperfect information, increasing the number of investors (or, in our terminology, increasing the amount of pooling) reduces a firm's cost of capital and increases its market value. This benefit arises through

---

8. Jensen (1993) argues that the largest firms may actually be less efficient than small firms, citing firms like General Motors with inadequate corporate governance systems that may have squandered shareholder money.

Table 3-6   Sources of Capital for Privately Owned Enterprises

Type	Debt Capital	Equity Capital
Internal Sources	Loans from owners	Capital stock of the founder(s) or the proprietor's equity Retained earnings of the firm
Informal External Sources	Loans from family members and friends Trade credit from suppliers and customers	Investment by individuals as informal participants
Financial Intermediaries	Lending by depository or nondepository financial institutions Secured or unsecured debt	Venture capital European-Style Investment Corporations (ESIC)
Public Markets	Bond issues Asset securitization	Common and preferred stock issues

Source: Adapted from *The State of Small Business: A Report of the President,* Washington, D.C.: United States Government Printing Office, 1992, p. 265.

improvements in the quality and quantity of information available to potential investors.

Other forces lead firms to seek narrow investor bases. Firms may face increasing marginal costs of identifying additional numbers of investors; at the extreme, the transactions costs of finding one million investors, each contributing $100, are likely to be substantially more than the costs of finding a smaller number of larger investors. Increasing the size of its investor base also tends to drive a firm toward ever-more-distant investors. As larger distances must be spanned—both in terms of geography and in terms of initial knowledge of the firm—the cost of raising funds increases. (Chapter 4 discusses the link between geographical separation and higher costs, and Chapter 7 deals with the relationship between informational distances and costs.)

There are a variety of specific means by which pooling is accomplished. Table 3-6 shows various pooling mechanisms, characterized by the source of pooled funds and the type of claim issued. To fund its needs, a firm may rely on some or all of these pooling vehicles. Fund sources differ by their increasing distance, crudely measured, from the current investor base. A firm can raise money from its existing owners, from noninvestors who have private knowledge about the firm or its owners, from financial intermediaries, from broad clienteles who respond to offerings in public markets, or from the government (which in turn raises its funds through taxation). Investors may be knowledgeable venture capitalists, family members or friends, traditional intermediaries like banks or insurance companies, a widespread clientele of households and mutual funds responding to a public offering, or the government (through specific research funding or issue of guarantees). These diverse institutions all fulfill the pooling function, albeit in different forms, benefits, and costs.

Table 3-7 presents a snapshot of extent to which firms rely upon external financing (or pooled funds) in the United States and in nine developing countries. An International Finance Corporation study finds that, to fund their growth, firms in less developed countries use far more external financing (pooling) than do firms in developed nations. In Korea, for instance, 85% of the large-firm growth between 1970 and 1984 was funded by externally generated funds, but externally generated capital (pooled funds) funded only 24% of large-firm needs in the United States [Singh and Hamid (1992)].

In communist and socialist regimes, governments are the primary pooling mechanisms, centralizing capital raising (taxation), investment (central planning), and management activities. This centralization of pooling has costs, most notably inefficient resource allocation and inadequate monitoring. Recent experience in privatizing much of the wealth in postcommunist Central and Eastern Europe shows that the transition away from government pooling mechanism has not been trouble-free. Poland's and Czechoslovakia's attempts to restructure their country's pooling mechanisms have had to contend with low private savings levels and an attendant disparity between household wealth and necessary enterprise size. Because households have insufficient resources to buy all of the national productive capacity outright, shares in the nation's firms have been distributed to households through asset sales, leases, and voucher systems.

These economies' pooling needs have been addressed by governmental fiat, as the government distributed enterprise ownership to its citizens through multiple bilateral contracts. At the same time, banks and private intermediaries resembling mutual funds arose to collect the households' vouchers and, in turn, issue them shares in funds—multilateral pooling vehicles. These mutual fund-like intermediaries deliver informa-

Table 3-7 Capital Structures and Funding Sources of Selected Countries

For the largest 50 companies in each country, the table lists the after-tax retention ratio and the percent of growth financed by internal funds (retained earnings), long-term debt, and external equity.[1] (The fractions do not sum to 1.00 across each row because funding of short-term liabilities is omitted.)

Country	Years	After-tax Retention Ratio	Internal Finance	External Long-Term Debt	External Equity
				Sources of Funds	
United States	1970–79	0.60[2]	0.52	0.21	0.03
Korea	1980–87	0.59	0.12	0.45	0.40
Pakistan	1980–86	0.46	0.58	0.16	0.12
Mexico	1984–88	NA	0.17	0.03	0.76
India	1980–88	0.67	0.36	0.46	0.11
Turkey	1982–87	0.24	0.18	0.16	0.61
Malaysia	1983–87	0.45	0.42	0.02	0.31
Jordan	1980–87	0.40	0.06	0.16	0.12
Thailand	1983–87	0.47	0.17	0.16	0.84
Zimbabwe	1980–88	0.61	0.58	0.00	0.43

Source: "Corporate Financing Decisions in Developing Countries," A. Singh and J. Hamid, Technical Paper, International Finance Corporation, 1992, p. 11 and p. 43.

1. The number of firms in Jordan and Turkey is 35 and 38, respectively. The data for the United States are for a larger (unspecified) number of firms.

2. These data are for 1970–1984.

tion gathering, monitoring, and liquidity services to their shareholders. The move from multiple bilateral contracts to multilateral pooling also illustrates the "innovation spiral," as the innovation of vouchers provided the raw material from which another new product (funds) was created.

Pooling's role in support of large-scale efficient enterprise is clear. Without a means to draw upon the resources of multiple households, firms would be forced to operate at considerably reduced and less efficient scales. Consumers and producers would suffer because prices would be higher and output lower than in a world where firms could expand by aggregating capital. Although it imposes costs due to the dispersion of ownership, pooling is the bridge between small households and large firms. It provides small firms with access to capital, and small savers with access to attractive investments.

The Demand for Pooling by Households: Efficient Liquidity and Diversification

Even if firms could operate at efficient scales without pooling, households' independent demands for pooling would ensure its role in the financial system. Without pooling, households could own only assets that they could buy in totality. All but the wealthiest households would have a single investment, or at most a few. We have already seen how, without pooling, poorer households would be denied opportunities to invest in the largest, most profitable, firms. Equally important, pooling permits households to have many small investments instead of a few large holdings, improves their ability to meet liquidity needs, and (through multilateral pooling vehicles) permits low-cost diversification and monitoring.

Diversification

Individuals tend to be risk-averse in that they prefer to bear less variation in return for any given expected return. Variation in return, or risk, can be reduced through diversification, whereby investors spread their wealth among a large number of imperfectly correlated ventures rather than concentrating on a small number of firms. Diversification lowers the overall variability or risk of a portfolio's return without lowering its expected return.[9] In a practical sense, diversification—especially low-cost diversification—would not be attainable without pooling as accomplished through multilateral contracts.

Without multiple bilateral contracts, real assets would be indivisible. As a result, households with modest wealth would be forced to invest in one, or at most a few, small enterprises, exposing themselves to significant nonsystematic risk.[10] They could not invest in a broad portfolio that

---

9. Diversification is an important component of portfolio theory, which was developed by Markowitz (1959). For diversification to be of benefit to investors, assets in the portfolio must be less than perfectly correlated. In general, the less correlated the assets, the greater the potential gains to diversification. A fully diversified portfolio is one that retains only market risk, which is the sensitivity of assets to economy-wide fluctuations. A fully diversified portfolio is insensitive to firm-specific events such as strikes and bankruptcies.

10. In a frictionless market described by the Capital Asset Pricing Model (CAPM), investors are not compensated for bearing diversifiable or nonsystematic risk, as the investors can

would permit them to shed firm-specific or idiosyncratic risk. It would appear as if asset divisibility alone—or the existence of multiple bilateral contracts—would provide households with the diversification they demand. To see this, assume firms issue debt or equity in denominations small enough to be purchased by most households. Households could diversify their holdings by purchasing claims of a large number of firms. Were there no transactions or information-gathering costs, were shares completely divisible, and were managing a portfolio of securities effortless, every household could create a fully diversified portfolio.

Yet there are a multitude of costs and other frictions.[11] Some costs arise from fixed costs of trading, such as processing and "ticket" charges by brokers who execute trades on behalf of clients. The presence of fixed charges makes it more expensive for an individual to buy $1,000 each of ten securities than $10,000 of one security. Other charges, like the bid–ask spread, are more subtle: the "lemons" problem, encountered by buyers and sellers of used cars, is a factor in the cost of buying securities too. Sellers of stock tend to have information about poor future prospects for that firm; buyers of stock will have the opposite. This leads naturally to an information-induced "spread" between the buy (ask) and the sell (bid) price for a security, a type of transactions cost.

If transactions costs are included in the pooling calculus, small households' ability to diversify on their own becomes more problematic. Households must trade off transactions costs associated with a large number of small holdings with the benefits that stem from full diversification. If a household puts all its wealth into one stock, it can minimize its direct transactions costs. Yet this household will fall far short of creating a diversified portfolio. Alternatively, holding its wealth constant, the household could buy small amounts of many tradable assets and incur larger transactions cost per dollar of wealth invested. *Gross of costs*, such a portfolio is more likely to deliver the mean and variance of a well-diversified portfolio; transactions costs, however, can offset or eliminate the benefits of diversification.

The *gross* benefits of diversification (before deducting transactions costs) are graphed in Figure 3-4. Using a historic series of returns on New York

---

eliminate this risk costlessly through diversification. In a market with transactions costs, asset returns may compensate investors for holding a poorly diversified portfolio [Mayshar (1979)]. Our analysis, however, assumes that investors are not adequately compensated for bearing diversifiable risk.

11. Academic theory has attempted to explore the effect of market imperfections on equilibrium asset prices, portfolio choice, and social welfare. For examples, see Mayshar (1979) or Merton (1987).

Figure 3-4   The Effect of Portfolio Diversification

The chart shows the standard deviation of a portfolio's return as the number of securities in the portfolio increases. After about 40 securities, the portfolio risk flattens out and approaches 19% per year.

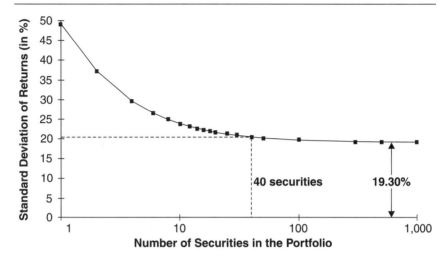

Stock Exchange equities as an example, we show how a portfolio's standard deviation of returns, which is a measure of its riskiness, falls as the number of securities in the portfolio increases. For example, with four stocks the portfolio has a standard deviation of 30% per year. Notice that, as the number of stocks increases, the standard deviation falls until it levels off at 19.3% per year, which is the variance of the equity market as a whole. The majority of the variance reduction is achieved by holding around 40 securities, the "minimum efficient scale" to form a fully diversified portfolio. This portfolio, on the basis of its standard deviation, is about as risky as a fully diversified market, and can be expected to deliver the same expected return.

   Can individual investors achieve this degree of diversification in a world with pooling at the corporate level, realistic transactions costs, and no multilateral pooling (financial intermediaries such as banks or mutual funds)?[12] To answer this question empirically, we examine the transactions costs borne by five representative households who each purchase a portfolio of 40 equities. Each representative household has total wealth (net worth) equal to each of the five net worth quintiles of the U.S. population.

---

12. The analysis here is in the spirit of Statman (1987).

Table 3-8   The Transactions Costs of Acquiring a Portfolio of 40 Common Stocks

The table tabulates the transactions costs of directly creating diversified equity portfolios of 40 stocks for households. The households are divided into quintiles based on median household income. The table shows family net worth, the amount invested per firm, number of shares per firm (assuming an average of $40/share), and commissions based on currently quoted discount broker rates.*

Quintile	Net Worth ($)	Investment Per Company (40 companies)($)	Number of Shares per Company	Round-trip Commission ($)	Commissions Paid per $ Invested (%)
bottom	$ 4,324	$ 108.10	2.7	$3,120	72%
2	19,694	492.35	12.3	3,120	16
3	28,044	701.10	17.5	3,352	12
4	46,253	1,156.33	28.9	3,972	9
top	111,770	2,794.25	69.9	5,956	5

*Households are grouped into five quintiles by income using data from the U.S. Department of Commerce's Survey of Income and Program Participation in *Household Wealth and Asset Ownership: 1988* (U.S. Government Printing Office, 1990). For each of these quintiles, median net worth is reported (Table B, p. 3), repeated above in the first column. This net worth was invested in 40 firms, assuming an average price per share of $40, before commissions, with a per-company dollar investment and number of shares purchased reported in the second and third columns. The round-trip commission costs for purchasing this number and dollar amount of shares are calculated on the basis of commission schedule for a major U.S. discount brokerage firm, using current rates, and reported in the fourth and fifth columns.

Thus, the poorest household has total net worth of $4,324, and the wealthiest has net worth of about $112,000. For each household, we calculate how many shares of each of the 40 firms they will own, given an average stock price of $40 per share. Round-trip commissions are reported on the basis of recent retail quotations given by a major discount brokerage.

The results are shown in Table 3-8; it shows that transactions costs to establish a 40-firm portfolio are high, in an absolute sense. For the median investor, over 12% of net worth is consumed in commissions alone. Were bid–ask spreads and recurring charges such as portfolio rebalancing costs and custodial fees included, the costs of creating a 40-stock portfolio would be even higher. Clearly a household with net worth less than $50,000 would pay dearly to attempt to create a 40-stock diversified portfolio.

Instead of buying shares in 40 firms, the five households might elect to buy stocks only in units of round lots (groups of 100 shares), thereby minimizing transactions costs, although at the expense of poorer diver-

Table 3-9 Household Wealth, Transactions Costs, and Diversification

The table presents the total cost of buying a portfolio of stocks, subject to the constraint that shares are only purchased in units of round lots. The second column lists the number of round lots purchased and the third column the standard deviation of the resulting portfolio. The fourth column presents the difference in expected return between this portfolio and a levered position in a fully diversified equity portfolio with the same total risk. It is essentially the market penalty for bearing undiversified risk. The return reduction and the commission costs are combined in the last column to give the all-in economic cost of holding such a portfolio compared to holding a costless fully diversified equity mutual fund.*

Quintile	Median Net Worth ($)	Number of Round Lots Purchased	Standard Deviation of Portfolio	Penalty for Undiversified Risk in (%)	Round Trip Commissions ($)	Round Trip Commissions (%)	Total Cost with 7-year Holding Period (%)
bottom	$ 4,324	1.1	48.0	9.26%	$ 170	3.93%	9.82%
2	19,694	4.9	28.3	2.91	$ 808	4.10	3.49
3	28,044	7.0	25.8	2.11	1,154	4.11	2.69
4	46,253	11.6	23.8	1.46	1,912	4.13	2.05
top	111,770	27.9	21.1	0.58	4,598	4.11	1.16

*Households are grouped into five quintiles by income using data from the U.S. Department of Commerce's Survey of Income and Program Participation in *Household Wealth and Asset Ownership: 1988* (U.S. Government Printing Office, 1990). For each of these quintiles, median net worth is reported (Table B, p. 3), and reported above in the first column. This net worth is divided into round-lots of 100 shares, at an average price of $40 per share, or $4,000 per round lot, giving the number of round lots purchased in column 2. The standard deviation of a portfolio with that number of different firms was calculated according to the methodology in Statman (1987) and is given in column 3. The fourth column reports the return that investors would demand if forced to bear this higher level of risk, calculated consistent with Statman's analysis. The fifth and sixth columns give the commissions paid to execute this strategy, using the current commission schedule of a major U.S. retail discount brokerage firm. The final column represents the annualized cost of the strategy, assuming a seven-year holding period. This cost is the annual return reduction (column 4) plus one-seventh of the round-trip commissions (column 6).

sification.[13] If this strategy is followed, the median investor could buy less than seven round lots (see Table 3-9). The median investor would face a standard deviation of 25.8% per year, higher than the risk of a fully diversified index. Assuming that the market does not price diversifiable

13. The existence of round-lot costs is a peculiarity of the U.S. institutional structure. More generally, any cost structure that has both a fixed and a variable component, such as a fixed "ticket" charge as well as a "per share" charge, will exhibit this concavity over order quantity.

risk, the household is uncompensated for being less than fully diversified; the additional 6.5% of variation is a cost borne by the risk-averse investor. Because of wealth constraints, the investor is unable to lower this residual excess risk.

We can quantify the cost of this additional risk by comparing the partially diversified portfolio of round lots to a fully diversified index portfolio constructed to entail minimal transactions costs, such as an index mutual fund. If we borrow money and invest in the index fund, we can achieve the same risk (standard deviation) as the investor's partially diversified portfolio. The partially diversified portfolio involves the same amount of risk as the levered index fund, but provides no additional return above the market return, because the risk arises through underdiversification, not leverage. The difference in returns is the economic cost of partial diversification.

To estimate the magnitude of this cost, assume a riskless rate of 2% per year, and a return on the S&P 500 of 6.2% per year above the risk-free rate. By borrowing 34 cents for every dollar invested in the index, we can construct a levered fully diversified portfolio with an identical standard deviation as the partially diversified one. The return of this portfolio is 10.3% (2% + 6.2% × 1.34). The difference of 2.1 percentage points over 8.2% is the cost of partial diversification; that is, an individual could lever the index portfolio by 34%, take on the same risk as produced in the partially diversified portfolio, and receive 2.1 percentage points more return. Notice in the fourth column of Table 3-9 that the penalty for undiversified risk then drops to as low as 58 basis points for the wealthiest individuals but is as high as 926 basis points for the lowest net worth category. The last two columns of the table show the estimated round-trip commissions for the position and the total annualized cost of investing, assuming a seven-year holding period typical of mutual fund investors.[14]

These back-of-the-envelope calculations have several immediate implications for businesses that provide pooling services, such as mutual funds or unit trusts. By comparing the multilateral pooling vehicles to the alternatives consumers can construct using only bilateral contracts, we can calculate how much consumers should be willing to pay to achieve a fully diversified portfolio. A provider of pure pooling services could, in the absence of competition, charge between 116 and 982 basis points of return *per year* for providing a diversified equity portfolio, and be cheaper than consumers' other alternatives. Because the average mutual fund account size is about $11,000, the extra charge would seem to be closer to

---

14. From Sirri and Tufano (1993a), this is taken as the ratio of aggregate annual mutual fund redemptions to the aggregate size of funds.

Figure 3-5 Relative Costs of Diversification, Commissions, and Mutual Funds

The chart illustrates the cost of producing diversification through the direct purchase of equity securities or through the purchase of indexed mutual funds for a U.S. investor seeking $100,000 of equity exposure. The costs of direct holdings include lack of diversification and commissions. The cost of the representative indexed mutual fund is simply the annual expense ratio of the fund.

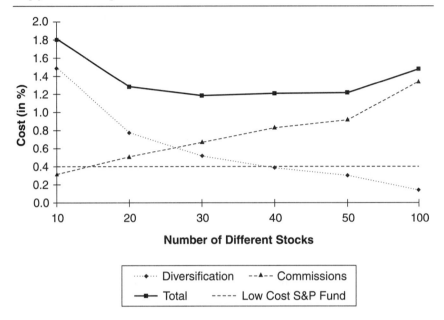

the high end of the scale.[15] For the median investor with net worth of $28,044, annual costs of 2.69% amount to $750 per year. With around 80 million households in the United States, this suggests that households seeking diversification on their own would incur costs of $60 billion per year, which could be reduced dramatically through multilateral pooling vehicles. The figure is meant to be suggestive rather than precise, but it explains some of the tremendous growth in retail asset management products.

The two experiments suggest a clear trade-off between transactions costs and inadequate diversification. Figure 3-5 graphs this trade-off for a hypothetical investor with $100,000. As she increases the number of different stocks held, her opportunity losses relative to a fully diversified index fall. At the same time, the round-trip commissions annualized over a seven-year holding period rise as the size of transactions falls. Taking

15. Investment Company Institute (1993).

both of these costs into account, she would minimize the total costs of synthetic indexing by holding approximately 30 stocks.[16] Thus, for the investor with $100,000 seeking broad equity exposure but lacking multi-lateral pooling vehicles, manufacturing a close substitute costs 150 to 200 basis points per year in total costs.

For all but the wealthiest investors, the pooled alternative has significantly lower costs. As a comparison point, Figure 3-5 also shows the costs (fees charged) for a pooled index portfolio offered by one leading mutual fund vendor. By joining with other investors through mutual funds or other financial intermediaries, an investor can diversify at relatively low costs. For our investor with $100,000, the fully pooled vehicle has costs roughly two-thirds lower than the optimal "direct" investment.

Although this analysis is cast in terms of the current institutional structure of the United States, the lesson has broader applicability: just as economies of scale in production technologies lead firms to demand pooling services, economies of scale in securities transactions cause households to do the same. Without access to pooling, all but the wealthiest households would find diversification impossible to attain.

Liquidity

Households face both predictable and unpredictable needs for cash, whether occasioned by medical emergencies, college tuition, or new home purchases.[17] Households could hold much of their wealth in cash to accommodate potential cash flow needs, but this would severely constrain the returns they could earn. Instead, households prefer to keep most of their wealth invested in real assets, but maintain the ability to make incremental investments or sell some amounts at low frictional costs, which we define as *liquidity*.

Without pooling, a household's ability to buy or sell incremental investments would be limited, as only purchases and sales of *entire* assets would be permitted. Unless its cash needs exactly match the size of its existing assets, the household would bear transactions costs to sell one asset, use a part of the proceeds to fund its immediate cash needs, and then bear additional transactions costs as it reinvests the difference in

---

16. This analysis ignores differential bid–ask spreads and costs of rebalancing, and places no value on the investor's time spent constructing, tracking, and monitoring the portfolio.

17. In the absence of pooling, the household's demand for liquidity is driven not only by its own needs, but also by the cash flow needs of the firms it finances. A household financing a firm that has seasonal or unpredictable cash flow needs, such as a farm or a toy manufacturer, would need to ensure that it has sufficient cash to fund the firm's peak cash needs.

another business. For example, without pooling, parents funding a child's college education might have to liquidate their investments in businesses.

From the perspective of a potential buyer, however, such a sale would be indistinguishable from a sale motivated by a realization that an investment has poor expected future returns. This is the "lemons" problem that afflicts products whose quality is difficult to discern by inspection.[18] The presence of "lemons" in the resale market lowers average prices for both quality- and liquidity-motivated sellers, making the consumption shocks more costly to households.

The all-or-nothing nature of transactions in a hypothetical no-pooling world precludes owners from sending credible signals that their sales are not motivated by their superior information. If pooling were permitted, the household could continue to hold a portion of the partially disposed asset, and thus signal its continued interest in, and optimism about, the business.[19]

Thus, pooling affects the provision of liquidity in three ways. It separates the liquidity needs of firms from their investors. It permits the partial purchase and sale of assets, which in turn allows households to hold small pieces of large, high-returning businesses. And it reduces the frictional costs of transactions caused by informational asymmetries. By supporting liquidity, pooling therefore reduces a household's needs to hold cash, or conversely increases their ability to fund productive investments.

Monitoring

In a world without multilateral contracts, households, as the sole providers of external capital, must conscientiously monitor the management of the firms they fund. Conflicts of interest will arise between the managers and the household providing the productive capital. For instance, managers, because they are employees, not owners, may not work as hard as the household wants. They may choose excessively safe projects in an effort to preserve their jobs, or they may consume the firm's resources disproportionately through managerial perquisites. These are "agency problems," documented in the work of Jensen and Meckling (1984). Remote owners cannot efficiently structure arrangements so that agents, the managers, will act in their interests. For the household, this complicates

---

18. See Akerlof (1976) for a formal treatment of this problem, or Glosten and Milgrom (1985) and Easley and O'Hara (1987) for application to securities markets.
19. In a world without pooling, other elements of liquidity might actually improve. Search costs to identify potential buyers of entire businesses might actually fall in a no-pooling world because of the strong incentives for private parties to develop efficient markets for the transfer of large investment blocks.

the choice of investment projects and makes risk management all but impossible.

Just as a centralized intermediary can provide efficient diversification and liquidity, so too can it provide low-cost monitoring. The evolution of early pooling ventures, such as nineteenth century New England banks studied by Lamoreaux (1991), demonstrates the relationship of pooling and monitoring. Unsure what investments were of high quality, and with their relatively small amounts of wealth, New England families invested in uninsured deposits of local banks that were dominated by insiders who controlled the boards and the lending policies. Even though these directors often elected to lend a high fraction of bank capital to themselves or their associates, they were known to local depositors to be of good standing, and thus depositors willingly entrusted their funds to these banks. The undoing of many of these banks occurred in the late nineteenth century, when the New England economy was transformed from a net demander to a net supplier of capital, and loans were required to be made at arm's-length. As their directors had never cultivated any credit analysis skills (and perhaps had little interest in depositors' welfare once their own personal firms were financed), their monitoring skills were inadequate, and these banks failed to survive.

Monitoring takes time, effort and skills, as investors must collect, process, and interpret timely information. Some of this monitoring activity is independent of the size of the investment, but economies of effort may be realized as the information gained from monitoring can be used and expensed over a larger investment base. Pooling lets households delegate the monitoring function to professionals who can devote substantial resources to overseeing their firms.

Pooling via multilateral contracts does not eliminate the household's need for monitoring; rather it changes the object of its attention. Instead of monitoring the managers of hundreds of diverse firms, households must watch the managers of a single pool. If this pool manager is in the business of producing information about their investments, the household will benefit if this information is credibly passed along to them at a relatively low marginal cost. If the financial institution is opaque, however, this benefit may not be realized, and the household will have to structure a contract with the pool manager to align their interests with those of the investors.

Summary

Household demands for pooling arise from three sources: a need for efficient risk management through diversification, a need for liquidity, and a need for efficient monitoring. These three rationales, in conjunction with firms' large capital needs, explain the prominent role pooling plays in virtually all economies—from very primitive to highly developed economies, in both capitalistic and socialistic societies.

Two Multi-level Pooling Mechanisms: Financial Institutions and Financial Markets

Multi-level or multilateral pooling mechanisms that link enterprises and households can be structured in many different ways. Two generic mechanisms are financial institutions (or intermediaries) and financial markets. To illustrate pooling through financial institutions we examine *delegated investment management*, where investors hire agents to identify and manage financial investments. An alternative to this actively intermediated process is pooling through the financial markets in the form of *asset securitization*. Securitization depends on the ability to segregate a collection of financial claims and to restructure their risky cash flows to increase their attractiveness to investors or to lower financing costs for issuers.

Two of many methods to accomplish pooling, these illustrations demonstrate how intermediaries or financial markets serve similar functions. Most pooling mechanisms lie between these two polar cases, incorporating both active intermediation and direct pooling through capital markets. Which method is most appropriate depends on its relative cost as determined by the nature of assets pooled and by the composition of the investor base.

Pooling and Investment Management Services

To obtain efficient diversification, liquidity, and monitoring, households holding lumpy, poorly diversified portfolios could enter into a series of financial swaps with one another. This approach has the disadvantages that monitoring and coordinating the actions of each of the participants is likely to be highly costly; contracting would require the simultaneous consent of many parties; rebalancing might be difficult to execute; and each household would be subject to the complicated, multi-party credit risk of all of the other households unless the contributed assets could be made bankruptcy-remote. Rather than each household dealing with tens, hundreds, or thousands of other households directly, it is more efficient for each household to contract with a single intermediary that provides investment management services, as we have defined multilateral contracting via pooling.

The intermediary may be a relatively transparent entity such as a mutual fund, whose assets and investment strategies are visible.[20] Or, the intermediary may be more opaque, such as a securities firm, commercial bank, or hedge fund. In either case, the role of the intermediary is to identify feasible investments, select those with suitable performance characteristics, execute the necessary transactions, and distribute the economic returns of these claims to investors. Such an intermediary may be an agent of either the investors, the business enterprise, or both.

Advantages of intermediate pooling. There are at least three conditions under which a financial intermediary or institution can prove to be an efficient pooling vehicle: (1) when the assets require extensive costly monitoring; (2) when the intermediary can acquire information unavailable to or costly to investors; and (3) when the institution can produce claims unavailable in the market.

First, intermediate pooling is effective when pooled funds are used to purchase an asset that requires *monitoring*. Suppose a small firm anticipates cash flow needs for two years to fund expansion, and wants funding from a financial institution in the form of a term loan. Monitoring this investment involves careful observation of the financial position and the actions of the borrower. Covenants may be broken and need to be renegotiated during the loan's life, which makes the loan more difficult to sell to a broad clientele that may lack the skills to monitor performance and renegotiate contracts as needed. Commercial banks regularly confront these problems as issuers of middle-market loans, as do insurance firms that hold privately placed notes. In contrast, Treasury securities require virtually no monitoring and negotiating.

Because the intermediary must actively represent the interests of the ultimate holders of the pool, its contract with investors must align its incentives with theirs, or reflect costs of possible misalignment. Opaque intermediaries, such as banks, for example, could fund themselves solely with equity. The quality of an institution's loan portfolio, however, is not observable, making it difficult for investors to distinguish between a "good bank" and a "bad bank." Townsend (1979) has shown that funding a financial institution through equity will result in inefficient risk-sharing. He shows that it is preferable for a loan originator to issue risky debt to the outside investors and retain a residual claim of the loan for itself. The originator thus reduces the burden of outside monitoring, and is free to

---

20. In the United States, regulations require mutual funds to disclose their holdings quarterly and to state their investment guidelines in a prospectus. These rules could be made more or less stringent depending on a regulator's objectives. In theory, the open-end mutual fund informs investors about the status of their investments with only the slightest delay.

invest in and enjoy the economic benefits of risky and somewhat opaque projects.[21]

Active intermediation may be preferred when intermediaries can *acquire or process information that investors find unavailable or costly*. This ability may arise from the intermediaries' past investments, scope economies arising from the collection and corroboration of real-time data from multiple sources, economies of scale of information collection, superior valuation models, or its ability to respond quickly to market anomalies. The belief that fund managers have superior information and investing skills is central to mutual fund marketing appeals [Sirri and Tufano (1993b)]. Venture capitalists market a similar set of skills both to investors and to young firms needing capital. Access to the "deal flow" provides a vantage point from which to identify superior investments, and their prior experiences, management skills, and contacts allow venture capitalists to provide entrepreneurs with benefits beyond the risk capital they deliver [Sahlman (1990)]. The case for delegated investment management is also made by hedge funds that profit by taking large arbitrage positions to exploit minute pricing discrepancies uncovered by continuously scanning global markets in real time. For many mutual funds, venture capitalists, hedge funds, and other delegated investment managers, an institution's *raison d'être* is its superior information skills.

Finally, pooling may take place through an institution when *the intermediary produces claims that are otherwise unavailable in the marketplace*. To manage risk, for example, a household may seek insurance against declines in an equity portfolio, or choose a contract that allows it to keep pace with rising college or housing costs. Were these claims not traded in the market, an institution might emerge as the vehicle for delivering them, either by executing a dynamic trading strategy on its customers' behalf or through underwriting, in which the intermediary takes principal risk. As an example of the former, early forms of portfolio insurance delivered equity holders protection against drops in their portfolio using dynamic trading strategies [see Kyrillos and Tufano (1994)]. More recently, risk management investments targeted to households have begun to appear in the form of "life-cycle" funds, with risk/return characteristics matched to the ages of targeted investors. A life-cycle fund may invest more heavily in high-risk securities early in investors' life, deferring capital gains whenever possible. As time passes, the fund's composition might shift to

---

21. We observe this solution in practice in Lamoreaux's (1991) study of New England commercial banking in the 1800s. Bank directors, who were insiders, were the ultimate equity holders in the intermediary, and the outside depositors were issued risky demandable debt.

lower-risk, fixed-income securities. Additionally, the fund might hedge against inflation, and other macroeconomic risks. The fund may trade only in listed securities, but it provides a dynamic mix of the securities that is unavailable otherwise, which gives rise to active intermediation.

In summary, intermediaries may be particularly well-suited to serving as a mechanism for pooling funds when the underlying investments require substantial ongoing information collection, monitoring, recontracting, or trading.

Costs of intermediated pooling. Pooling via intermediaries is not costless. The separation of principals and agents gives rise to predictable and costly conflicts between intermediaries and their customers. Managers of mutual funds have the potential to engage in self-dealing by trading against their own funds. Conflicts of interest among investors and managers of financial pools are perhaps even more pronounced in the banking and savings and loan industries. Here, the existence of a guarantee on the face value of deposits weakens depositors' incentives to monitor management, and the division of claims between depositors and equity holders leads to additional conflicts of interest among the various investors.[22]

Esty (1994) studies these conflicts of interest in savings and loans institutions, focusing on how organizational form affects the propensity of the pool managers (the managers of the savings and loans) to take on additional risk. Increased riskiness benefits shareholders at the expense of depositors (or, in the case of insured deposits, the government insurer).[23] In theory, high levels of equity ownership by managers of savings and loans give them incentives to increase risk, which transfers value from depositors/insurers to shareholders. Esty's evidence is consistent with this hypothesis. He finds that the structure of organizational claims affects risk-taking behavior: Managers of stock institutions and those with greater leverage assumed greater risks than mutual savings and loans and less levered firms.

Judging whether an investment manager has earned a sufficient return for the investment risk borne is a difficult task. The ongoing debate over whether there are any skilled investment managers at all [e.g., see Grinblatt and Titman (1989) or Ippolito (1989)], or whether good performance is just an artifact of an inaccurate measurement technique [Brown,

---

22. Such a guarantee may be explicit, as it is in the United States at present, or it may be implicit, as in some of the Scandinavian countries and Japan.
23. Equity holders in a levered firm essentially hold a call option on the firm, with an exercise price equal to the face value of the debt. By increasing the volatility of the firm, they will increase the value of their call, leading to what is typically referred to as the "asset substitution" problem, in which equity holders prefer to substitute more risky assets for less risky ones.

Goetzmann, Ibbotson, and Ross (1992)] attests to the difficulty of measuring the investment performance of intermediaries. This performance measurement task is complicated when intermediaries undertake investment strategies as principals by underwriting the financial claim on the firm's own account.

As an example, consider an index-linked savings certificate sold by an investment bank, which promises to pay depositors a return linked to the performance of a stock index, such as the S&P 500 or Dow Jones Industrial Average. These contracts are principal obligations of the issuer, yet the way the issuer funds the obligation is opaque to the investor. An index mutual fund, by contrast, can deliver a similar payout, with the fund manager buying and holding a portfolio of securities in a trust on behalf of the client.

The return to both investments will depend on the level of the S&P, but the return to the investor in the savings certificate also depends on the solvency of the issuer. As Merton (1993) points out, intermingling these risks may be inefficient and costly, and many customers of financial intermediaries prefer their claims to be relatively insensitive to the fortunes of the issuer. As the demand for more finely tailored investment products rises, an increased reliance on principal contracts will make this aspect of intermediated pooling's costs of increasing concern to investors. The market's recent response to these concerns has been to establish high-credit-quality subsidiaries to offer certain products, such as derivatives.

Pooling and Securitization

Though institutions such as banks or mutual funds may play an active and ongoing role in the pooling of household investments, pooling can also be performed more directly in the capital markets through *asset securitization*. Asset securitization is an example of the financial markets' ability to satisfy the pooling function without an ongoing intermediary. In this case, financial intermediaries play an important role in setting up a capital market pool, but typically play a minor role throughout its later life.

In broad terms, a securitized instrument is a traded financial asset representing a direct claim on the cash flows of a segregated collection of assets held in a special-purpose trust. Although this definition is broad enough to include trusts whose underlying assets are liquid claims, such as closed-end mutual funds, we focus on underlying assets that are not actively traded in efficient and liquid markets. Securitization facilitates the pooling of wealth in three instances: (1) when the assets pooled are homogeneous in nature; (2) when assets do not require substantial ongoing monitoring and servicing; and (3) when liquidity can be added to otherwise illiquid assets through liquidity stripping.

To create a securitized asset, an underwriter or originator initially collects a portfolio of financial assets, segregates them into a trust, and then writes a collection of financial claims against this trust. Identifying appropriate claims to be placed in the trust involves considerable skill, as does the process of distributing the resultant securitized claims to investors. Once these processes end, the originator or underwriter generally has only a minimal role in the management of the pool. Most often the role is administrative, and quite often the underwriter bears no risk after the pool is distributed.

The types of assets amenable to securitization as a pooling mechanism are somewhat restricted. First, the assets to be securitized must be of a *relatively homogeneous nature*. Because there is no investment manager to act as the investors' agent and as an intermediary, the probability distributions for the cash flow from the pool must be transparent. In one instance, a relatively small number of assets are securitized so that investors in the trust can assess the riskiness of each asset individually. For example, investors in a real estate investment trust that holds a few properties can observe them, assess their condition, and verify the likelihood of the future promised cash flows. More frequently, however, a securitized pool includes many assets whose risk/return characteristics are homogeneous so that investors can rely on statistical information to estimate the pool's cash flows. Issuers and underwriters of such securitizations generally provide investors with data about the historical realizations of payments, default rates, and credit status.

The most important example of such a vehicle is the mortgage-backed security (MBS), which has revolutionized housing finance in the United States. The pooling of groups of similar home mortgages into a trust, in part bypassing costly intermediation by depository institutions, allows investors to fund housing directly. Prepayment and default rates, which are important in determining a mortgage security's value, can be modeled from historical data.

The second instance in which securitization facilitates pooling is when the underlying assets require *little individual servicing or monitoring*. It is difficult to structure a contract giving agents the proper incentives to service and monitor the assets in a securitized pool. The holders of the securitized claim are the beneficiaries of the servicing or monitoring, but all the costs are incurred by the servicer, who may have limited financial interest in the pool. At the same time, a large number of assets makes it impractical for investors to verify servicing quality. Thus, securitization seems most applicable when ongoing servicing is quite limited, such as for home mortgages. The mortgage holder collects and distributes payments, and initiates default procedures if payments are not made. Renegotiation of such a loan is quite rare. In addition, third-party guarantees of the securitized pool, provided by the government or private parties, eliminate servicing quality from investors' concerns about the security.[24] Securitization has been used successfully to finance a wide range of assets, including accounts receivable, and loans for autos, boats, and mobile homes.

One place asset securitization has failed to date to make much headway because of the need for ongoing monitoring is in financing commercial bank portfolios of commercial and industrial (C&I) loans. As of mid-1994, U.S. commercial banks had $603 billion worth of C&I loans on their portfolios. Banks, which are opaque financial institutions, could potentially lower their costs of funding high-quality C&I loans if they could segregate and fund them separately from the rest of their assets. Although banks might like to segregate loans and sell them to the capital markets, these loans require detailed and continuous monitoring by the lender, and typically involve renegotiation of contract terms, security, loan covenants, and loan maturity over their life. Incentive contracts may provide for banks to share in the loan losses, but such an arrangement requires loans to remain on the banks' regulatory accounting books, increasing capital charges.[25]

A third instance when pooling may take the form of securitization is when bundling assets *enhances the liquidity* or lowers the cost of trading securities. Large bid–ask spreads represent payments from buyers and sellers, as a group, to compensate market makers for holding inventory and for bearing losses resulting from trading with informed buyers and sellers. The market maker must not only finance these shares held in inventory, but also bear the risk of adverse price movements. Market makers will also lose in trading with informed parties, and because of adverse selection, traders will be drawn disproportionately from those who are informed.

For infrequently traded securities, and for those with high degrees of informational asymmetry, large bid–ask spreads are common. Traditionally, intermediaries served as the vehicle to fund these types of firms and projects. We have recently begun to see asset securitization accomplish

---

24. An important innovation in this market was issuance by the government of a guarantee on the ultimate payment of the principal of the mortgage. For a discussion of such guarantees, see Bodie and Merton (1992).

25. One place C&I loan securitization has been successful is in the case of Fremont Financial Corporation, a small non-bank intermediary that lends to middle-market borrowers on a fully secured basis. For a discussion, see Sirri (1994).

this pooling task and, in so doing, enhance liquidity in these assets through the process of liquidity-stripping. The bundling of many illiquid assets diminishes the market maker's risk of suffering by trading with informed traders, as the informed must have superior information about the *entire bundle* of assets. Furthermore, bundling increases the traded asset's unit scale of and frequency of trading, reducing the relative inventory a market maker must hold. These factors can reduce the required bid–ask spread.[26]

Consider an investor who would like to invest in a diversified portfolio of international securities for one month, but finds the round-trip spreads charged on national exchanges too large to justify the investment.[27] As an alternative, the investor can purchase the securities, place them in a trust, and then sell over-the-counter claims against the entire portfolio of illiquid stocks to shed all or some of the exposure. The claims sold can be equity swaps, options, or pure equity participations in the pool. The sale is executed on a diversified portfolio so that informational concerns vanish (it is improbable for an investor to have credible private information about a large group of firms). Liquidity problems are minimized as well, because the diversified portfolio claim is an attractive and often traded security among passive and quantitative international equity managers. A clear example of this can be seen in formation of a diversified portfolio composed of individually purchased shares of stock in the S&P 500. Buyers of stocks encounter spreads of 50 basis points, but buyers of a pooled substitute (index futures) face 3 basis point spreads.

This form of securitization immobilizes the underlying assets once purchased, and subsequent trading can be accomplished through securitized OTC or exchange-traded claims. We see this structure used by Leland O'Brien Rubinstein in their SuperTrust products. The underlying asset purchased is a basket of S&P 500 stocks, and against these immobilized assets a variety of claims are carved out.[28] The immobilized basket of 500 stocks need never be traded, but the claims written against them could trade freely—at far lower transactions costs and higher liquidity than the underlying basket.

Limits to Multilateral Pooling

Will financial systems ultimately be populated with mammoth multilateral pools? Focusing on the benefits and costs of pooling, increasing size

---

26. See Merton (1993).
27. Perold and Sirri (1994) document that one-way all-in cost for a U.S. investor trading a portfolio of EAFE stocks is 1.39%.
28. See Kyrillos and Tufano (1994).

beyond a certain point may not be economical. The benefits of diversification level off after a certain point: Adding additional securities to an already well-diversified portfolio has virtually no impact on the reduction in risk. In the case of monitoring, larger pools may have greater bargaining power in negotiations with the firms in which they invest, although these gains must be offset by costs that households bear in overseeing a large pool manager. To capitalize on security selection skills, larger pools may be efficient in that they allow a skilled investment manager to identify mispriced securities and buy more of them rather than less. It has been shown that excessively large pools may be disadvantaged, however, facing higher costs of executing trades, especially for thinly traded securities.[29] Finally, beyond some point, identifying investors may become prohibitively expensive, especially given that marketing costs can account for perhaps as much as half of a fund's expenses [Sirri and Tufano (1993b)].

We should recognize, however, that the activities undertaken by pools need not be accomplished in one organization, and thus it might be oversimplistic to discuss the "size" of a pool. For example, the pooling of capital to fund home mortgages has been decomposed: Loan origination, loan servicing, and capital raising have been separated. The optimal size for each of these activities within the multilateral pool might be different.

Has pooling progressed to its most "mature" form? No, continuing evolution is almost certain. Shortcomings in legal structure and contract rights continue to be impediments to advances in pooling. Although we might tend to overlook the impact of the legal system on pooling, effective pooling technologies like securitization require an ability to freely transfer ownership of assets such as mortgages and to pass the attendant cash flows and legal obligations through the securitization structure.

In some countries and market sectors, laws and regulations on the transfer of property stymie the development of securitization. In Japan, for example, one step toward facilitating securitization was the 1993 passage of a law that simplified the transfer of property: through this law, perfection of the transfer is expedited, doing away with some of the formalities of the general law.[30] Though securitization is thought to be well-developed in the United States, laws and regulations in certain sectors prevent further advances. In the health care field, for example, laws and tax regulations make the transfer of receivables difficult. Some critics have argued that changes in these laws will facilitate securitization and in turn lower health care costs.[31] The future evolution of pooling,

---

29. See Perold and Salomon (1991).
30. See Lawden (1993).
31. See Salathe (1994).

especially through securitization, cannot be separated from legal and regulatory developments.

Perhaps more important, advances in information technology and financial engineering technology will support evolution of pooled vehicles. Improvements in information technology have driven certain types of transactions costs to the point that structures are now possible that could not have even been imagined 30 years ago. For example, a single credit card securitization might pool several million accounts; the flows to investors represent the ongoing receivables charged to each of the accounts included in the pool. This transaction is only feasible given low data-processing costs to assemble timely information on credit card payments and balances.[32] If the widely distributed communications technologies such as the Internet become the primary means of moving both information and funds, the costs of marketing, reporting, transfer, and customer service of most financial transactions would likely fall dramatically.

While we cannot predict the exact changes that these shifts in costs will have, almost certainly they will give rise to new means of pooling. Even today, we see financial services firms and information service providers positioning themselves to capitalize on new means of marketing financial products to consumers. With a new and low-cost channel to household saving, we could witness future innovations as dramatic as last decade's pooling of millions of credit card receivables.

Financial engineering technology is also likely to have a great impact on pooling. Traditional multilateral pools such as banks or mutual funds have offered investors relatively standardized investments. For example, most mutual funds offer investors a single claim: a pro rata claim in the equity of the pool. One could imagine an indexed pool that is more customized: The pool would hold a broad-based index and each investor could choose whether to incorporate downside protection or to limit or augment exposure for rises in the index. Obviously, the investor could create these positions by investing in the pure index fund and then acquiring puts and calls separately. Or, the pool could offer the customized index claims by aggregating the demands of investors and buying or manufacturing the necessary derivatives to manage the net exposure of the pool. Although individuals could create these customized investments on their own, institutional investors are likely to enjoy lower costs of designing, monitoring, and executing the necessary derivative trades, especially for customized products such as those indexed to real (as opposed to nominal) returns.

---

32. For a case of asset-backed receivables, see Mason et al. (1995), pp. 287–330.

The future of pooling may be toward "mass customization," where the efficiency gains of large size are combined with the benefits of tailoring products to individuals' needs. Mass customization has been a topic of great interest among strategists, manufacturing experts, and marketers, and may describe future developments in pooling as well. Continued development and validation of pricing and risk management models will support this latent trend toward tailoring financial products to the needs of suppliers and demanders of capital. Of course, these developments must be supported by—or at least not be impeded by—laws and regulations.

Summary

Pooling is so pervasive in financial systems that it can easily be taken for granted. It aggregates wealth and facilitates large indivisible investments, benefiting both owners of productive firms and investors. Without access to multiple investors through multiple bilateral contracts, owners of firms that demand capital would be forced to operate their businesses at scales far below the optimum level for productive efficiency. Hence, the ability to pool wealth is a requirement for efficient production, and firms require well-developed pooling mechanisms to access sufficient low-cost funds.

Investors need to put their surplus funds to work and manage the risks of their portfolios. If restricted to investing in whole operations, investors would hold inferior investment portfolios, deprived of the benefits of diversification and liquidity that arise from investing in a large number of different firms. Thus, their desire to modify the risk/return characteristics of their investments at low cost forces investors to seek pooling, particularly the multi-level form of pooling, in which they join with other investors to fund many enterprises simultaneously.

If firms need external funds to produce efficiently, and individuals need investments to earn high returns per unit of risk, the two parties share a desire to reduce costs. At its core, pooling achieves these tandem goals. From a firm's perspective, pooling allows production at levels of technology and scale so that unit costs are minimized. From an individual's view, pooling helps achieve the highest return per unit of risk because it permits economical risk-sharing.

Although pooling can primarily be thought of as a means to minimize costs, both of firms and of individuals seeking diversification and monitoring, it serves other functions. Pooling provides households and firms with liquidity, facilitating the purchase and sale of incremental amounts of firm ownership. Furthermore, it plays a role in the distribution of wealth, by allowing the less well-to-do a chance to join with others to invest in profitable assets that otherwise would be out of reach.

Pools can be designed in many different ways. When extensive monitoring, renegotiation, and servicing are required, pooling may best be accomplished through a financial intermediary that maintains an active role throughout the life of the investment. In other cases, where the assets require less ongoing maintenance, direct pooling through securitization may be preferable.

The evolution of pooling has been shaped by legal and technological developments. Nations' laws have clearly affected the type of pooling that has taken place. Pooling as we know it presumes that entities such as corporations can be endowed with certain legal rights, including the rights to hold and to transfer property. Important legal developments centuries ago supported bilateral contracting through the creation of the corporate form. Important legal developments today remove impediments to the transfer of title to pooled vehicles.

Technological developments have also affected pooling. Most recently, computing technology has made possible securitization in which literally millions of individual claims are bundled together and sold to investors. Further developments in information technology and financial engineering are likely to affect pooling in the near future. Of these, the possibility of "mass customization" of multilateral financial pools presents an intriguing possibility combining the efficiency gains of large pools with the delivery of tailored financial services such as risk management.

Appendix A: Household Wealth and Enterprise Funding Needs, 1991

Data on individual/family wealth and total financial claims on public firms are collected from several sources. For individual and family wealth, data come from *Fortune* [Losee (1992)] and *Forbes* [Seneker (1992)]. The combined set contains 326 family groups residing in 42 countries. Where dollar amounts differ for the same family or individual, the *Forbes* number is used. All individuals within the same family group (immediate family, related by marriage, or related and having the same last name) are combined. *Forbes* and *Fortune* estimate "net worth" and "wealth" using estimates of the market value of the families' wealth.

Data used to calculate the total amount of financial claims on a given company are compiled from Global Vantage, a financial reporting package similar in form to COMPUSTAT, but including financial accounts from many of the largest non-U.S. companies. By its construction, Global Vantage includes data only on the larger foreign companies and those with accessible financial accounting. Since our analysis is concerned mainly with publicly traded companies having total financial claims of $1 billion or more, this limitation should not produce any significant bias.

To collect company-specific data, the database of over 8,000 companies is first screened to eliminate those companies without any publicly available market value (i.e., those without any publicly traded securities or without publicly available price quotations on the securities). From this subset (over 7,000 companies in 35 countries), the value of all financial claims on each company is calculated.

Total financial claims are defined as all external debt and equity of the consolidated company. The variable DT (defined as long-term debt plus short-term borrowings) is used for total external debt valued at book value. For total equity, the variables PCAPT, MIB, and MKVALI are summed. PCAPT, or total preferred capital, represents the total book value of all types of preferred stock outstanding. As with debt, book value is considered the closest available proxy for market value. MIB, or minority interest as a balance sheet item, captures the value of any external financial claims or subsidiaries. Finally, the variable MKVALI represents the total market value of the company's common equity. All values are translated into dollars at the first fiscal year-end rate. Where separate market values for different classes of equity of the same company are listed, these are combined into one aggregate market value data item.

Available company data are then compared to family wealth data. Twenty-two countries have both available company information and families or individuals with wealth of $1 billion or more.[33] The full data set for these 22 countries includes 2,218 companies with total financial claims of $1 billion or more, and 269 families or individuals with wealth of $1 billion or more.

A family or individual is considered able to finance a given firm if the total wealth of the individual/family is equal to or greater than the total value of financial claims on that firm. The individual or family is always considered able to finance the largest firm possible (ranked by total financial claims). If more than one individual/family is able to finance a firm, the wealthiest individual/family is used, and the remaining individuals/families are able to finance the next-largest-claims company, and so on. Where one individual/family is able to finance more than one firm (as in the case of Liechtenstein), all firms able to be financed are noted.

---

33. For 20 countries, the *Forbes* and *Fortune* lists note the presence of billionaires, although no firms appear on Global Vantage as having publicly traded shares and external claims of $1 billion or more. These countries are: Argentina, Brazil, Brunei, Chile, Colombia, Greece, India, Indonesia, Israel, Jordan, Kuwait, Lebanon, Macau, Morocco, Philippines, Saudi Arabia, Taiwan, Turkey, UAE, and Venezuela. Thirteen countries had firms with publicly traded claims and external funding in excess of $1 billion, but no billionaires according to the *Forbes* and *Fortune* lists. These are: (Netherlands) Antilles, Belgium, Bermuda, Cayman Islands, Finland, Ireland, Liberia, Luxembourg, New Zealand, Norway, Panama, Papua New Guinea, and the (British) Virgin Islands.

In the case of several individuals/families all having exactly $1 billion in wealth, companies under $1 billion in total claims are included in the "$1 billion +" category until the individual/family list is exhausted, with the sole exception of Mexico, where there are more families/individuals than firms with $1 billion in wealth/claims and less. Accordingly, one individual and one family are not used, each having total wealth of $1 billion.

Appendix B: Household Wealth and Enterprise Funding Needs, 1924

Data on individual/family wealth and total financial claims on public firms come from several sources. For individual and family wealth, a data set is compiled from Lundberg (1937). Lundberg estimates the gross fortune of each individual or family group as of 1924. Total calculated fortune is derived from aggregate income disclosed on 1924 tax returns. Lundberg characterizes his estimates as conservative, given the other sources of hidden income common at the time. The total data set includes 60 families.

The largest 100 companies from 1917, ranked by total asset size, are identified using a list compiled by *Forbes* (1987). The largest 50 railroads of 1917, as reported by the U.S. Interstate Commerce Commission (1919), are then determined. The two lists are combined, yielding 146 data items (four railroads are included in the *Forbes* list).

Total financial claims are defined as total debt plus equity, measured at book value. Book value is defined as capital stock (both common and preferred) plus any surplus account. The companies' 1917 financials come from Poor's Manuals, the Interstate Commerce Commission report on railroads, and, in some cases, actual annual reports.[34] Each company is then ranked by total financial claims.

A family or individual is considered able to finance a given firm if the total wealth of the individual/family is equal to or greater than the total value of financial claims on that firm. The individual or family is always considered able to finance the largest firm possible (ranked by total financial claims). If more than one individual/family is able to finance a firm, the wealthiest individual/family is used, and the remaining individuals/families are taken as able to finance the next-largest-claims company, and so on.

To determine which families/individuals would qualify as billionaires

---

34. Data for four banks (First National City Bank, Guaranty Trust Co. of N.Y., Chase National Bank, and National Bank of Commerce) are obtained from annual reports, year ending 1917.

in 1993, the CPI index is used to adjust each wealth figure to 1993 dollars. Given this methodology, only those individuals/families with 1924 wealth of $125.6 million or more are considered equivalent to today's billionaires.

References

Akerlof, George (1976), "The Market for Lemons: Quality Uncertainty and the Market Mechanism," *Quarterly Journal of Economics*, 84, (3): 488–500.

Compustat Global Vantage. *Automotive News*, (1993), May 26: 3.

Bodie, Zvi, and R.C. Merton (1992), "On the Management of Financial Guarantees," *Financial Management* (Winter): 87–109.

Brown, S.I., W. Goetzmann, R. Ibbotson, and S. Ross (1992), "Survivorship Bias in Performance Studies," *Review of Financial Studies*, 5: 553–580.

Dewing, A.S. (1934), *Study of Corporate Securities*, New York: Ronald Press.

Easley, David and Maureen O'Hara (1987), "Price, Trade Size, and Information in Securities Markets," *Journal of Financial Economics*, 19: 69–90.

Esty, Ben (1994), "Organizational Form, Residual Claims, and Incentives: A Study of Risk-Taking in the S&L Industry," Harvard Business School Working Paper, Boston.

Glosten, Larry, and Paul Milgrom (1985), "Bid, Ask and Transaction Prices in a Specialist Market With Heterogeneously Informed Traders," *Journal of Financial Economics*, 14: 71–100.

Grinblatt, Mark, and Sheridan Titman (1989), "Mutual Fund Performance: An Analysis of Quarterly Portfolio Holdings," *Journal of Business*, 62: 393–416.

Investment Company Institute (1993), *Mutual Fund Fact Book*, Washington, D.C.: ICI.

Ippolito, Robert (1989), "Efficiency with Costly Information: A Study of Mutual Fund Performance, 1965–84," *Quarterly Journal of Economics*, 104: 1–23.

Jensen, Michael C. (1993), "The Modern Industrial Revolution, Exit, and the Failure of Internal Control Systems," *Journal of Finance*, 48 (3): 831–880.

Jensen, Michael C., and William H. Meckling (1984), "Theory of the Firm: Managerial Behavior, Agency Costs and Ownership Structure," in *The Modern Theory of Corporate Finance*, Michael C. Jensen and Clifford W. Smith, Jr., eds., New York: McGraw-Hill.

Kyrillos, Barbara, and Peter Tufano (1994), "Leland O'Brien Rubenstein Associates: SuperTrust," Harvard Business School Case No. 294-050, Boston.

Lamoreaux, Naomi (1991), "Information Problems and Banks' Specialization in Short-Term Commercial Lending: New England in the Nineteenth Century," in *Inside the Business Enterprise*, Peter Temin, ed., Chicago: University of Chicago Press.

Lawden, James (1993), "Japanese Securitization—In for a Major Boost?" *International Financial Law Journal*, (9): 29–31.

Losee, Stephanie, and Ani Hadjian (1992), "The Billionaires List," *Fortune*, September 7: 98–138.

Lundberg, Ferdinand (1937), *America's 60 Families*, New York: The Vanguard Press: 26–27.

Markowitz, Harry M. (1959), *Portfolio Selection*, New Haven, CT: Yale University Press.

Mason, Scott, Robert C. Merton, André Perold, and Peter Tufano (1995), *Cases in Financial Engineering*, Englewood Cliffs, N.J.: Prentice Hall.

Mayshar, Joram (1979), "Transaction Costs in a Model of Capital Market Equilibrium," *Journal of Political Economy*, 87 (4): 673–700.

Merton, Robert C. (1993), "Financial Intermediation: A Functional Perspective," Harvard Business School Working Paper No. 93-020, Boston.

——— (1987), "A Simple Model of Capital Market Equilibrium with Incomplete Information," *Journal of Finance*, 42 (3): 483–510.

Perold, André (1993), "BEA Associates: Enhanced Equity Funds," Harvard Business School Case 293-024, Boston.

Perold, André, and Robert Salomon (1991), "The Right Amount of Assets Under Management," *Financial Analysts Journal*, 47 (May/June): 31–39.

Perold, André, and Erik Sirri (1994), "The Cost of International Equity Trading," Harvard Business School Working Paper (May) Boston.

Rhys, Garel (1989) "Smaller Car Firms—Will They Survive?" *Long Range Planning*, 22 (5): 22–29.

Sahlman, William A. (1990), "The Structure and Governance of Venture-Capital Organizations," *Journal of Financial Economics*, 27 (2): 473–521.

Salathe, Gregory (1994), "Reducing Health Care Costs through Hospital Accounts Receivable Financing," *Virginia Law Review*, 80 (2): 549–576.

Scherer, F.M. (1980), *Industrial Market Structure and Economic Performance*, Chicago: Rand McNally College Publishing.

Scott, W.R. (1911), *The Constitution and Finances of English, Scottish, and Irish Joint Stock Companies to 1720*, Cambridge: Cambridge University Press, 3 volumes.

Seneker, Harold, ed. (1992), "The World's Billionaires," *Forbes*, July 20: 148–224.

Singh, A., and J. Hamid (1992), "Corporate Financing Decisions in Developing Countries," Technical Paper, International Finance Corporation: 11–43.

Sirri, Erik R. (1994), "Fremont Financial Corporation," Harvard Business School Case 294-054, Boston.

Sirri, Erik R., and Peter Tufano (1993a), "Buying and Selling Mutual Funds: Flows, Performance, Fees, and Services," Harvard Business School Working Paper 93-017, Boston.

——— (1993b), "Competition and Change in the Mutual Fund Industry," in *Financial Services: Perspectives and Challenges*, Samuel L. Hayes, III, ed., Boston: Harvard Business School Press.

Statman, Meir (1987), "How Many Stocks Make a Diversified Portfolio?," *Journal of Financial and Quantitative Analysis*, 22 (3): 353–363.

Thygerson, Kenneth (1993), *Financial Markets and Institutions*, New York: Harper-Collins.

Tirole, Jean (1988), *The Theory of Industrial Organization*, Cambridge: MIT Press.

"The Top 100—1917" (1987), *Forbes*, July 13: 122–123.

Townsend, Robert (1979), "Optimal Contracts and Competitive Markets with Costly State Verification," *Journal of Economic Theory*, 21: 265–293.

U.S. Interstate Commerce Commission (1919), *Statistics of Railways in the United States for the Year Ended December 31, 1917*, Washington: Government Printing Office.

Ward's Automotive Yearbook 1993, Ward's Automotive International, Southfield, MI: 59. Compustat Global Vantage.

CHAPTER FOUR

The Transfer of Economic Resources

DWIGHT B. CRANE

A well-developed financial system facilitates the flow of resources from "savers" to "users" so that there is an efficient allocation of capital to its most productive applications. Financial institutions such as banks and insurance companies perform this function, acting as intermediaries in the transfer of resources from savers and investors to borrowers. The transfer function is also performed through the activities involved in issuing and distributing securities to investors.

Individuals, geographic regions, and industries all experience phases in which funds are either needed or available. Often there is a life-cycle phenomenon at work. Younger households typically need to borrow to purchase housing and other assets, but later begin to accumulate financial assets to provide resources for their nonearning years. Newly emerging industries or countries often require substantial amounts of capital to support their growth, while mature entities and economies may be looking for new investment opportunities. Many other factors besides life cycle are at work: the emergence of a new technology; the discovery of a natural resource; a change in political environment; and so on. China is one of the oldest countries, for example, but it is in an emerging phase and is actively seeking capital inflows.

The ability to shift economic resources for long periods of time over long distances has existed for some time. When railroads in the United States faced a capital shortage in the 1830s and 1840s, they were financed by long-term sterling bonds issued in London. By 1844, for example, the Philadelphia and Reading Railroad had over $6 million worth of sterling bonds outstanding (roughly $100 million in 1994 dollars). These railroad bonds typically had initial maturities of 20 or 30 years, were secured by the railroad's property, and were convertible into equity in the railroad at the holder's option. This type of bond issue became the standard for railroad bonds throughout the nineteenth century.[1]

Such bonds were typically purchased by wealthy investors, but long-distance investments were made available to investors of moderate means when the Foreign & Colonial Government Trust was formed in March 1868 in the United Kingdom. In this early example of pooling, certificates with a face value of £100 and an income yield of 7% were sold to investors. The £1 million proceeds of the offering were invested in bonds issued by foreign and colonial governments and traded on the London Stock Exchange. They included bonds issued by Argentina, Brazil, Egypt, Italy, Turkey, and the United States, among others. The yield on these bonds averaged 8%, providing enough extra income for the trust to repay investors' principal over 24 years. Although *The Economist* and other newspapers at the time were skeptical about the quality of the trust's portfolio, shares traded at a premium after the offering, and only one of the original 18 bonds in the portfolio defaulted.[2]

There are many other examples of long-distance transfers of economic resources to productive uses. When oil or gold was discovered, when a new geographic frontier was being developed, or when a new supply of funds emerged, people developed ways to take advantage of these opportunities. Such flows of resources, however, tended to be episodic rather than routine.

Furthermore, it has often been costly and sometimes quite difficult to transfer economic resources over longer distances. Lending practices during the period of sharply rising oil prices in the late 1970s illustrate both the episodic nature of long-distance flows and some of the costs. During this period, oil-producing countries accumulated large U.S. dollar reserves that were deposited with banks in the Eurocurrency market. A substantial share of this increased bank liquidity was recycled as loans to Third World countries. Lenders believed that countries had substantial incentive to manage their economic affairs so they could maintain access to the capital markets, and that the capital markets would continue to provide new funds. Eurocurrency credits to the six most indebted Latin American countries more than tripled from $8.8 billion in 1977 to $27.0

---

1. The use of railroad bonds is discussed in Chandler (1954), pp. 250–251.
2. See McKendrick (1993).

billion in 1981.[3] A short time later many of these countries were in crisis, the flow of new funds had dropped dramatically, and several large commercial banks experienced great difficulty with losses on outstanding loans.

The 1970s' increase in oil prices also led to domestic lending difficulties within the United States. The oil-led economic boom in the southwestern region encouraged several U.S. banks to expand their lending to enterprises in this area, even though their home offices were hundreds or thousands of miles away. These distant institutions relied at least partly on loans originated by local banks whose lenders presumably knew nearby business firms well and would share the best credits with their northern correspondent banks. The Penn Square Bank of Oklahoma, for example, originated and sold more than $2 billion in loan participations to larger distant banks, including the Continental Illinois Bank in Chicago and Seattle First National Bank in the state of Washington.[4] Both banks failed when the oil boom faded and the loans sold by Penn Square Bank turned sour.

In spite of the difficulties illustrated by the Penn Square debacle, there is an important need for interregional or long-distance lending, the primary subject of this chapter. To be efficient, these transfers depend heavily on the performance of other financial functions, including an efficient payments system, the effective management of risk, and ways to manage the incentive problems that arise in financial contracts when one party has information the other party does not.

Management of risk, as well as the information and incentive problems are particularly important. Lending is usually thought of as a single homogeneous activity, but, as discussed in Chapter 1, it can be split conceptually into two components. One is a default-free transfer of economic resources, and the other is an implicit guarantee of the loan.[5] In this view, when an entity makes a loan, it receives interest for the risk-free transfer, and it receives a fee for bearing the default risk. Often the risk-free rate and guarantee fee are combined into a single interest rate that reflects the perceived default risk. In fact, the lender is being compensated for a transfer function and a risk management function that are quite different, both conceptually and practically.

Managing this guarantee component through evaluation and monitoring is a critical aspect of lending. Early financial intermediaries dealt with this issue by staying local, receiving funds from and lending to nearby

---

3. Morgan Guaranty Trust Company, *World Financial Markets,* January 1984.
4. See Fraser and Richards (1985).
5. In the language of Chapter 1, a default-free loan is equivalent to a risky loan plus a loan guarantee. Thus, a risky loan is equivalent to a default-free loan less a loan guarantee. This means that, whenever lenders make loans to borrowers who have some chance of defaulting, they are implicitly selling loan guarantees.

and well-known customers. Such practices, of course, did not provide an effective solution to the long-distance transfer of economic resources. In order to transfer efficiently over longer distances, it has been necessary to develop other institutional arrangements that allow guarantee problems to be managed at greater distances from the source of funds.

After a number of false starts, institutional changes in the U.S. mortgage market transformed a highly localized market into an international market in which the source of funds is completely independent of the location of the home being financed. This has been accomplished by developing ways to package mortgage loans into a pool of assets that could be subdivided and sold as securities to interested investors. Similar techniques have been successfully applied in lending to large corporations, but have had only limited success applied to medium-size and smaller companies.

Lending to middle-market companies remains a predominantly local market phenomenon; nearby institutions have an advantage in the guarantee function because of better information and lower monitoring costs. Some lending institutions, however, extend their geographic base by doing asset-based lending. In this case, control of the collateral reduces the information advantage of the borrower and lowers the cost of the guarantee function. In addition, there has been a successful securitization of mid-market loans in the United States. Securitization of these loans may not follow the path of securitized mortgages, but, as discussed in the final section of the chapter, new ways to manage the guarantee function may lead to some restructuring of the mid-market lending activity.

Role of Local Institutions

Municipal savings banks in Germany, agricultural credit cooperatives in France, and building societies in England and the United States are all examples of early institutions that played an important role in their country's financial system. Patterned after the English building societies, the original savings institutions in the United States illustrate how the local nature of these early institutions served to help manage the incentive problems.[6] These institutions were peer associations in which participants were required to pool their savings through regular membership payments. When the pool was large enough, a member borrowed funds to build a house. As this loan was repaid and the savings pool continued to grow, the next member borrowed, and so on.

---

6. Institutions in other countries could serve equally well as relevant examples of locally oriented intermediaries. The municipal savings banks in Germany, for example, invested deposited funds in the same district that provided the funds. See Welfling (1968), p. 237.

The first such U.S. organization was the Oxford Provident Building Association, which was organized in Frankford, Pennsylvania, in January 1831. It made loans for homes only within five miles of Frankford, so there was very limited movement of resources across space. The maturity of the loans must have been quite short as well, since all member loans were repaid within ten years, and the association was dissolved in 1841.[7]

Early U.S. commercial banks were also local in character. They were similar to the building associations in that they provided a vehicle for local business people to pool their resources and provide short-term loans to each other. The funds of these early banks were provided by business people in the community, with a large share in the form of equity capital. The loans were unsecured, short-term, and very local in nature; many of the loans were extended to directors of the bank. It was virtually impossible for a Providence business person to obtain a loan from a Boston bank in the early nineteenth century, and vice versa, even though these cities are only sixty miles apart.[8]

With limited territorial reach and short maturities, these local institutions had only rudimentary ability to transfer economic resources. Their capabilities, however, reflected the reality that the other functions of the financial system were also performed in limited ways. The short loan maturities, for example, were a way to help manage risk. In addition, the payments mechanisms needed to transfer resources were not well-developed. Gold and silver were readily accepted as payment, but the costs and risks of transferring coins were significant, to the carrier as well as to the owner. One estimate for the early 1830s is that there had to be a 1% spread in the value of silver to justify shipping it between New York and Boston, a distance of about 200 miles. Notes or currency issued by individual banks could be transferred more easily than specie, but in the early nineteenth century these notes lost their value quickly as the distance from the issuing bank grew and knowledge of the bank diminished. After about 50 miles they lost virtually all of their value.[9]

The Management of Information and Incentive Problems in Lending

A strength of local institutions is always their ability to manage the incentive problems that arise in financial contracts when there are disparities in information among the parties. First of all, when the parties to a transaction are familiar to each other, as they were in these local institutions, the disparity in the amount of information known is kept to a

---

7. See Ornstein (1985).
8. See Lamoreaux (1991).
9. See Klebaner (1990), p. 25.

minimum. Lending only to well-known individuals was once so in-grained it was sometimes considered inappropriate to undertake a credit investigation. A U.S. bank president schooled in nineteenth century bank-ing told an employee that ". . . under no circumstances ought we to ask anybody about our own customers."[10]

When there is an information disparity, two main incentive problems arise. "Adverse selection" refers to the possibility that the building and loan association would attract risky applicants whose true status would be hard to detect from the information available. The early associations met this problem by lending only to members, and the members them-selves were further screened by the regular payments of savings they were required to make to the association. The early U.S. commercial banks handled adverse selection in a similar manner, as the borrowers were equity investors and depositors.

"Moral-hazard problems" occur once funds are lent. For example, bor-rowers have an incentive to invest in relatively risky endeavors, because they receive all the upside benefits if high returns are achieved. The lenders receive no benefit beyond the stated interest and principal. Yet, if the risky endeavor fails, lenders suffer the consequences. A related issue is that borrowers may underinvest; for example, they may undermaintain their equipment if they face a cash flow problem. Monitoring borrowers to deal with these issues can be costly, but the cost is lessened by lending only to local, well-known customers. Peer pressure also acted as a low-cost enforcement mechanism in the early institutions.

Because well-run local institutions are able to manage information and incentive problems effectively, they still play an important role in both developed and emerging financial markets.[11] Local savings institutions, community banks, and cooperative associations exist along with nation-wide financial firms in many countries. By themselves, however, local institutions cannot transfer resources over longer distances.

Their limitations are clearly seen in the interest rate differentials pre-vailing in the United States in the nineteenth century. Surplus savings accumulated in the northeastern part of the country, but when the de-mand for capital shifted to the southern and western parts, substantial differences in interest rates were seen. It was difficult for the locally based

---

10. Klebaner (1990), p. 68.
11. An interesting example of a local institution is the Grameen Bank in rural Bangladesh. The bank was set up in 1977 with the support of the Ford Foundation to provide credit in small amounts to the landless poor. It operates much like the early building and loan associations. Borrowers are required to join a peer group and make small deposits. After the first two borrowers start to repay, others may borrow from the pool. Loan losses have been quite small. See Ford Foundation (1991).

banks to mobilize the transfer of capital over these distances. Measured by gross returns on earning assets of banks, interest rates were several hundred basis points lower in the northeastern states than in the distant western and southern states. In 1900, for example, the return on earning assets at New England banks was 6.34% as compared to 8.95% at western banks in the Great Plains and Mountain states.[12]

Extending Distance in the Transfer of Resources

The barrier to funds mobility in the United States was overcome primarily by the development of a national commercial paper market late in the nineteenth century. "Commercial paper" in this context means bills of exchange or notes issued in the course of commercial transactions. For example, when a manufacturer sold goods on credit to a wholesaler, the trade credit took the form of a note issued by the wholesaler and endorsed (i.e., guaranteed) by the manufacturer.[13]

Commercial paper dealers operated primarily in the Northeast, but they spread to several midwestern cities by 1880 and to the West Coast by the turn of the century. These dealers competed with local banks in the Midwest, for example, by placing commercial paper from the region with northeastern banks, obtaining lower interest rates for the borrower. This forced the midwestern banks to reduce their interest rates on local business loans. As would be expected, the result was a trend toward equalization of interest rates across the country as funds moved more efficiently outside local regions.[14]

The commercial paper market proved to be a successful means of transferring resources because it provided a cost-effective way to deal with some of the information and incentive problems.[15] A distant bank that purchased the note might not have much information about the wholesaler, but the manufacturer knew the wholesaler well enough to take the credit risk. Furthermore, the need for the wholesaler to continue to purchase from the manufacturer provided an incentive to pay off the note, and these repeated business transactions lowered the cost of monitoring for the manufacturer.

Not all of the information disparity problems were solved in this

---

12. See Davis (1965) for a discussion of the interest rate differentials.
13. Bills of exchange have a long history. They were first created in Europe in the thirteenth century in the Italian cities of Genoa, Florence, and Venice. Their origin may be even earlier in the Islamic nations. See Braudel (1982), pp. 113 and 556.
14. See Davis (1965) for a discussion of the development of the commercial paper market.
15. Because the notes were short-term and were "self-liquidating" as the wholesaler paid for the goods, the notes were also considered less risky. See Lamoreaux (1991).

process. Adverse selection was still an issue because the manufacturer might endorse risky notes in a last-ditch effort to move inventory, or the commercial paper dealer might try to sell riskier paper to an uninformed bank. These problems, however, were not sufficient to prevent the commercial paper market from developing as a more effective means to transfer resources, thus reducing the interest rate differentials that existed in the United States.

The commercial paper market shows that the development of securities markets played a key role in making the transfer of economic resources more efficient. The use of secured debt to fund U.S. railroads in the 1830s, mentioned above, is another example. Early railroads in New England were typically financed locally through equity investments of nearby residents who could follow the construction progress and who would benefit from the railroads. As railroads covered greater distances, and it became necessary to attract funds from more distant investors, the form of financing shifted to secured debt.[16] This form of financing lowers the high cost of gathering information and monitoring investments from a distance, since it restricts the borrowers' use of the funds. A lien on assets, for example, prevents borrowers from selling the assets and investing the proceeds in riskier endeavors.[17]

Development of the U.S. Home Mortgage Market

One of the most important recent examples of an improved capability to transfer economic resources across regions is the development of a securitized market for home mortgages. Even as the early building associations evolved into savings and loan associations and other types of savings institutions, they retained their local nature. This happened partly because of tradition and because of prohibitions against out-of-state lending, but it occurred also because there is an important local aspect to mortgage lending. People with knowledge of local market conditions need to participate in the mortgage application and appraisal process, as well as deal with the loan and property in the event of default. Thus, "agents" of the lender need to be locally based, so they will have access to much more information than a distant provider of funds would normally possess. This factor means that the possibility of information and incentive problems increases as the distance between the borrower and the lender grows. One study of mutual savings banks, for example, finds

---

16. Tufano (1994) made this observation based on the historical analysis of Chandler (1954).
17. See Stulz and Johnson (1985) for a discussion of how secured debt lowers the cost of monitoring.

a direct correlation between loan loss rates on mortgages and the distance of the loan from the home office.[18]

Early Attempts at Interregional Lending[19]

Several attempts to develop interregional mortgage markets were made in the last century, but each of them failed after a relatively short period of time. "National" building associations, for example, began to be formed in the mid-1800s to compete with the local intermediaries. These groups paid solicitors to recruit members in areas that were hundreds of miles away and set up local boards to originate and monitor loans in those locations. This movement grew to 240 national associations, but a wave of closings began in 1896, and by the early 1900s only six remained. These six had restricted their lending business to local areas.

Lending agents also emerged as a way of providing the local contact and information needed. These agents played a significant role in originating and servicing mortgages, primarily for individual investors in the mid-1800s. They tended to be local lawyers, real estate promoters, or bankers who knew the local market much better than distant lenders. There was a substantial incentive problem here, since the agents were paid a commission for new loans. In some instances they received other benefits as well. Real estate promoters, for example, had a clear incentive to obtain loans for their customers.

Mortgage companies formed in the mid-1800s brought an increased level of professionalism to the market. They supervised the origination and monitoring activities of loan agents through a traveling supervisory force, and they serviced the mortgages, collecting payments and transmitting them to the lender. To give added reassurance to lenders, the mortgage companies began to guarantee their loans, first informally and then formally during the land boom of the 1880s. This package of services proved to be an effective way of attracting mortgage funds, perhaps to the extent that it contributed to the boom in land prices. In any event, when land prices collapsed in the next decade, the mortgage company structure collapsed as well.

After the failure of almost all of the national building associations, insurance companies were the only traditional financial intermediary that

---

18. Lintner (1948) studied foreclosure costs for mortgages made by Massachusetts mutual savings banks between 1918 and 1931. The net loss on loans close to the home office was 3.8%. This increased to 7.1% for loans made two to three cities distant and to 10.0% for loans four or more cities away. The study is quoted in Snowden (1995).
19. This section relies heavily on Snowden (1995). See his work for a further discussion of the development of the interregional mortgage market.

actively provided mortgage funds interregionally. They suffered like other participants when land prices crashed in the 1890s, for example, but they began to put in place a number of mechanisms that dealt more effectively with the incentive problems involved in long-distance lending. Some hired loan agents as salaried employees to reduce the incentives posed by the commission structure. Although mortgage companies still played an important role, insurance companies began to put safeguards in place. These included restricting mortgage companies to exclusive relationships, the specification of criteria for acceptable loans, and the right to return loans to the mortgage company after one year. Insurance companies also strengthened their property management skills so that they could better handle defaults.

The Development of Securitized Mortgages

Even the insurance companies' efforts failed under the weight of the Great Depression. Although it would still take several decades before a fully functioning securitization process was in place, the U.S. government made some key decisions as a result of this traumatic period. An important first step was formation of the Federal Housing Administration (FHA) in 1934. It offered credit insurance on mortgages that met the underwriting standards it established. In addition, it developed the long-term, self-amortizing mortgage that became the standard loan structure in residential financing. Thus, the FHA not only provided a means to reduce credit risk to lenders, but it also took the first steps in standardizing the underwriting criteria and the mortgage design, both of which were critical to the later securitization process.[20]

While these are significant advances in facilitating the transfer of resources, they did not shift the mortgage market from a local to an interregional or long-distance market. Savings institutions and commercial banks still accounted for 73% of the outstanding home mortgages in 1970, as shown in Table 4-1. Virtually all of these institutions provided mortgage loans only within their home state, and often within a more narrowly defined home region or community. The volume of mortgage loans available within a particular region was still limited by the funds available to the local depository institutions.

This began to change after rising interest rates in the late 1960s and the resulting increase in lending institutions' costs of funds caused yet another crisis in the thrift industry. The Federal National Mortgage Associa-

---

20. Fabozzi and Modigliani (1992) make this point in their discussion of the development of the U.S. mortgage market.

Table 4-1 Home Mortgage Debt Outstanding, by Holder, 1950 to 1993[a]
(percentages of total)

	1950	1960	1970	1980	1990	1993
Thrift Institutions (Savings and Loan Associations and Mutual Savings Banks)	37%	52%	58%	50%	22%	15%
Commercial Banks	22	14	15	17	18	18
Life Insurance Companies	20	18	10	2	1	0
Government Agencies	4	5	8	8	6	8
Federal-Related Mortgage Pools				11	38	43
Others[b]	17	11	2	12	15	16
Total	100%	100%	100%	100%	100%	100%

Sources: Data for 1950–1970 taken from the *Statistical Abstract of the United States*, 1976, 96th Annual Edition. Data for 1980–1993 taken from the *Federal Reserve Flow of Funds Accounts*, First Quarter 1994.

[a]Mortgages on one- to four-family structures.

[b]Includes mortgage companies, real estate investment trusts, state and local retirement funds, noninsured pension funds, state and local credit agencies, credit unions, and finance companies.

tion (Fannie Mae) and the Federal Home Loan Mortgage Association (Freddie Mac) were authorized in 1970 to purchase pools of mortgages and to issue securities collateralized by the pools. Fannie Mae and Freddie Mac, federally sponsored entities, guaranteed the payment of interest and principal. The Government National Mortgage Association (Ginnie Mae), an agency of the government, also supported securitization. It guaranteed securities issued by private entities that pooled mortgages guaranteed by the FHA and other federal agencies.

While mortgage pools in which the government plays some role still dominate the mortgage-backed securities market, private securitization has also emerged as an important factor. Commercial banks, investment banks, and others package nongovernment-guaranteed loans and issue securities backed by pools of mortgages. In order to obtain a high credit rating from rating agencies such as Moody's and Standard & Poor's, the credit quality of the mortgage-backed securities is enhanced in any of several ways. The issuer of the securities can provide a corporate guarantee to back the security if it has a sufficiently high credit rating of its own, or credit insurance can be purchased from one of the firms in this business. Alternatively, a mortgage pool can be structured so that there are senior and subordinate securities. The senior debt holder has priority on the cash flow. The subordinated debt is held by the issuer or sold to investors willing to take the higher risk. The amount of the subordinate debt is selected so that the senior debt receives a high credit rating.

The Impact of Mortgage Securitization

Mortgage securitization has transformed a highly localized lending market into one in which interregional and even international lending is commonplace. Of the $1,056 billion of mortgages originated in the United States in 1993, $665 billion or 63% were securitized.[21] The largest originator of mortgages in the United States is not a savings institution or other financial intermediary. It is a mortgage banking firm, Countrywide Credit Industries, Inc., which originates and then sells mortgages to investors. With offices in 41 of the 50 states, this company originated over $50 billion of mortgages in 1993, for a market share in excess of 5%.[22] Savings institutions still originate and hold mortgage loans for homes in their communities, but by 1993 they held only 15% of the mortgages outstanding, down from 58% in 1970. (Total mortgages held by savings institutions are more than this because they also own mortgage-backed securities.)

The securitization process, particularly for mortgages, has made the transfer of economic resources much more efficient by eliminating the tight link between the origination and the funding of the loan. For example, a savings bank in a young, rapidly growing community might have had difficulty in the past funding the demand for mortgages from its customers, while a bank in a mature community with an established housing stock might well have had excess liquidity. With securitization, loans can be originated in the growing community and sold to savings banks with weak loan demand or to any institution with funds to invest. The tight geographic link between deposit taking and lending is no longer the constraint it was in earlier years, as the securitization of various types of consumer loans, including credit card receivables, automobile loans, home equity loans and others, is now routine in the United States.

Moreover, the movement of resources through time has been enhanced by the securitization process. The typical mortgage loan in the United States, a long-term amortizing instrument with a fixed interest rate, offered advantages to borrowers. History has shown that this is not an

---

21. Inside Mortgage Finance (1994).
22. Countrywide Credit Industries, Inc. (1994).

attractive security for investors, however, or even for the savings institutions that typically held the instrument. By splitting mortgage pools into cash flows with differing maturities, it has been possible to structure separate mortgage instruments, each of which appeals to a specific type of investor.

Indeed, this is one of the important motivations supporting the development of the market. Pension funds, for example, have a need for long-duration assets to match their long liabilities. With mortgage-backed securities, it is possible to create long-duration assets by separating out appropriate cash flows from the mortgage pool. Similarly, instruments were created to meet the interests of commercial banks, mutual funds, and so on. As of mid-1993, pension funds owned 12.7% of the outstanding mortgage-backed securities, banks owned 25.4%, and non-U.S. institutions owned 10.4%. Savings and loan associations, the traditional mortgage lender, owned only 10.6%.[23]

While the government played a key role in this transformation of the mortgage market, many other enabling factors affected the ease of securitization. What kept the early mortgage market local was the substantial disparity in information available to the lender on the one hand, and that available to the other parties—the borrower, the local agent, and the mortgage company. This disparity created substantial incentive problems. In the modern mortgage market, the information required about a loan applicant is highly standardized, readily available, and easily checked. Estimating the market value of the property requires judgment, but the appraisal process is routine, and data on comparable home sales are a required part of the process.

In the language of Chapter 7, which is devoted to a discussion of information and incentive problems in financial contracting, the value of the residential property is not "information-sensitive." That is, the borrower has no special information that will not become available in the lender's approval process. Furthermore, there is minimal moral hazard. The use of the funds is restricted to the purchase of the home, and the buyers have an incentive to maintain the property since they retain ownership.

While adverse selection was a serious problem with early loan agents, in the modern market the criteria for loan approval are easily spelled out in terms of appropriate loan-to-value ratios and other variables. Criteria used for mortgages to be put in the pool are also clearly specified, and there is an audit process that checks for compliance. In addition, the issuer of the securities has an incentive to manage the quality of mortgages put into the pool because a good reputation allows future deals to be done.

---

23. Inside Mortgage Finance (1994).

The Large Corporate Market

Current lending to large corporations contrasts sharply with earlier mortgage and business lending, when being close to the borrower was the only way to reduce the disparity in information and manage the incentive problems. Large corporations around the world now disclose a substantial amount of information to financial institutions and markets. Even though the extent of disclosure varies, depending upon practices in the home market of each company, the desire to access international financial markets has encouraged both increased and more standardized disclosure. This information is processed and analyzed by credit analysts at major rating agencies and at numerous lending institutions around the world. It is digested by equity analysts at financial firms and institutional investors. Any new information about a firm, either released by the firm or uncovered by the news media, is immediately available through modern communications systems. Furthermore, individuals who trade a company's securities watch intently for changes in trading volume or price that might signal new information about the company.

The role of the home bank has changed considerably as a result of the improved flow of information concerning these large corporations. Once upon a time, a bank close to a large borrower had a substantial information advantage that gave it an especially important role in extending credit and playing the lead role in loan syndications and other debt issues. Today, this information advantage has virtually disappeared for corporate customers with high credit ratings. Companies with AAA ratings can issue debt securities at the same price as a similarly rated bank, and they do. Highly rated companies regularly issue debt securities in both domestic and international markets, in lieu of bank borrowing. Home country banks still have a competitive edge *vis-à-vis* outside institutions because of historical ties, local regulations, and other services they provide to the customer. But, when competing for a lead management position on a financing deal, the ability of a banking firm to distribute securities in the desired currency may be much more important than any information advantage of the home bank.

In spite of the improved information flow, corporations are still somewhat opaque to outsiders. Managers at any business have more information about the firm's problems and prospects than lenders and investors outside the firm. This affects their cost of external financing, so they seek ways to lower the cost by using assets that are more easily understood. This is the modern version of borrowing from a "local banker" who knows your firm well enough to understand that you are a low-risk borrower. Setting up a captive finance company and using it as a borrowing vehicle is one example. Securitizing receivables is another. American

Express, for example, securitized its charge card receivables in the first financing of this type.[24]

Large commercial and universal banks have assisted in this process by establishing a new kind of financial institution, called a multi-seller conduit, that finances accounts receivable of large international companies. As the name implies, each conduit is used to securitize the receivables of multiple companies, not just a single seller of receivables.[25]

Deutsche Bank, Citicorp, and Union Bank of Switzerland (UBS), among others, have established such conduits. In its second conduit, UBS established Mont Blanc Capital Corporation (MBCC) as a multi-seller, multi-currency securitization conduit for large corporations with accounts receivable from European companies. The corporations can fund receivables denominated in any European currency by selling a pool of these receivables to MBCC, the conduit. Or, they can borrow from MBCC using a pool as collateral. MBCC funds itself primarily by issuing A-1+/P-1-rated $U.S. domestic commercial and Euro-commercial paper, as well as AAA/Aaa-rated medium-term notes. Hedging programs are used to minimize interest rate or currency risk.[26]

The high credit rating is obtained by using two layers of credit protection. Each seller of receivables provides some form of credit enhancement for its specific pool, such as overcollateralization or cash collateral. Then UBS provides an additional layer of credit protection that is programwide and covers 10% of the total program. It also maintains liquidity facilities in various currencies to assure adequate financing.

Mont Blanc Capital Corporation and other conduits are essentially special-purpose "wholesale banks" that have a much lower cost structure than traditional wholesale banking. A study of the conduits estimates the following cost structure:[27]

Distribution and administration	15 basis points
Liquidity enhancement	20
Structuring cost (annualized)	10
Credit enhancement	10
Total	55 basis points

Conduits are able to borrow at an average of 7 basis points (bp) below the London Interbank Offering Rate (LIBOR). Adding the 55 bp of ex-

---

24. Perold and Singh (1993).
25. The forerunner to multi-seller conduits was single-seller conduits in the United States. The first such conduit was Premium Funding Inc., formed by Citibank and Merrill Lynch in 1991. See Gage (1991).
26. Union Bank of Switzerland (1994).
27. This discussion of multi-seller conduits draws on a study by Dobson (1993).

penses brings the all-in cost to the seller up to 48 bp above LIBOR, still 14 bp cheaper than single-seller securitization programs because of economies of scale in the multi-seller programs. For sellers with A+ to BBB-ratings, the cost of conduit securitization is roughly comparable with the cost of raising medium-term finance directly on the balance sheet.

Thus, a lower all-in cost is not usually the primary motivation for investment-grade companies to use these conduits. The major advantages are the ability to raise off-balance sheet financing and to diversify sources of funds. In some instances, this form of financing is also an incremental source of funds that otherwise would be difficult to obtain. The selling corporation is able to fund on an anonymous basis through the conduit, thus avoiding use of bank or investor limits for its direct debt obligations.

For corporations below investment-grade, conduits could potentially reduce the cost of borrowing, although conduits in Europe retain some credit exposure to the seller during the time that accounts receivable payments are in transit from customers. In the United States, conduits are able to receive these payments directly via post office mail boxes rather than have them pass through the selling corporation. There is a relative lack of lock-box systems and daily settlement capabilities in Europe that would provide this protection to the conduit, so most programs exclude subinvestment-grade sellers.

Middle-Market Lending

While home mortgage lending and the financing of the receivables of investment-grade corporations are dramatically different market segments, they do share a common characteristic. In both segments, there are identifiable assets that are not especially information-sensitive. As a result, it is possible to structure transactions in which borrowing needs can be met by selling securities to investors in distant locations. The result is an efficient transfer of resources over long distances.

In contrast with other advances in these market segments, the institutional arrangements for lending to smaller and medium-size companies remain comparatively unchanged. The information disparity between these mid-market borrowers and their lenders is relatively large, leading to significant adverse-selection and moral-hazard problems. When a new prospect shows up to apply for a business loan, how does the banker know if the applicant meets the risk criteria of the bank and qualifies for the bank's standard terms? It is relatively costly to gather the data and analyze them to answer this question and prevent adverse selection.

If a loan is granted, the monitoring costs in dealing with moral-hazard problems are also high. Smaller companies, for example, often seek rapid growth, which requires ever-increasing investments in working capital and fixed assets, financed with the lender's funds. If a company gets into difficulty, the incentive problem may worsen as the firm seeks to work its way out of difficulty by extending excessive credit to weaker customers. Or, the owners may seek to take funds out of the business to invest in other activities. These moral-hazard problems can be dealt with to some extent by restricting the loan maturity so that management must frequently reapply and provide updated information to the bank, by imposing covenants that restrict management's flexibility, and by taking collateral. Each of these actions, however, increases the monitoring costs.

Nearby intermediaries have a substantial information advantage when dealing with these customers, much like the nineteenth century local institutions. Institutions that are physically close are much more likely to have knowledge about the borrower, whether through personal contact or general reputation. The cost of monitoring the borrower on a regular basis is also lower if the lending institution is nearby. This is particularly true if the borrower is using the lending bank for its payments transactions. The pattern of cash inflow and outflow often contains important information about a borrower's financial condition.

While the local bank has a clear information advantage, it is technically possible for a credit guarantee to be separated from the funding. A local bank or other institution can carry out the credit approval process and agree to monitor the borrower. Then, instead of providing funds itself, it could guarantee the loan for another lender. This happens regularly in the United States and Europe when a bank provides a credit enhancement that allows noninvestment-grade borrowers to issue securities in the commercial paper market. It has not yet happened on a regular basis for the smaller loans involved in U.S. mid-market lending. The relatively small size of these loans makes it uneconomical unless a way can be developed to package these loans into a pool, as in the securitization of home mortgages and other consumer credit.

Mid-Market Securitization: The Case of
Fremont Financial Corporation

There is one successful example in the United States of the securitization of mid-market commercial loans. Fremont Financial Corporation is a relatively small commercial finance company that specializes in middle-market lending. In 1992, the company had a $282 million loan portfolio of 190 borrowers, for an average loan size of about $1.5 million. All of its loans are secured by accounts receivable and inventory, with the amount of the available loan tied by formula to these assets. The borrowing clients and their collateral are monitored very closely. All cash receipts of the clients are made through Fremont, and about 75% of the company's personnel are employed solely for the monitoring function.[28]

Fremont normally financed its lending by borrowing from commercial banks. In 1993, however, it successfully structured and sold securities backed by its pool of company loans. The structure is similar to that for other securitized loan pools. A separate finance subsidiary was set up to purchase loans from Fremont Financial. This subsidiary then placed the loans in a Master Trust that issued securities secured by the pool of loans. Fremont enhanced the credit quality of these securities by providing a large enough pool of loans to overcollateralize the senior securities and by purchasing nontransferable subordinated certificates.

For the first issue of these transactions, Fremont was able to obtain an AAA rating from Standard & Poor's Corp. and Duff & Phelps Corp. Just prior to Fremont's second issue later in the year, however, Moody's Investor Services gave an unsolicited rating on the earlier issue of only Baa1, well below the AAA rating given by the other rating services. Moody's was reported to have concerns that the deal structure did not give investors enough protection should Fremont Financial fail. Since Fremont was the major lender to most of its borrowers, there was concern that its failure would trigger a chain of borrower defaults.[29] This added 25 basis points to the cost of the second issue.

Other Nationwide Mid-Market Lending

While securitization is one way to transfer funds over long distances, another is for a financial intermediary to lend through widespread branches and fund the loans by issuing deposits or securities in the name of the intermediary. Commercial banks, while they have extended their reach in the United States through out-of-state acquisitions, have not achieved true nationwide lending through branches. The more common widespread lending to mid-market companies is by commercial finance companies, such as Heller Financial and GE Capital. Their lending to middle-market companies is typically secured by accounts receivable, inventory, or machinery and equipment. They also provide funding by factoring accounts receivable and by leasing equipment to mid-market companies. Heller established its business credit group to build a national presence in asset-based lending. All of the group's financings are secured by accounts

---

28. See Sirri and Zeitung (1994). Other securitizations of small business loans have occurred, but they are based on loan assets guaranteed by the Small Business Administration of the U.S. government.
29. See Coleman et al. (1994).

receivable, inventory, or plant and equipment. The company also has an equipment leasing business in which it works with both equipment manufacturers and end users in selected industries such as health care and communications.[30]

It is not surprising that a large share of long-distance lending to the mid-market is tied to specific assets. The use of collateral reduces the cost of monitoring, and, for the assets being financed, the borrower has little if any information advantage. GE Capital's extensive experience with the purchase and sale of assets in its market segments provides it with very useful knowledge. In fact, it may have more information than any one borrower about the economic value of the assets being financed. In addition, GE Capital is positioned in some cases to control the value of the assets over time. The company's railcar leasing business includes six wheel-repair shops scattered over six states to help maintain the cars it rents.[31]

Looking Ahead: Will Mid-Market Lending be Securitized?

The securitization process in home mortgage lending, large corporate lending, and other areas has greatly transformed the institutional arrangements used to transfer resources from lenders to borrowers in these market segments. In these instances, proximity between the borrower and lender is no longer important, and funds are transferred efficiently over long distances. Mid-market lending so far has resisted this structural change, as traditional financial intermediaries have maintained their role in this market. An interesting way to think about the future performance of the transfer function is to consider whether the current institutional arrangements for mid-market lending will continue to stand.

Barriers to Change

There are reasons why commercial banks and other traditional intermediaries play the key role that they do. The incentive problems resulting from information disparities are particularly strong in mid-market lending. Institutions with a local presence have an advantage in gathering information to manage adverse selection and in monitoring the borrower to deal with moral hazard. Institutions that handle the payments transactions of borrowers have an added information advantage as a result of their knowledge of the borrower's cash flow pattern.

Furthermore, some of the techniques used to securitize mortgages and other loans are more difficult to apply in the case of mid-market lending.

30. Heller Financial Inc. (1993).
31. See Paré (1994).

A high degree of standardization has developed in the home mortgage market, both in terms of the information gathered in the approval process and in the nature of the mortgage contract. This standardization makes it relatively easy to specify the mortgages that are put into a mortgage pool. A few key variables such as loan-to-value ratios can be used to define the quality of the mortgages, and straightforward analysis is applied to gain an understanding of the loan loss experience for different quality levels.

Standardization is more difficult to achieve in mid-market lending. There are various types of borrowers, structures of loan arrangements, and underwriting standards across lenders. This makes it much more difficult to specify the criteria and quality of loans to be put into a securitized pool. Perhaps credit-scoring models will prove to be adequate, but it is hard to measure quality by looking at a selected set of ratios. The monitoring process is also more difficult for mid-market loans because the amount and quality of each loan changes over time.

Finally, there are regulatory issues to be resolved before the business loan market can be readily securitized. For example, if a bank sells a pool of loans with partial recourse to the bank, the bank's capital requirements are based on the size of the whole pool, not just the amount of the recourse.[32] This greatly reduces the motivation for U.S. commercial banks to securitize their loans.

Motivations for Change

In spite of these barriers, the technology for securitizing mid-market loans has been successfully developed and utilized. Fremont Financial demonstrates that it can be done. Although there has not yet been a ground swell of similar issues, there are analogues. Heller Financial securitizes the portion of small company loans that is guaranteed by the Small Business Administration (SBA). And, Chrysler Financial Corporation has successfully securitized the nonguaranteed portion of SBA loans by using loans that have real estate as collateral.[33]

The motivation for continued progress in the securitization of mid-market loans stems from the public policy interest in assuring an adequate flow of resources to small- and medium-sized businesses and from competitive pressures on traditional intermediaries. In the securitization of home mortgages, the need for public policy concern was clear-cut because of repeated crises in the local thrift institutions. These institutions have

---

32. Rosenberg and Kravitt (1993).
33. Capasse (1993).

proven to be very inefficient in the task of mobilizing resources over longer distances, and they face substantial interest rate and liquidity risk when they use short-term deposits to fund long-term fixed-rate loans. There has not been a similar crisis in mid-market lending, but there has been a continuing public policy interest, as illustrated by formation of the Small Business Administration and giving it a role in providing credit support for these loans.

Governmental interest grew in 1993 because of a concern that mid-market borrowers were having difficulty obtaining loans. Commercial bank lending to commercial and industrial companies was growing very slowly. Some felt this was because of banks' reluctance to lend rather than because of weak loan demand. U.S. Congressional hearings on the topic, "Secondary Market for Commercial Business Loans," were held by the House Subcommittee on Economic Growth and Credit Formation. There was also a House of Representatives proposal to create a new agency, Venture Enhancement and Loan Development Administration for Small, Undercapitalized Enterprises (Velda-Sue), that would sponsor secondary market transactions. Other proposals did not go so far, preferring to liberalize regulations and encourage the private sector to create a secondary market on its own.[34] Although these efforts lost momentum by 1994 as Congress turned its attention to other matters and the pace of business lending picked up, the seeds of regulatory and legislative change have been planted.

Middle-market lending remains an attractive market segment for commercial banks, so there is little motivation for commercial bankers to develop a securitized market for these loans. On the other hand, with increased competition on many fronts, there is pressure on banks to reduce operating costs and an incentive to develop more standardization in mid-market loans. Bankers are reducing the amount of loan officer time required to tailor individual loan agreements by designing a small number of standardized loan contracts for smaller business loans. Although this approach will not necessarily lead to securitization, standardization is a necessary step.

The biggest pressure for change comes from the fact that securities have proved to be a very efficient way to transfer economic resources over long distances—for home mortgages, lending to large corporations, and other purposes. If the information and incentive problems can be dealt with, securities provide a means to unlink the location of the source of funds from their use, allowing the efficient movement of funds to their most productive purposes.

---

34. Cushman (1993).

What Role for Institutions?

It is too early to tell if securitization of mid-market loans will become widespread, or what form it will take if it develops, but there is reason to anticipate pressures on the current institutional arrangements for transferring resources to this market. Instead of securitization, an alternative model to broaden the geographic scope of funding for mid-market loans in the United States would be nationwide banking, an event likely to occur. Then a giant bank could tap its deposit sources in the Northeast, for example, to fund mid-market loans in the West. Will this be the most efficient way to transfer resources to mid-market borrowers?

Perhaps it will be more efficient for a bank or other lending institution located in the West to originate mid-market loans and structure pools of these loans for securitization. An institution's ability to manage the information problems involved in originating and monitoring the loan portfolio over time may be a more important competitive advantage than the widespread funding capability of a giant nationwide bank.

References

Braudel, F. (1982), *The Wheels of Commerce: Civilization and Capitalism, 15th–18th Century,* Volume II, New York: Harper & Row.

Capasse, T.E. (1993), "Growing Market for Commercial Loan Securitization," House of Representatives Subcommittee on Economic Growth and Credit Formation of the Committee on Banking, Finance and Urban Affairs, April 21, Washington, D.C.: U.S. Government Printing Office.

Chandler, A. Jr. (1954), "Patterns of American Railroad Finance, 1830–50," *Business History Review* (September) 28: 248–263.

Coleman, C., S. Davis, M. Peltz, and I. Picker (1994), "Anything and Everything," *Institutional Investor,* 28 (1): 70–78.

Countrywide Credit Industries, Inc. (1994), *1994 Annual Report,* Pasadena, CA.

Cushman, J.H., Jr. (1993), "Investing in Loans to Businesses," *New York Times,* March 29, D: 1.

Davis, L.E. (1965), "The Investment Market, 1870–1914: The Evolution of a National Market," *Journal of Economic History,* 33: 355–393.

Dobson, A. (1993), "The Prospects for Conduits in European Asset-Backed Financing," *International Securitization Review* (October): 19–31.

Fabozzi, F.J., and F. Modigliani (1992), *Mortgage & Mortgage-Backed Securities Markets,* Boston: Harvard Business School Press.

Ford Foundation (1991), *Investing for Social Gain: Reflections on Two Decades of Program-Related Investments,* New York: Ford Foundation.

Fraser, D.R., and R.M. Richards (1985), "The Penn Square Bank Failure and the Inefficient Market," *Journal of Portfolio Management* (Spring): 34–36.

Gage, T.J. (1991), "Wall St. Rapunzel Offers Access to Capital Markets Tower," *Corporate Cash Flow* (September): 7.

Group of Thirty (1989), *Clearance and Settlement Systems in the World's Securities Markets*, New York: Group of Thirty.

Heller Financial, Inc. (1993), *Form 10K*, Chicago.

Inside Mortgage Finance (1994), *The Mortgage Market Statistical Annual for 1994*, Washington, D.C.: Inside Mortgage Finance Publications.

Klebaner, B.J. (1990), *American Commercial Banking: A History*, Boston: Twayne Publishers.

Lamoreaux, N.R. (1991), "Information Problems and Banks' Specialization in Short-Term Commercial Lending: New England in the Nineteenth Century," in *Inside the Business Enterprise: Historical Perspectives on the Use of Information*, Peter Temin, ed., Chicago: The University of Chicago Press, 161–203.

Lintner, J. (1948), "Mutual Savings Banks in the Savings and Mortgage Markets," Harvard University, Boston.

McKendrick, N. (1993), *The Birth of Foreign & Colonial: The World's First Investment Trust, 19 March 1868*, Cambridge.

Morgan Guaranty Trust Company of New York (1984), *World Financial Markets*, January.

Ornstein, F.H. (1985), *Savings Banking: An Industry in Change*, Reston: Reston Publishing.

Paré, T.P. (1994), "GE Monkeys with its Money Machine," *Fortune* (February): 81–87.

Perold, A.F., and K. Singh (1993), "American Express TRS Charge-Card Receivables," Harvard Business School Case 293–120, Boston.

Rosenberg, R., and J. Kravitt (1993), "How Feasible Is the Securitization of Loans to Small and Medium-Sized Businesses?" *Commercial Lending Review*, 8 (4): 4–15.

Sirri, E.R., and A. Zeitung (1994), "Fremont Financial Corporation," Harvard Business School Case 294–054, Boston.

Snowden, J.A. (1995), "The Evolution of Interregional Mortgage Lending Channels, 1870–1940: The Life Insurance-Mortgage Company Connection," in *Information and Coordination: Historical Perspectives on the Organization of Enterprise*, N. Lamoreaux, and D. Raff, eds., Chicago: University of Chicago Press.

Stulz, R.M., and H. Johnson (1985), "An Analysis of Secured Debt," *Journal of Financial Economics*, 14 (4): 501–521.

Tufano, P. (1995), "Securities Innovations: A Historical and Functional Perspective," in *Cases in Financial Engineering: Applied Studies of Financial Innovation*, S. Mason, R. Merton, A. Perold, and P. Tufano, eds., Englewood Cliffs, NJ: Prentice Hall.

Union Bank of Switzerland (1994), "Mont Blanc: Multi Seller Securitisation Programme for European Currency Trade and Financial Receivables," Zurich (August).

Welfling, W. (1968), *Mutual Savings Banks: The Evolution of a Financial Intermediary*, Cleveland: The Press of Case Western Reserve University.

CHAPTER FIVE

The Allocation of Risk

SCOTT P. MASON

Traditional characterizations of the financial system emphasize its role in facilitating the efficient allocation of *capital* in the economy. But an equally important function of the financial system, the efficient allocation of *risks* in the economy, is less well understood. Indeed, the risk allocation function is rapidly evolving due to increased financial innovation. Most notably, innovations in the area of derivatives have significantly increased both the efficiency and the complexity of the risk allocation function. But many question the overall benefits of financial innovations like derivatives. For example, there are fundamental questions over the role of derivatives in past major market dislocations and firm failures. And the debate on government regulation of the global over-the-counter derivatives markets is emblematic of the general concerns about the impact of financial innovation on the stability of the financial system. The objective of this chapter is to inform this debate through a comprehensive description and discussion of the risk allocation function.

This chapter is specifically concerned with the financial system's role in enhancing overall risk allocation in the economy. What is driving the significant financial innovations in the area of risk allocation? First, individuals and firms are not indifferent to the risks they bear, and therefore are made better-off by enhanced risk allocation facilities. Second, higher levels of volatility for interest rates, foreign exchange rates, and commodity prices have increased the potential benefits associated with improved risk allocation. (See Figures 5-1, 5-2, and 5-3.) And third, advances in

Figure 5-1 Percent Difference Five-Year U.S. Treasuries

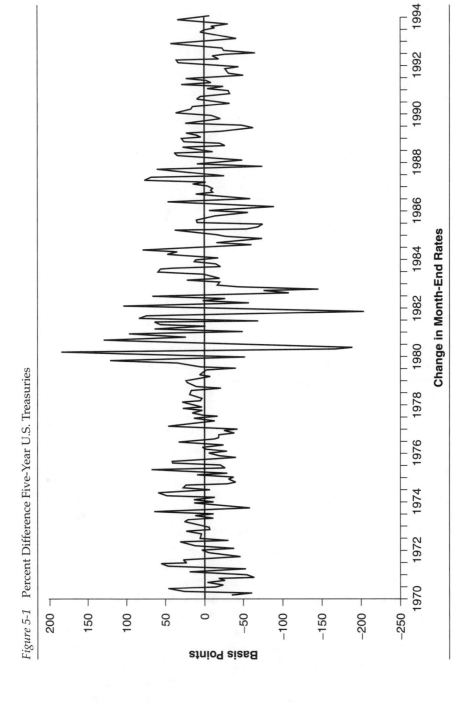

Source: Adapted from Reuters PLC and Smithson and Smith (1995).

Figure 5-2 Percent Change in Deutschemark–U.S. Dollar Exchange Rate

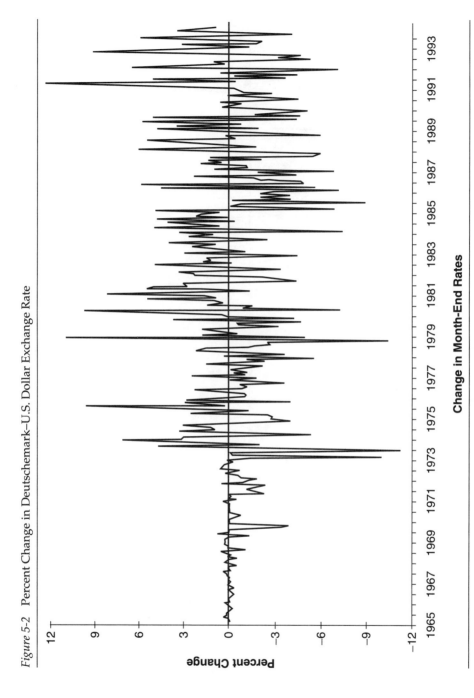

Source: Adapted from Reuters PLC and Smithson and Smith (1995).

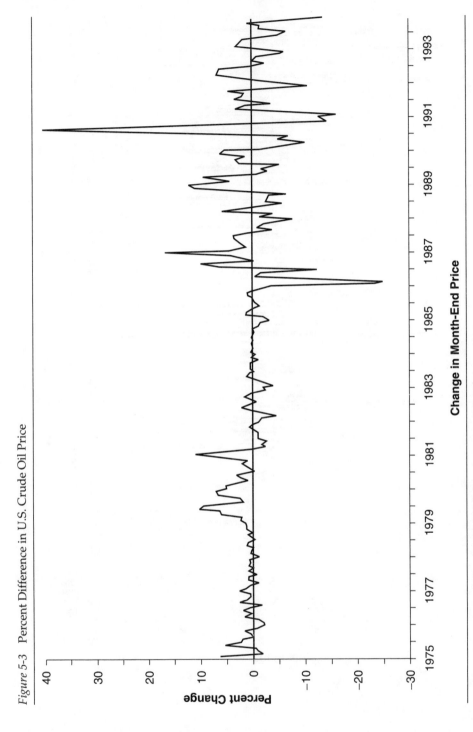

Figure 5-3 Percent Difference in U.S. Crude Oil Price

Source: Adapted from Reuters PLC and Smithson and Smith (1995).

computer and finance technologies have lowered transactions costs, which in turn has enabled a broader range of risk management strategies. The resulting enhanced risk allocation facilities allow for the further separation of the funding and risk-bearing components of financial transactions. Thus individuals and firms are increasingly able to choose the precise risks they wish to bear, and to shed unwanted risks.

The extent of risk allocation in the economy is significant, but not all of this activity involves the financial system. For example, education can be viewed as a means of managing the risks associated with one's human capital. The collective work arrangements of families or tribes have the effect of reducing each individual's risks. Firms reduce workers' risks through implicit lifetime employment agreements. Firms can manage their overall risks through real investment decisions involving, say, plant locations or flexible production technologies. And governments can, given their tax and legal powers, reduce individuals' risks through social insurance programs.

But it is the financial system that is central to the broad-based management and allocation of risks in the economy. Traditionally through securities and insurance markets, and more recently through derivatives markets, the financial system brings the benefits of efficient risk allocation to both individuals and firms. For individuals, insurance affords financial protection from the unanticipated loss of income or wealth. Individuals also use the securities markets for managing risks. For example, the stock market gives an individual the ability to shed or acquire exposure to a company's risk by selling or buying its stock.

Firms also use insurance and securities to manage risks. But, it is probably firms' use of derivative instruments that has attracted the most recent attention. Firms, including financial firms, use both listed and over-the-counter derivative instruments to manage many different types of risks. Options, futures/forwards, swaps, caps/floors, and their many permutations are used to manage firms' equity, commodity, currency, and interest rate exposures. Organized exchanges offer standardized contracts to a variety of end users, while at the same time financial firms create highly customized derivative contracts in the over-the-counter market to meet the special needs of a single customer.

There do exist theoretical arguments against a positive role for risk management at the firm level, based primarily on the availability of essentially equivalent risk management opportunities for individuals. But whether motivated by tax, costs of financial distress, or agency issues, firms are increasingly using complex financial instruments and techniques to address both their operating and strategic exposures. And this is particularly true of financial firms, given the central role of creditworthiness in relationships with their customers.

Despite the wide variety of securities, insurance, and derivatives markets, and the significant advances in risk management techniques in the past 20 years, in some circumstances the private financial system lacks the ability or the willingness to provide certain risk allocation facilities. In many of these situations, the government will promote financial programs that support the desired spreading of risks. Most of these programs involve some form of insurance or loan guarantee that is difficult or impossible for the private financial system to provide. Prominent examples in the United States are Social Security, the insuring of bank deposits through the Federal Deposit Insurance Corporation (FDIC), and the insuring of private defined benefit pension plans through the Pension Benefit Guaranty Corporation (PBGC).

Thus, individuals and firms depend on the financial system in many ways (such as the direct use of the securities, insurance, and derivatives markets) to help manage their risks. In addition, financial transactions and arrangements like fixed versus floating-rate mortgages, defined benefit versus defined contribution pension plans, and lease versus buy all have significant risk allocation components. And government also has a role in the overall risk allocation function, often providing risk-bearing services in the absence of private market alternatives. But it is government's role as regulator that potentially has greater implications for the workings of the financial system generally, and the risk allocation function specifically.

Our purpose in this chapter is to provide a comprehensive treatment of the risk allocation function and thereby offer more insight into the issues underlying the ongoing debate on the systemic implications of financial innovations, like derivatives, for the health of the financial system. First we set forth the economics of risk allocation and describe the role of the financial system in facilitating efficient risk-bearing in the economy. We then describe the three generic means by which the financial system actually affects risk management in the economy. We discuss the role of risk management at the firm level (including the special role of risk management within financial firms) as well as the growth of risk-bearing by the government. We conclude by addressing the debate on the implications of financial innovations like the global over-the-counter derivatives markets for the stability of the financial system and the potential role of government as regulator.

The Allocation of Risk and the Real Economy

Understanding precisely (1) how enhanced risk allocation benefits the economy, and (2) how the financial system facilitates the efficient allocation of risks, is key to the debate on the net effect of financial innovations like derivatives. Yet, much of the observed structure of risk allocation activities is due to market imperfections, such as taxes, regulations, and transactions costs, or agency and asymmetric information issues as discussed in Chapter 7. And while it is important to understand the structural details of risk management in the presence of market imperfections, this institutional understanding will not necessarily make clear the fundamental real economic benefits of enhanced risk allocation.

It is perhaps easiest to see how expanded risk management opportunities affect the real economy if we examine the role of risk allocation in a simple neoclassical, or perfect markets, economy. In a perfect markets economy, individuals derive their ultimate welfare from consumption and are viewed as *the* fundamental real economic unit. Individuals manage the resources such as tangible wealth and human capital, which support consumption, through their investment decisions. Indeed, all institutional (and financial) structure in a neoclassical economy theoretically exists for the *sole* purpose of enhancing overall welfare through the facilitation of individuals' consumption and investment plans.

In a world of *certainty*, the existence of financial securities and markets can improve the allocation of resources in the economy since an individual's savings need not equal the individual's investments on a period-by-period basis. Furthermore, the existence of riskless bonds of every maturity is sufficient to assure an efficient allocation of resources for the overall economy and to provide the appropriate information "signals" to support the separation of consumption and production decisions in the economy (as discussed in Chapter 6). Thus, even in a simple riskless economy, the financial system facilitates the efficient allocation of resources through time.

The individual's consumption investment problem is significantly more complex in the presence of uncertainty because individuals as the ultimate owners of all resources are collectively the ultimate bearers of all risks. Uncertainty affects an individual's welfare through its unexpected consequences for lifetime consumption or the wealth that supports this consumption. The presence of risk has a negative effect on individuals' welfare if we assume that individuals are *risk-averse*.[1] A risk-averse individual will pay an insurance risk premium to avoid an actuarially fair gamble,

---

1. It may seem natural to associate the term *uncertainty* with all unexpected consequences, and the term *risk* with specifically *negative* unexpected consequences. But risk, defined in this relative manner, would then have to be viewed in context; that is, a given change in a particular asset's price could have different unexpected consequences for different individuals' consumption and wealth. A more relevant definition for our purposes is a nonreferential, or absolute, measure of risk. Therefore we will associate both the terms *uncertainty* and *risk* with *all* unexpected consequences of an asset's return.

and will have to be paid a compensatory risk premium to undertake such a gamble willingly. It is precisely in this sense that individuals are not indifferent to the risks they bear.

Arrow (1953) and Debreu (1959) were the first to consider how, in an uncertain economy, both resources and risks get allocated efficiently. They show that the key to an efficient allocation is the existence of securities and markets for all future contingencies, i.e., a *complete market*. In this model uncertainty and time are partitioned into a set of *states*. Associated with each state is a tradable state security that pays a known fixed amount of money only if that state occurs. In the Arrow–Debreu model, an individual uses wealth to fund a lifetime consumption program by forming a portfolio of these state securities.

While elegant by theoretical standards, the Arrow–Debreu complete markets model is so general as to be untestable. And the cost and moral-hazard implications of the number and type of necessary markets make the model of little direct prescriptive or practical use. For example, one implication of the existence of a complete set of state security markets is that individuals need trade only once in order to achieve their most efficient allocation of resources and risk-bearing. But while being an abstraction, the Arrow–Debreu model does suggest, relative to other models, a more comprehensive interpretation of individuals' investment decision-making under uncertainty.

For example, in the Capital Asset Pricing Model (CAPM) the only uncertainty affecting an individual's consumption is that introduced by the portfolio investment decision.[2] In this model allocational efficiency requires only that individuals can choose between two mutual funds: a riskless bond fund and a fund containing all risky assets in proportion to their value. Here the individual decides not which risks to bear, but how much risk to bear (market risk, that is, since all nonmarket risk is assumed to be diversified away in the market portfolio). The result is that while different individuals may decide to bear different amounts of risk, all individuals bear the same type of risk. That is, all individuals hold risky assets in the same proportion. Here securities are viewed primarily as a means for individuals to achieve an efficient risk/return trade-off in their investment activities.

The Arrow–Debreu model suggests that securities serve an additional role. Arrow interprets an individual's portfolio choice of state securities as determined by not only an investment objective, but also by the degree to which that individual prefers to bear various risks. Thus securities are seen by Arrow as providing a general means of managing risks for individuals.

---

2. See Sharpe (1964), Lintner (1965), and Mossin (1966).

This expanded risk management role for securities in the individual's consumption-investment problem is developed fully in Merton (1973b). Merton shows that when individuals' lifetime consumption is affected by uncertainties, in addition to market risk, individuals will register different relative demands for risky investments. Important common sources of uncertainty might include interest rates, the characteristics of the investment opportunity set (e.g., market volatility), or the price of consumption goods.

While in the CAPM the availability of two funds (the riskless asset and the market portfolio) assures individuals of efficient risk-bearing, Merton describes a model where multiple funds corresponding to a set of important common sources of uncertainty provide this same service.[3] In this model, capital markets are posited as "dynamically complete" with regard to these important common sources of uncertainty; that is, it is possible through dynamic trading strategies to "hedge" these sources of uncertainty. This is consistent with Arrow (1953) and Radner (1972), who first pointed out that an Arrow–Debreu equilibrium allocation can be achieved without a full set of state securities if individuals can use dynamic trading strategies to replicate the payoffs to the missing securities. *Thus, with the appropriate financial system infrastructure to support low-cost continuous trading, Merton shows that it is feasible to approximate the risk allocation benefits of the idealized complete markets world of Arrow–Debreu.*[4]

Thus the overall objectives of individuals' investment decisions are to achieve (1) a higher expected level of consumption through a return to capital, (2) a better lifetime allocation of resources, and (3) a lower level of risk by providing hedges against common and idiosyncratic risks. Risk-averse individuals are made better-off by the expansion of risk management facilities in the economy because they are not indifferent to the type, or the amount, of risk they bear. Risk-sharing opportunities allow individuals to choose the risks they wish to bear and to shed unwanted risks.

To the extent that the financial system increases both the efficiency and breadth of risk management in the economy, its risk allocation function enhances economic welfare. Specifically, welfare is enhanced when individuals can use risk management to fashion preferred contingent patterns

---

3. See Merton (1975, 1977b).
4. Besides managing their exposure to common sources of risk, each individual could also register differential demand for risky assets as a means of managing idiosyncratic risks such as specialized human capital, personal tastes, or age of death. Since different individuals could view a long or a short position in the same security as an effective hedge against these personal risks, this type of demand for risky securities should not have a systematic effect on equilibrium expected rates of return. Therefore, we would observe individuals registering different relative hedging demands for the same risky asset.

of lifetime consumption and to manage the risks associated with real investments that they might not otherwise make in the absence of risk-sharing.

The Three Dimensions of Risk Management

The complexity of many risk management activities often serves to mask the fundamental real benefits that enhanced risk allocation provides in the economy. This same complexity also obscures the fact, as touched on in Chapter 1, that risk management services can be viewed in terms of just three generic approaches to risk management; *hedging, diversification,* and *insurance.*[5] *Hedging* allows for the elimination of a risk through the spot sale of the risk, or through a transaction in an instrument that represents an obligation to sell the risk in the future. *Diversification* reduces risk-bearing through the combining of less than perfectly correlated risks. And *insurance* here refers to a set of securities or contracts that limit risk in exchange for the payment of a premium. Despite the myriad of complex institutional arrangements and securities transactions given over to risk management in today's economy, all risk allocation activity can be analyzed in terms of this taxonomy.

Hedging

A risk exposure can be eliminated through a hedging transaction. Hedging mechanisms in the financial system include spot markets, forward/futures markets, and swap markets, as well as special structured arrangements like leasing. Spot markets represent one of the most fundamental means by which the financial system facilitates the management of risks. To give an example of the size of these types of markets, worldwide equity markets in 1992 featured trading volume in excess of $5.5 trillion, with the United States accounting for $2.7 trillion. Computer and finance technologies have lowered the transactions costs associated with trading and therefore expanded the use of hedging markets.[6] Spot markets allow individuals to sell the risks they do not wish to be exposed to and to purchase those risks they prefer to bear. Entrepreneurs can thus separate their personal investment and risk-bearing problems from the capital investment decisions of their enterprise, and consider risky investment

---

5. See Merton (1990). Consistent with the treatment in Merton (1990), we will take risk management in this section to mean the elimination or reduction of risk. More generally, risk management, and the risk allocation function, is also associated with the *acquisition* of selected risk exposures.
6. See Figures 5-4 and 5-5.

Figure 5-4 Ratio of Annual Dollar Trading Volume to Year-End Market Capitalization

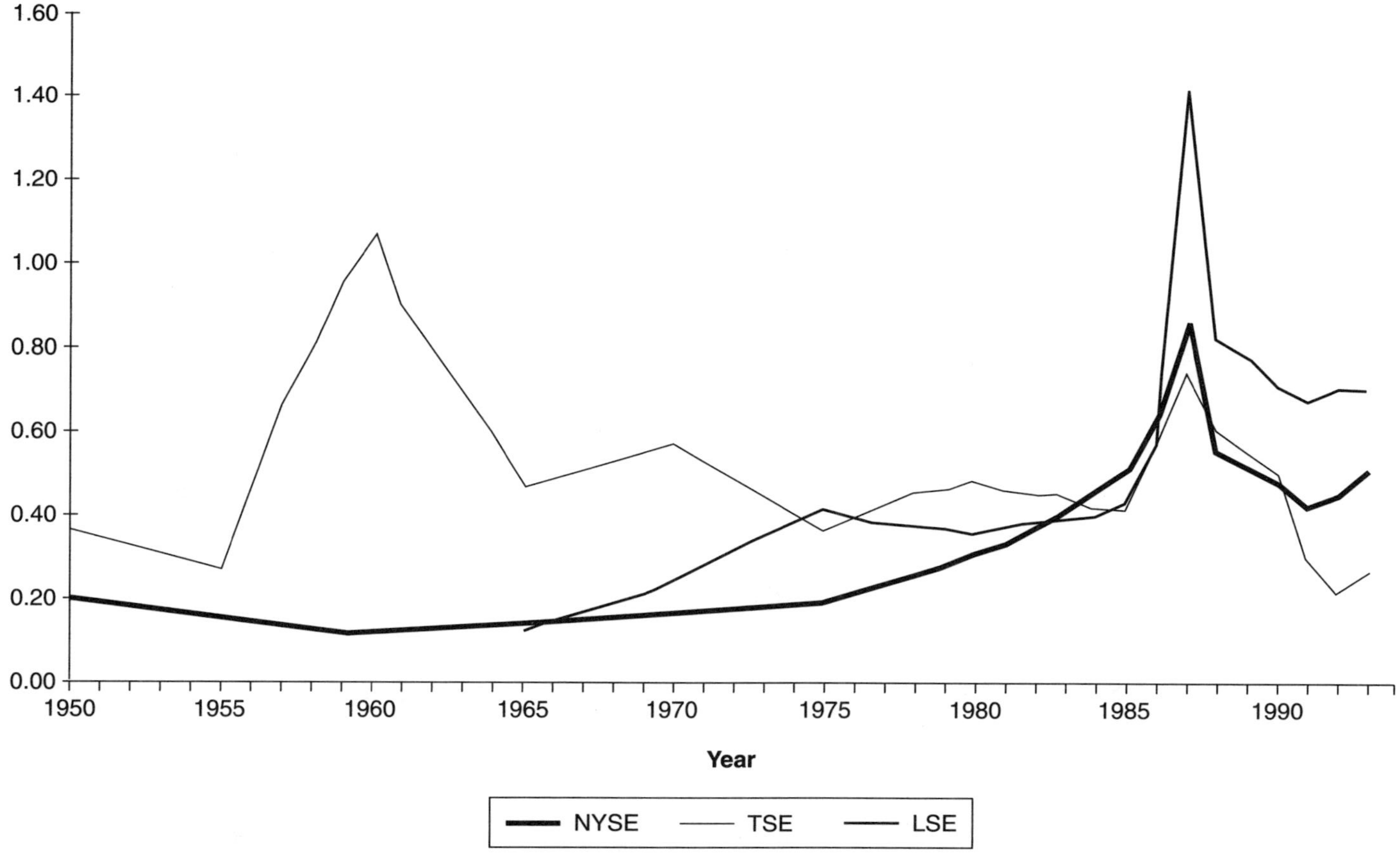

Source: London Stock Exchange, New York Stock Exchange, Tokyo Stock Exchange.

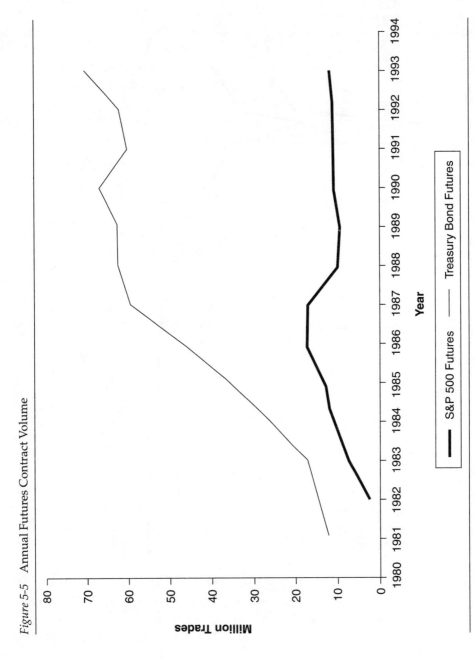

Figure 5-5   Annual Futures Contract Volume

Source: Chicago Board of Trade, Chicago Mercantile Exchange.

opportunities for the firm that might not otherwise have been considered in the absence of risk-sharing.

In the presence of transactions costs, there may be more efficient means than the spot markets to accomplish the same risk management goal. And primary securities may be an imprecise means of managing certain risks.[7] *Forward* and *futures* contracts are derivative instruments that provide an alternative means of hedging risks. The buyer (seller) of a forward or futures contract is obligated to buy (sell) a specified asset on a specified expiration date for a specified contract price. Forwards trade in a few very large institutional over-the-counter markets. The global daily turnover in forward transactions in the foreign exchange market, for example, is estimated at $420 billion.[8]

Consider an example involving a farmer selling and a baker buying a forward contract on wheat so as to hedge their respective exposure to future wheat prices.[9] This simple transaction demonstrates several important points:

1. The opposite sides of the same transaction can be risk-reducing for both individuals. That is, being short (long) the forward contract on wheat is risk-reducing for the farmer (baker), and being long or short the same forward contract on wheat could be risk-increasing for anyone whose wealth is not so directly tied to the price of wheat.

2. In theory, both the farmer and the baker can accomplish the same risk reduction through the use of the spot markets. The farmer could lock in the price of wheat one year from now by "borrowing" wheat today, selling it spot, and promising to replace the borrowed wheat with the future harvest. Similarly, the baker could lock in the price of future wheat purchases by borrowing money, buying the wheat today, and storing it. But it is not difficult to imagine that the transactions costs associated with these spot market solutions—borrowing wheat, borrowing money, and storing wheat—could be high enough to make the forward contract the more efficient means of risk reduction.

3. It is true that either the farmer or the baker will be seen, *ex post*, as having locked in, via the forward transaction, a disadvantageous price for wheat relative to the spot price that will hold on the delivery date for the contract. But this does not alter the fact

7. See Arrow (1953).
8. See Bank for International Settlements (1993).
9. This example is taken from Bodie and Merton (1995).

that both the farmer and the baker achieved an *ex ante* reduction in their overall risk, and therefore both were made better-off by the forward transaction.

4. While the forward contract itself is risky, it does not add to aggregate real risk. The forward contract has the marginal effect of facilitating the efficient pooling of previously existing real risk exposures.

The net result of combining a risk exposure and a sold forward position is to eliminate the risk exposure. The contract price is by convention initially set such that neither the buyer nor the seller requires payment in order to enter the contract. Therefore the economic cost of eliminating any possibility of a loss associated with a risk exposure is the elimination of the possibility of a gain. Selling a forward contract written on the risk exposure is thus equivalent, in risk management terms, to the outright sale of the risk exposure. But, in many instances, issues like explicit and implicit transactions costs, regulation, or tax will argue for the use of the forward market instead of the spot market for risk management purposes.

Futures contracts, which are essentially standardized forward contracts, trade on a wide variety of organized exchanges around the world. The size and the standardization of futures contracts make the futures market accessible to individuals who are unable to trade in the institutional over-the-counter derivatives markets such as the forward market. By the end of 1991 a total of $2.25 trillion (notional amount) of exchange-traded financial futures contracts were outstanding globally, written on interest rates, currencies, and stock market indexes.

While futures perform essentially the same risk management function as forward contracts, many contract features of futures are designed to address the management of the credit risks inherent in the trading of forward-like-contracts in a public market. These features include initial margin, variation margin, maintenance margin, and a central clearing mechanism. And in order to assure that these public markets will operate at volumes sufficient to justify their costs of operation, futures contracts are written on sources of uncertainty important to a vast number of individuals and firms. As a result we observe, for example, futures markets in U.S. Treasury bonds, the Eurodollar, the S&P 500, and the yen/dollar exchange rate.

Given forward and futures contracts, it is possible to disaggregate aggregated risks and to allow for more precise management of risks than through the use of primary securities. So, for example, a businessperson can sell yen futures, as an alternative to selling shares in her firm, to manage a foreign currency risk exposure, or a farmer can sell wheat futures, as opposed to an interest in his farm, as a more direct means of managing exposure to wheat prices.

A *swap* is another type of over-the-counter derivative instrument that facilitates the hedging of risks. A swap contract obligates two parties to exchange two defined cash flow streams at specified intervals, for a specified period of time. The interim contractual cash flows are either fixed or calculated by multiplying the notional amount of the swap by specified reference rates or prices. The great majority of these transactions are classified as either interest rate, currency, equity, or commodity swaps.

Swaps can be thought of as a structured set of forward contracts. Consistent with this characterization, swaps typically have an initial value of zero, with the periodic rate of exchange between the two cash flow streams and/or the associated notional amounts set so that neither party requires a payment in order to enter into the agreement. Given transactions costs, tax, regulations, and accounting standards, however, swaps often prove to be a more efficient means of managing risks than the equivalent set of hedging transactions in either the spot or forward/futures markets.[10] By the end of 1992, the total notional amount of interest rate and currency swaps outstanding globally was $4.7 trillion.[11]

There are structured securities and transactions in the financial system that also facilitate the management of risks through hedging. For example, leasing an automobile can be viewed as separating the use of the automobile from the risk of owning the automobile. In this sense, an automobile lease is equivalent to the simultaneous purchase and forward sale of the automobile. The purchase of a fixed annuity to provide retirement income or the refinancing of a floating-rate mortgage with a fixed-rate mortgage are other examples of using financial transactions to hedge risks. Finally, there are structured debt securities whose payouts are indexed to quantities like the price of oil or the level of the stock market that are used to manage risk via hedging.

Hedging is the elimination of a risk exposure through a spot or a forward transaction in the financial markets. Yet transacting in primary securities like equities may be, relative to the ideal of pure state securities, an imprecise means of managing risk. And more cost-efficient hedging vehicles, like forwards/futures or swaps, can also prove to be imprecise in the presence of exact risk management objectives. In the discussion of insurance, the third dimension of risk management, it will be shown how insurance contracts, options, and the dynamic trading of spot markets address these issues of imprecision.

---

10. See Perold (1992).
11. International Swaps and Derivatives Association (ISDA).

Diversification

The risk-pooling benefits of diversification are the functional justification underlying institutions such as mutual funds and insurance companies. These organizations use diversification to reduce, but not totally elimi- nate, risk through the combining of less than perfectly correlated sources of risk. The fundamental efficiency gains due to diversification are well known. We can demonstrate this in the classic risk management problem of a group of individual ship owners.

Imagine a group of risk-averse merchants, each of them owning a trading ship. We assume that each ship owner faces the same type of uncertainty; i.e., if the ship returns safely the owner will realize $100,000, but there is a 0.2 probability that the ship will sink, in which case the owner receives nothing. Therefore, each ship owner faces the probabilistic payoff:

Probability	Payoff
0.2	$ 0
0.8	$100,000

The expected payoff associated with each ship is $80,000. There is a 0.2 probability of a complete loss and a 0.8 probability of a maximum payoff of $100,000. Therefore the risk of the payoff, measured as the standard deviation, is $40,000.[12]

Assume that the probability of one ship sinking is independent of another sinking; each ship follows a different trade route. Now note what happens when two owners securitize the payoffs to their ships, and then swap one-half of the payoff from their own ship for one-half of the payoff from the other's ship. Each of the two owners will now face a new probabilistic payoff:

Probability	Payoff
0.04	$ 0
0.32	$ 50,000
0.64	$100,000

Since the probability of one ship sinking is independent of the other sinking, the probability of both sinking is 0.04, and the probability of both returning safely is 0.64. Note that the expected payoff to each of the

---

12. Standard deviation = $40,000 = $[(0.2) (0 - 80,000)^2 + (0.8) (100,000 - 80,000)^2]^{1/2}$.

merchants, with this risk-pooling arrangement, remains at $80,000, the same as the expected payoff to one ship. But the probabilities associated with the extreme outcomes—of losing everything or making $100,000—have decreased. As a result, the standard deviation has become $28,284, that is, the payoff has become less "risky."[13]

Owners who prefer less uncertainty about the future value of their ships' investment will value reducing the probability of losing a dollar more than the symmetric loss from reducing the probability of gaining a dollar.[14] As a result, each owner benefits from the arrangement, and in this sense, the collective risk associated with the two ships is borne more efficiently. Such an arrangement is also likely to affect aggregate investment behavior (such as the number of ships engaged in trade), as each individual's risk exposure to shipping has decreased.

These efficiency gains due to diversification can be increased by extending the risk-pooling arrangement to more ship owners. Assume there are N ship owners, all of whom securitize the payoffs to their ships. Now assume that each ship owner swaps, in turn, $1/N$th of its own for $1/N$th of the payoff from each of the other ships. Or, alternatively, assume that the ship owners form a company, and each contributes one ship to the company for $1/N$th of the ownership of that company. Each ship owner still faces an expected payoff of $80,000, but the uncertainty, again measured as the standard deviation, has gone to $40,000/(N)^{1/2}$.

N	Individual Standard Deviation
1	$40,000
2	$28,284
3	$23,094
10	$12,649
100	$ 4,000
10,000	$ 400
1,000,000	$ 40

Here we see the power of broad-based risk reallocation, although it is important not to misinterpret this result. Note that diversification, or any other method of risk management, does not change the amount of real risk in the economy. Instead it reallocates the risk.

---

13. Standard deviation $= $28,284 = [(0.04) (0 - 80,000)^2 + (0.32) (50,000 - 80,000)^2 + (0.64) (100,000 - 80,000)^2]^{1/2}$.

14. See Rothschild and Stiglitz (1970, 1971).

It would appear from our example that as N becomes very large, risk for the individual ship owner tends to zero. While this is strictly true, what is *not* true is that the aggregate risk associated with shipping in the economy tends to zero. As more and more ships are added, i.e., N is increased, the amount of risk borne by each individual decreases on the order of $1/N^{1/2}$, but the aggregate risk in the economy associated with shipping *increases* on the order of $N^{1/2}$. Specifically, aggregate shipping risk, as a function of N, is $40,000\ N^{1/2}$.

N	Aggregate Standard Deviation
1	$ 40,000
2	$ 56,569
3	$ 69,282
10	$ 126,491
100	$ 400,000
10,000	$ 4,000,000
1,000,000	$40,000,000

Although the standard deviation of each individual's payoff is lower with the risk-pooling alternative to single ship ownership, it is always true that individuals *collectively* bear all shipping risk in the economy, irrespective of the organization of ship ownership. This point is made most simply by considering the case of two ship owners. In this case, aggregate risk is simply the standard deviation of the payoff associated with two ships, i.e., $56,569 in the last example. The risk borne by each of two single ship owners, again measured as standard deviation (SD), is $40,000 as given in the previous two-ship example. Since these risks are independent, the aggregate risk borne collectively by the two owners, i.e., the "economy," is

$$\text{Aggregate Risk} = [(SD_1)^2 + (SD_2)^2]^{1/2}$$

$$\text{Aggregate Risk} = [(\$40,000)^2 + (\$40,000)^2]^{1/2} = \$56,569$$

Now consider the case where the two owners pool their risks. As demonstrated previously, the standard deviation (SD) of each merchant's payoff for this case is $28,284. How can it be then that these two owners collectively bear the aggregate risk of $56,569? The reason is that the risk exposures of the two owners are now perfectly correlated and therefore the risk borne collectively by the two owners is calculated as

$$\text{Aggregate Risk} = [(SD_1)^2 + 2(SD_1)(SD_2) + (SD_2)^2]^{1/2}$$

$$\text{Aggregate Risk} = [(\$28,284)^2 + 2(\$28,284)(\$28,284) + (\$28,284)^2]^{1/2}$$

$$\text{Aggregate Risk} = \$56,569$$

Therefore, in the risk-pooling case, individuals continue collectively to bear the aggregate risk associated with shipping in the economy, *but in a more efficient manner as measured by the standard deviation of each individual's exposure.*

This simple example demonstrates two distinct means by which N individuals can bear, collectively, aggregate shipping risk of $\$40,000\ (N)^{1/2}$; that is, each individual can own a ship and face a standard deviation of payoff of $\$40,000$, or each individual can own $1/N$th of all ships and face a standard deviation of payoff of $\$40,000/N^{1/2}$. As long as risk-averse individuals are not indifferent to the amount of risk they bear, they are made better-off by the availability of a financial system, i.e., a securities market, which allows for the pooling and reallocation of risks through diversification.

But of course, uncertainties need not be statistically independent, as in the ships example, for individuals to benefit from diversification. It is necessary only that risks be less than perfectly correlated in order to derive risk management benefits from the combining of uncertainties. Perhaps the best example of this is the common stock mutual fund, described more fully in Chapter 3, which pools the monies of a large number of individuals and invests these funds in a broad portfolio of equities. The uncertain returns to equities are not statistically independent. They share exposure to common sources of uncertainty such as the level of economic activity or interest rates, so we would not expect the holders of mutual funds to realize the same dramatic reduction in individual risk through diversification as do the ship owners.

But that is not to say that the reduction of uncertainty to the individual holder of shares of a mutual fund is zero or of insignificant benefit. To see this, imagine that uncertainty surrounding the returns to equities is made up of two parts: exposure to a set of common factors such as economic activity or interest rates, and exposure to idiosyncratic uncertainty, that is, the risks specific, or unique, to only that equity. Therefore, when a mutual fund combines a large number of equities together into a portfolio, the portfolio does not lose the individual equities' collective exposure to such common factors as the economy. But there is a powerful diversification effect on the set of idiosyncratic uncertainties present in the portfolio, because these risks are, by definition, statistically independent of one another. Therefore, as more equities are added to a portfolio, idiosyncratic uncertainty tends to zero, while there remains an irreducible component of uncertainty associated with the equities' common sources of uncertainty.

As a practical matter, it generally takes no more than 30 to 40 equities to reach the point where a portfolio's idiosyncratic uncertainties are diversified away. Again, aggregate uncertainty has not been reduced by structuring the holding of equities as a mutual fund, but risk-bearing has become more efficient through the diversification of idiosyncratic risks.

Insurance

Insurance is a precise approach to risk management. The most common examples of insurance, for our purposes, are actuarial insurance, guarantees, and options. These contracts make it possible, through the payment of a premium, to limit risks and at the same time structure completely generalized contracts as to the pattern of contingent payoffs. Thus insurance contracts are a highly discriminating means of managing uncertainty, because they allow not only the precise isolation of a risk, but also the flexibility to structure arrangements that manage specific portions of a risk. And while in theory the dynamic trading of spot markets, if they exist, can achieve these same results, in practice insurance contracts are often a significantly more cost-efficient means of risk management.

Actuarial insurance is the traditional product offered by insurance companies that helps individuals manage risks associated with their tangible wealth or human capital, e.g., life, health, homeowners, or automobile insurance. Actuarial insurance also helps firms manage such risks as liability or catastrophe. By 1990, worldwide direct insurers had total premium income of $1.3 trillion and direct investment volume of over $4.0 trillion. As with all insurance arrangements, actuarial insurance contracts pay a known amount contingent upon the occurrence of certain specified events. Actuarial insurance typically exists for risks that cannot be readily hedged through the securities markets. But, as will be shown, diversification plays a central role in enabling insurance companies to offer efficiently priced actuarial insurance contracts to their customers.

To understand the role of diversification in the production of actuarial insurance, consider the previous ships example. Assume now that the merchant ship owners form a mutual insurance company to insure each ship for $100,000 against sinking. If there is to be absolute certainty that this insurance company will be able to fund all possible claims against it, the company would have to charge a premium of $100,000 per ship. Of course, any money remaining in the insurance company after all claims have been satisfied would be returned, equally, to all original policyholders. That is, the $100,000 premium can be thought of as being made up of a pure insurance premium and an equity investment in the insurance company.

At a minimum, tieing up this amount of capital in this manner would be impossible for some and inefficient for most. But notice what happens, due to the power of diversification, if the merchants structure the insurance company so that it can fully cover all claims against it with a probability of at least 0.999999, i.e., that the company will fail once in a million times. The premiums that N merchants would have to pay to fund such an insurance company are:

N	Premium
1	$100,000
10	$ 80,083
100	$ 39,000
1,000	$ 26,008
10,000	$ 21,900
100,000	$ 20,601
1,000,000	$ 20,190

Of course a number of factors that make insurance companies complex and expensive to run are ignored in this simple example. Adverse selection, moral hazard, capital, investment performance, and operating expenses all play a major role in actual insurance companies. But this example does serve to demonstrate the basic point. As it is well-known that risk-adverse individuals are made strictly better off by the purchase of actuarially fair insurance, we see that it is possible, through diversification, to fund a "riskless" insurance company through premiums that, in the limit, approach being actuarially fair, i.e., (0.2) ($100,0000) = $20,000. Clearly this is a more efficient arrangement than a fully funded, truly riskless, insurance company. This example demonstrates not only the central role of diversification in the provision of actuarial insurance, but also once again how diversification enhances the efficiency of risk-bearing in the economy.

It is important not to interpret this result in too restrictive a manner. That is, the result is not dependent on one company insuring statistically independent but otherwise identical risks. To see this, imagine the merchant ship owners form N insurance companies, each of which is to insure one ship. Clearly, in order to assure the same level of performance as in the last example, each of the N insurance companies would have to charge a premium of $100,000. But if each company were able to exchange $1/N$th of its potential liability with each of the other companies (reinsure), then each company would be able to charge the same single-ship premium ($20,190) as in the last example.

Most important, this result is not dependent on the insurance companies exchanging similar risks, i.e., ships, lives, or automobiles. What is central to the result is that the risks are independent, or largely independent. Therefore the companies could be exchanging risks of a significantly different nature, say, major catastrophes, personal injuries to entertainment figures, or the theft of an important piece of art. What is gained by the spreading of these independent risks among the N pools of insurance capital, in this case aggregate premiums paid, is that the insurance companies are able to charge each insurance buyer a significantly lower premium. Or, equivalently, insurance capital deployed in the most efficient risk-bearing manner through the reinsurance market assures the most efficient premiums for insurance buyers.

Guarantees provide the same pattern of risk protection as actuarial insurance. Financial guarantees provide insurance-like protection against credit or other sorts of financial risks. Examples of *explicit* financial guarantees include lines of credit, a parent company's guarantee of a subsidiary's debt, a government's guarantee of the debt of a financially distressed private enterprise, or a government's guarantee of private deposits and pensions. But *implicit* financial guarantees are even more common.

There is an implicit guarantee, or insurance component, present in every risky loan. To see this, assume that for a risky loan it is possible to purchase a riskless guarantee as to the repayment of the loan. It is definitionally true that:

$$\text{Risky Loan} + \text{Loan Guarantee} = \text{Riskless Loan}$$

Or, equivalently:

$$\text{Risky Loan} = \text{Riskless Loan} - \text{Loan Guarantee}$$

What this simple expression says is that for the lender, holding a risky loan is analogous to holding a *riskless* loan and selling a loan guarantee. The borrower's position is equivalent to owning a loan guarantee and having borrowed risklessly. And just as actuarial insurance helps manage specific risks, e.g., a ship sinking, implicit and explicit guarantees help manage the risk of default.

Options, like calls and puts, are another example of a type of insurance contract. Through different combinations of options it is possible to create securities and to reshape the payoffs to uncertain assets in a wide variety of ways. These factors help explain the growth and success of the organized exchanges and over-the-counter markets given over to options. Listed options (standardized exchange-traded options) are written on common stocks, common stock indexes, U.S. Treasury debt, foreign exchange, and commodities. Over-the-counter options are written, with highly customized features, on a wide range of financial and physical assets. By the end of 1992, $1.25 trillion notional amount of exchange traded options and $0.6 trillion notional amount of over-the-counter options were outstanding.

The way options facilitate risk management is quite straightforward. Recall the example of the wheat farmer and the baker. Using options, instead of forwards, the farmer can manage exposure to low wheat prices by buying a put on wheat. And the baker can guard against high wheat prices by buying a call.

Notice here that options allow the farmer and the baker to manage precise portions of the overall uncertainty of wheat prices. Compare this result with the net result of the farmer selling a forward contract, which is to eliminate *all* the risk associated with wheat prices, whether low prices or high prices. Therefore the cost to the farmer of eliminating the risk of low wheat prices through a forward contract is the elimination of the beneficial risk of high wheat prices.

A put option in contrast both protects the farmer from the risk of low wheat prices and still allows him to benefit from high prices; where the premium paid for the put option is the cost of eliminating the risk of low prices. It is in this exact sense that insurance, options in this case, is a more discriminating means of managing risk than hedging, as the farmer is able to eliminate a precise portion of the overall risk of wheat prices.

It is theoretically possible to create virtually any security, including state securities à la Arrow–Debreu, from *static* combinations of options.[15] But it is also possible to replicate, through the *dynamic* trading of hedging markets, the payoff to a wide range of securities, including options.[16] Thus, in theory, given continuous and costless trading, the risk management and other benefits of options can be duplicated through the hedging markets. In practice, however, the current cost and difficulty of pursuing the relevant dynamic trading strategies often makes options the more cost-efficient means of realizing these benefits. But it is in this sense that continuing advances in the financial system's infrastructure (such as payments and settlement systems, consistent legal, accounting, and regulatory treatments of transactions, and communication and computation

---

15. See Hakansson (1976), Ross (1976), Banz and Miller (1978), and Breeden and Litzenberger (1978).
16. See Black and Scholes (1973) and Merton (1973a, 1977a).

capabilities) will continue to expand the risk allocation capabilities of the financial system.

Risk Management at the Firm Level

Even in a perfect-markets world, individuals will delegate their real investment decisions to firms. The existence of firms, that is, the separation of ownership and management, is consistent with the neoclassical view that the only institutional structure that will evolve in an economy is one that improves efficiency. The potential efficiency gains associated with business firms are well-known and are related to issues like comparative advantage, division of labor, and economies of scale. These benefits derive from the organization of the firm's real, not financial, activities, so managers in a perfect economy need not concern themselves with issues like firm capital structure and risk management.

Despite the theoretical irrelevance of firm risk management in a perfect economy, firms in an imperfect economy engage in risk management activities for a variety of reasons. Not surprisingly, these reasons are related to economic imperfections, such as transactions costs, taxes, and the issues of agency and asymmetric information. Efficiency considerations related to the implementation of a firm's investment and strategic decisions provide additional rationale for transacting in risk management instruments.

Yet we hear now, at a minimum concern, and at most outright criticism, of the growing risk management activities of business firms. It has been suggested that not all firms fully understand the consequences of their risk management transactions, particularly those involving derivatives. This is an especially important issue for financial firms, given the central role of creditworthiness in the provision of financial services. Determining under what circumstances firms should be involved in risk management activities is therefore central to the ongoing debate on the suitability of derivatives for firm use.

Decisions ranging from the term and denomination of borrowings to the purchase of business insurance require managers of firms to consider the extent to which they should manage risks. Risk management is central, for example, to today's multinationals. Coca-Cola engages in a variety of efforts to manage its exposure to currency fluctuations, given that 81% of its $1.9 billion in 1992 operating income came from countries other than the United States. Indeed, at the end of 1992, Coca-Cola had $4.9 billion face amount of financial instruments on its books in order to manage this exposure.

However, corporations as varied as Metallgesellschaft and Dell Computer have recently reported sizable losses from attempted hedging activities. And Procter & Gamble, Barings Brothers, and Kashima Oil are but three firms to report equally large losses due to the speculative use of derivatives. While such losses might make some boards of directors question whether their firms should engage in "risk management" activities at all, at least one court decision suggests they increasingly have no choice. When an Indiana grain cooperative reported a loss as the result of an unanticipated swing in grain prices, shareholders (local farmers) successfully sued management and directors for negligence for failing to hedge adequately in the grain market.[17] Therefore, some would argue that risk management is not only a vital management tool but also a fiduciary responsibility.

Firm risk management activity is indeed at odds with normative finance theory, which states that financial decisions, including risk management, cannot create value at the firm level and are therefore irrelevant to shareholders.[18] Firms are seen as creating value exclusively from their real investment decisions and not from their financial decisions. Since it is assumed that individual shareholders can replicate at their level any financial decision made by the firm, shareholders are at best indifferent to, and in the presence of costs made worse-off by, firm-level financial policy decisions. Therefore, all capital structure and dividend decisions, and all risk management activities, including asset/liability matching, insurance decisions, diversification, and hedging activities, are viewed as irrelevant to the welfare of the shareholder. But if all these activities are irrelevant, why are firms' risk management activities growing so rapidly, and why are shareholders demanding that managers pursue risk management?

Why Firm-Level Risk Management?

The theoretical result that suggests that firms' financial decisions are irrelevant to the welfare of their shareholders is based upon an assumption of perfect financial markets. In a perfect financial market, there are no regulations, taxes, or transactions costs of any type, including information costs. In the absence of these imperfections, financing and investment decisions are entirely *separable* at the firm level, meaning management can and should focus only on the investment decisions of the firm and not on irrelevant financial decisions.

One argument for risk management at the firm level suggests that while

---

17. See Anonymous (1993) and Dodd (1993).
18. See Modigliani and Miller (1958) and Miller and Modigliani (1961).

risk management may not yield benefits to well-diversified shareholders, managers stand to gain from engaging in hedging activities. This argument proposes that, like the owners of closely held firms, managers may hold a large fraction of their wealth in company stock. Reduction in risk thus aids them despite its presumed neutral impact on other shareholders.[19] Another explanation suggests that managers may stand to gain by smoothing performance in order to convince potential employers of their capability as managers and to improve their own prospects and valuation in the labor market.[20]

Another argument suggests that the presence of certain tax structures can create an incentive for firm-level risk management. In particular, if effective tax rates rise as pretax income rises (i.e., the tax schedule is "convex"), shareholders can benefit from risk management. The firm saves the difference in taxes between the expected tax payment without hedging and the lower taxes payable with hedging.

While the narrow range of marginal corporate tax rates makes this argument questionable, other factors can contribute to the convexity of tax schedules. For example, the Alternative Minimum Tax (AMT) and the presence of tax shields such as tax loss carryforwards and tax credits can make effective tax rates convex despite the limited progressivity of corporate tax rates.[21] While hedging can create value under a convex tax schedule, other considerations may eclipse these benefits and make hedging a tax-disadvantaged activity.

Hedging activity is now subject to a number of ambiguous tax treatments. The Internal Revenue Service has argued that hedging gains and losses should be treated as capital income rather than ordinary income. While the tax rates for capital and ordinary income are currently the same, the inability to offset capital losses against ordinary income creates a tax asymmetry that may overshadow the benefits of a convex tax schedule.[22]

There are two forms of transactions costs that are argued to be relevant to hedging or risk management at the firm level. The first has to do with the well-known trade-off between the tax benefits of debt financing and

---

19. This argument is due to Stulz (1984). Froot, Scharfstein, and Stein (1993) counter that this is really a transactions costs argument, as for managers to engage in hedging at the firm level instead of the individual level they must face significant costs when trading for their own account.

20. See Breeden and Viswanathan (1990) and DeMarzo and Duffie (1991).

21. The tax argument is put forth in Rawls and Smithson (1990) and Smith, Smithson, and Wilford (1990), Chapter 17.

22. See, for example, *Corn Products Refining Company v. Commissioner of Internal Revenue (1955), Arkansas Best v. Commissioner of Internal Revenue (1988), Federal National Mortgage Association v. Commissioner of Internal Revenue (1993)*. While the IRS position has been rejected in the most recent *FNMA* decision, the IRS will likely appeal.

the costs of financial distress. These costs can take the form of direct costs (primarily the legal, accounting, and related advisory fees of bankruptcy) or indirect costs. Indirect costs, which can dwarf the direct costs, include the higher costs of contracting demanded by credit-sensitive customers, employees, and suppliers. Together these costs prompt managers to avoid, via risk management, outcomes where these costs might be incurred.[23]

The second form of relevant transactions costs concerns the relative ability of firms and individuals to implement risk management efficiently. Transactions costs impact the ability of individuals to hedge or create diversified portfolios and the ability of firms to execute their risk management strategies. The preference for firms to undertake risk management rather than individuals depends on these relative costs and, more important, on the presence of information asymmetries. If managers have access to information about risks facing a firm that is not available to shareholders, shareholders cannot construct an optimally diversified portfolio. In this case also, risk management at the firm level yields real value for shareholders. As an offset, however, shareholders must be able to monitor the risk management activities of firms in order to adjust their own portfolios in response.

Most conflicts between bondholders and shareholders stem from the differing nature of their claims. While bondholders hold claims that are fixed, the claims of shareholders are residual and have no upward limit. As a result, shareholders may choose to increase the riskiness of the firm's activities. By undertaking extremely risky projects, shareholders can increase the value of their claims and reduce the value of fixed claims. Bondholders, in turn, will attempt to exact higher rates if managers attempt to transfer wealth from them to shareholders in this manner. Firm risk management can be used to balance the conflicting concerns of these claims.[24]

Theoretically, firms should pursue attractive investment strategies regardless of the variability of cash flows generated by existing assets. They need not manage this variability by buying insurance or using hedging techniques. This theory, however, assumes that firms can raise additional external financing or can cut dividends, without incurring any additional costs.

In the world of perfect financial markets, this may be so. In reality, however, significant informational asymmetries will increase the costs of suffering from shortfalls. In industries of any complexity, management will understand the true value of investment opportunities better than the

---

23. See Smith and Stulz (1985).
24. See Smith and Stulz (1985).

broader financial markets. Accordingly, the providers of external financing will exact additional costs for this informational disadvantage, and these costs will be highest during periods of shortfalls, when the value of the firm's further investment options will seem even more uncertain to outsiders.

Informational asymmetries therefore make external financing costly, providing an impetus for managers to reduce the variability of internally generated cash flows through risk management activities.[25] This argument for firm-level risk management based on agency issues and informational asymmetries is treated in greater detail in Chapter 7.

These arguments suggest that the central risk management issue for firms is whether to hedge, diversify, or insure away existing risks. In fact, it is difficult to rationalize many firms' use of risk management instruments in these terms. To see this, recall that individuals use the risk allocation function of the financial system to shed unwanted risk and to *acquire* preferred risks. Firms also use instruments like derivatives as a cost-efficient means of acquiring, or increasing, exposure to a particular risk. Therefore, it is sometimes difficult to infer a firm's fundamental risk exposures from its use of risk management instruments.

To see this, suppose a firm has determined that interest rate increases adversely impact its business. Accordingly, the management chooses a fixed/floating liability mix heavily weighted toward fixed-rate debt. At the time the firm plans to issue a fixed-rate bond, however, it projects rates to decline considerably, and chooses instead to issue a floating-rate bond, planning later to swap that into fixed-rate debt at some more opportune time. Or the firm could issue fixed-rate debt now, and simultaneously assume a separate speculative position in the interest rate derivatives market. The firm has assumed this risk due to its conclusion that such an exposure is attractively priced, even given management's knowledge of the overall impact of interest rates on the firm's core business.[26] While, strictly speaking, these decisions represent the management of the firm's risk exposures, it is more in the spirit of efficient speculation than the management of existing risks.

Firms also use risk management transactions to implement strategic or competitive plans more efficiently. While a firm's competitive positioning is impacted by a number of risks, the traditional strategic planning response to risk exposures is to alter *operating* decisions. Implementing "natural" hedges as a competitive response has a number of disadvan-

---

25. This argument is advanced in Myers and Majluf (1984), Lessard (1990), and Froot, Scharfstein, and Stein (1993).
26. This example loosely parallels the case presented in Tufano (1993).

tages compared to "synthetic" hedges implemented through financial contracts. These include the lags implicit in such "natural" hedges, large implicit spreads in trading such positions, and the sticky and inflexible nature of these commitments. Synthetic hedges, or financial risk management, can provide the same competitive advantages without similar lock-ins and at much less cost.

Consider the decision of a firm to backward integrate in order to help manage risks related to suppliers, or forward integrate to manage risks related to distributors. An example is an oil refinery considering the purchase of an oil producer or a distributor of oil-based products. How would the efficiency of implementing such a decision compare to achieving similar positioning by entering into a variety of financial contracts, such as derivatives on crude oil or refined products? Informed use of risk management instruments at the firm level can be a source of value through creating possible competitive advantage more efficiently.

Risk Management of Financial Firms

While the presence of certain market imperfections can motivate non-financial firms' risk management activities, financial firms engage in risk management for an additional set of reasons. Financial firms play a central role in the *provision of* risk management services, among other financial services, to both individuals and firms. Financial firms facilitate the allocation of risk in a number of ways. They play a principal role in the derivatives markets and in the provision of actuarial insurance, diversification, and guarantees. Financial firms also provide structured financial services like savings/investment products (life insurance, annuities, defined benefit pension plans, and savings accounts) and payments/custodial facilities (demand deposits, securities accounts, money market funds, and electronic funds transfer). The essence of *creditworthiness* in the provision of all of these services gives risk management within financial firms a special significance.

It is important to distinguish between *investors in* and *customers of* a financial firm in order to highlight the importance of creditworthiness to such a firm.[27] Investors put capital at risk in the expectation of earning a return commensurate with the risk they bear. Equity investors, who bear more risk than debt investors, demand a higher expected return, just as subordinated debt investors demand relatively higher expected returns than senior debt investors. Investors want to understand a firm's creditworthiness because it represents the risks inherent in investing in the firm.

---

27. See Bodie and Merton (1992b).

Indeed, the decision to invest can be seen as the decision to intentionally bear the risk of a firm's creditworthiness.

Customers are another issue. It is generally not difficult to distinguish between investors and customers in the case of nonfinancial firms: Investors provide the firm capital, and customers purchase the firm's product. Even when customers hold a financial claim on a nonfinancial firm, such as a product warranty, these claims are far smaller than those of the firm's investors. It is different for financial firms. Customers are often significant liabilityholders of financial firms, almost always much larger than investors. Policyholders of insurance companies, depositors of banks, and investors in mutual funds are examples of customers who hold far larger financial claims than investors on financial firms. Besides the size of their financial claims, customers of financial firms also differ from investors in their view of a firm's creditworthiness.

Customers of financial firms purchase services that perform important economic functions. A customer who purchases property insurance wants a financial claim that pays off if her house is destroyed by fire, not a financial claim that pays off if her house burns *and* the insurance company is solvent. Similarly, a customer deposits money in a bank as a means of savings. Such a customer strictly prefers a financial claim that will pay, with certainty, the specified amount of money on the specified date. Customers of financial firms are thus very concerned with creditworthiness.

In theory, customers could manage the risk of default on the part of financial firms through diversification or through the purchase of third-party guarantees. Or financial firms could offer actuarially fair price reductions to reflect the possibility of default on their contracts. However feasible, these solutions ignore the fact that customers of financial firms have a strict preference for default-free contracting of financial services. Unlike investors, customers consider the bearing of financial firm risk extraneous to the central reason they contract with the financial firm. It is simply more efficient for the financial firm to address the issue of creditworthiness than for each individual customer to do so. And a significant element in the approach of financial firms to the management of their creditworthiness is the use of risk management techniques.

Financial firms, however, have difficulty communicating their creditworthiness to customers (and regulators). Their actions and their financial condition are difficult to monitor or observe; financial firms are relatively opaque. To preserve a competitive advantage, financial firms must carefully manage the amount and type of information that they share with other parties. But this works directly against keeping customers and regulators fully informed. Another factor is that financial firms can move into and out of activities more quickly than non-financial firms, which has direct consequences for the size and composition of their balance sheets. While this flexibility is a competitive necessity, it further aggravates the monitoring problem for customers and regulators. Finally, there is the issue of complexity. Recent years have seen an unprecedented amount of financial innovation that makes understanding financial firms more complicated. A case in point is the use of esoteric, over-the-counter derivatives.

The combination of information sensitivity, operating fluidity, and instrument complexity makes the problem of monitoring financial firms' creditworthiness difficult, if not impossible, for most customers and regulators. Customer responses to these realities are limited. Large, sophisticated customers can use master agreements or other netting arrangements to help manage their exposure to any one financial firm. Or customers can limit their business to AAA-rated financial firms or special-purpose subsidiaries. Smaller clients can limit their dealings to financial firms whose creditworthiness is guaranteed, say, by the government. To the extent that these alternatives do not prove adequate to address customer concerns about financial firms' creditworthiness, we would expect either more innovations, such as AAA-rated special-purpose subsidiaries, or more regulation.

Regulation is much more prevalent with financial firms than with nonfinancial firms. Whether its focus is the stability of the financial system or the protection of individual customers, regulation is often tied to maintaining creditworthiness. The regulations relative to the federal guarantee of deposits and of defined benefit pension plans, and state regulation of insurance companies, in particular, are motivated by concerns over creditworthiness. And related concerns over maintaining the stability of the financial system are seen in the general debate over the systemic implications of financial innovation and the specific calls for more regulation of the global over-the-counter derivatives market.

But government's role in the financial system goes beyond that of regulator. As another example of an endogenous institution, government improves the efficiency of the financial system not only by ensuring market integrity, but also by promoting competition or managing public-good type externalities. And when the private financial system is unable, or unwilling, to provide needed risk allocation services to individuals and firms, the government often provides the ultimate risk-bearing service.

Government Risk-Bearing

The failure of the private financial system to provide complete risk allocation services has created a large and increasing role for government risk-bearing in most developed countries. This role has been made even greater by a growing belief that some societal risks are imposed upon people without their consent and that individuals deserve to be protected by the government against them.[28] As a result, the government has become a major player in the financial system as both an explicit and implicit insurer, obligor, and guarantor.

The risk-bearing role of the government can take a variety of explicit forms, including insurer of bank deposits or pensions, or the guarantor of government-sponsored enterprises (GSEs) operating in sectors like housing or agriculture. In the United States alone, approximately three-fifths of all *nonfederal* credit outstanding is assisted by some form of federal program.[29] And government also implicitly bears society's exposure to catastrophic financial and nonfinancial risks.

With the assumption of student lending directly by the government and a proposal for a new GSE to assist in the securitization of middle-market loans, the explicit role of the government in the U.S. financial system will likely continue to grow. On a global scale, the dramatic demographic shifts expected throughout Organization for Economic Cooperation and Development (OECD) countries in the next 50 years will press many governments to rationalize their criteria for implicitly bearing financial and nonfinancial risks.[30]

Despite the prominence of the government as a bearer of risk in today's economy, an appreciation of the myriad of risks that government assumes is only beginning to develop. The Office of Management and Budget (OMB), for example, has just begun a formal evaluation of the government's contingent exposures. The rationale for the government's assumption of these risks is usually the inability or unwillingness of the private financial system to provide appropriate risk allocation services.[31] But, of course, government risk-bearing is not "free," and it is important to appreciate the costs and benefits of the government entering into such explicit, or implicit, contracts.[32]

---

28. In this view, risk is not a wager taken willingly in hopes of gain, but a danger not run out of choice.
29. See Sniderman (1993).
30. See Willman (1993) for an exposition of the consequences of the increasing age dependency ratio (measured as the population over 65 as a percentage of the population aged 15–64) throughout the OECD. For the entire OECD, the age dependency ratio is predicted to rise from 19% in 1990 to 28% by 2020 and to 37% by 2040. Overall, OECD estimates are for the doubling of pension burdens over the next 50 years, requiring real economic growth rates of up to 1.5% per year to pay for pensions alone.
31. We do not address here the risk-bearing by the government that has the explicit purpose of redistributing wealth or subsidizing certain activities or persons (e.g., VA mortgages).
32. OMB estimates the total present value of the costs of federal guarantees in force in 1993

One approach to understanding the rationale for government risk-bearing is to consider how risk management can privately fail. Many risks are not directly securitized, and highly correlated instruments may not exist, making it impossible to hedge or diversify these risks away. And private actuarial insurance for a particular risk may not exist because of the severity or scale of the risk being insured or a lack of reliable data on the probabilities associated with the risk.

The scale of certain risks—nuclear accidents or earthquakes, for example—may make the state the only possible and credible provider of insurance.[33] Accordingly, private markets, even if they argue that they can price and absorb the likelihood of such large-scale catastrophes, will not be seen as credible. Similarly, risks where "bad" outcomes can feed into more "bad" outcomes are difficult to price, and again lead to credibility problems for private insurers. For example, deposit insurance by the government is often justified by the fear of widespread panic and the possible contagion of bank failures. In this case, a private insurer could price the possibility of contagion into an insurance contract, but credibility and the scale of such risks remain issues.

The lack of reliable actuarial data can also lead to private market failures for large-scale, low-frequency risks.[34] Man-made disasters and natural catastrophes can impact large populations and entail great costs. There are huge difficulties associated with pricing these risks, as such events occur rarely, and there may be a long period between the risky event and the realization of damages. And if private insurers do not have accurate actuarial data, they cannot prudently provide contract coverage.

The unique strengths of the government also make it the ultimate risk bearer when adverse-selection and moral-hazard problems are particularly severe.[35] Adverse selection refers to the difficulties inherent in writing insurance; that is, the riskiest parties are often the parties most interested in obtaining insurance. Moreover, as an insurance firm raises its premiums, the least risky clients are likely to drop out of a pool, thereby worsening the overall quality of the pool. In this case, the government's ability to compel membership can serve to control the quality of pool. Moral-hazard problems occur when insured parties have less of

---

at between $123 to $224 billion, of which $62 to $104 billion relates to federal insurance of deposits and pensions. See Budget of U.S. Government (1993), pp. 49–51.

33. See Connolly (1993) for an excellent analysis of the Price–Anderson Act and the importance of "loss control" in assuring funding for nuclear projects.

34. See Ringleb and Wiggins (1993).

35. See Stiglitz (1993).

an incentive to avoid the risk covered by the purchased insurance. While private insurers often mitigate moral-hazard problems through restrictions and price discrimination, the greater monitoring and coercive powers of the government can favor it as a provider of insurance in some cases.

Because some insurance coverage can *credibly* be provided only by the state, customers may choose not to contract with private providers of insurance for some risks, as the company's ability to fulfill its obligations is suspect. Therefore, any private entity is, at least theoretically, at a disadvantage relative to the government as a provider of insurance. So why are insurance contracts not most effectively and efficiently provided by the government?

The government faces a number of issues that make it an inefficient and suboptimal provider of most forms of insurance. These include its inability to price-discriminate effectively, the tendency of regulators to become "captive" to the entities they should be monitoring, and the historic failure of governments to budget and account for guarantees appropriately.

While private markets function to differentiate price and quality, the political constraints on the government make such discrimination problematic. As an insurer, the government should objectively assess risks and price them accordingly. But this process is open to unfairness, and political expediency will tend to favor flat-rate pricing. Accordingly, governments will likely rely on simple rules that do not reflect all available information about a class of risks.

Regulators have a tendency to becoming "captive" in some way to the industries that they regulate.[36] Regulators quickly come to identify with their clients, become dependent on their survival, and actively work to insure their perpetuation. Regulators as insurers may thus be more than willing to show forbearance when dealing with "clients" as their own interests are not best served by revealing problems. This issue of forbearance was most clear in the S&L crisis as "acting promptly was not in the authorities' individual and collective interests, because the costs of whistle-blowing tend to be very high. When an official first calls attention to a severe public policy problem, the whistle blower is likely to be blamed for causing the mess."[37]

Finally, the government has historically relied on insurance contracts and guarantees as an effective channel for subsidies. Such indirect subsidies are politically attractive because, unlike more direct cash subsidies, they are not captured in the standard budgetary process. They thus

---

36. See Stigler (1971), Posner (1974), and Grundfest (1990).
37. Kane as quoted in Bodie and Merton (1992b), fn. 62.

provide political gains without imposing explicit costs on the government. Only within the last few years have regulators begun to attempt to recognize the myriad of guarantees and other credit activities on the government books in order to discipline the dispensation of such subsidies.[38]

A final cost of government risk-bearing is the impact that such intervention has on the market's allocational efficiency.[39] When the government bears risk, the discipline and judgment of the private capital markets is abandoned in favor of the decisions of regulators. As a result, government guarantees and other credit activities will channel funds to projects that would otherwise go unfunded, thereby depriving worthy projects of funding. These costs and distortions, while difficult to quantify, are possibly the largest costs of government risk-bearing in the financial sector.

The unique powers of government and the failure of the private financial system can be used to justify government risk-bearing in certain circumstances. However, the boundary between public and private risk-bearing is defined, in part, by the capabilities of the private financial system. These capabilities are rapidly expanding, due to the current pace of financial innovation. Whether, in certain instances, the risk allocation function of the private financial system will supplant government risk-bearing remains to be seen. Regardless, the government's roles as regulator and implicit bearer of catastrophic financial risks assure that private innovations in risk allocation will not go unscrutinized.

Innovations in Risk Allocation and the Stability of the Financial System

An enhanced risk allocation function results in real economic benefits. Predictably, financial innovation has led to economic organizations and mechanisms designed to facilitate the efficient allocation of risk. But not everyone is convinced of the overall welfare implications of ever-expanding risk-sharing facilities, particularly in the form of derivatives markets. Some recognize the real benefit of the risk-shifting function of the financial system, but see some derivatives markets as redundant, allowing speculators and arbitrageurs to achieve greater leverage, and consuming private and public resources to monitor.[40] Others point out that, in theory, much of what derivatives do can be accomplished in the primary mar-

---

38. See Phaup (1993) and Rodriguez (1993).
39. See Bodie and Merton (1992a) and Stiglitz (1993).
40. See Tobin (1984).

kets.[41] Finally, derivatives and derivatives markets have been likened to "financial hydrogen bombs" and "casinos."

In many ways, the global over-the-counter derivatives markets symbolize both the progress and the concern often associated with innovations in the financial system. The impact of derivative securities on the volatility of other markets, the redundancy of derivatives markets, the suitability of derivatives for certain organizations, and the impact of derivatives markets on the stability of the financial system are prominent examples of some of the concerns.[42] Because of these concerns, Congress and several agencies have called for increased government regulation of the global over-the-counter derivatives markets.[43] The decision whether to regulate the derivatives markets should, of course, be well informed. For the time being, public debate on this issue has revealed a fundamental misunderstanding of derivatives and, what is more important, the role of risk allocation in the economy.

The role of both dealers and users in the derivatives markets has attracted recent attention. Concerns about the creditworthiness of dealer

---

41. While this is strictly true in a perfect market, in an imperfect market characterized by costs, some market participants, such as financial firms, are able to transact more efficiently than other economic agents. Financial firms may be able to replicate the benefits of derivatives through the primary markets, but less efficient participants are unable to do so. Therefore derivatives markets, both organized and over-the-counter, bring the benefits of efficient risk management to those unable to replicate these services in the primary markets.

42. Damodaran and Subrahmanyam (1992) summarize the theoretical and empirical work on the effects of derivative securities on the markets for the underlying assets. The theoretical literature suggests that, in addition to the completion of markets [see Hakansson (1976), Ross (1976), Banz and Miller (1978), and Breeden and Litzenberger (1978)] and enhanced risk-pooling, derivative securities have a beneficial impact on markets because of reductions in transactions costs and enhanced informational efficiencies [see Diamond and Verrecchia (1987)]. Contrasting theoretical arguments claim that derivatives markets encourage speculation in the underlying asset market, with negative side effects accentuated by information and trading technologies. Stein (1988, 1989) presents a model showing that the use of derivatives markets by speculators with inferior information can have the effect of increasing the volatility of other markets, although Grossman (1988) describes an information-based model where the introduction of options dampens market volatility. And some have argued that the over-the-counter derivatives markets have reduced systemic risk due to the shifting of risks to those willing or better able to bear them [see Darby (1994)]. The empirical evidence indicates that, with the possible exception of stock index futures, trading in derivatives actually dampens the volatility of the market for the underlying asset. Finally, research on micromarket structure issues suggests that the introduction of derivatives appears to be associated with a decrease in the bid–ask spread and increased trading volume and liquidity in the market for the underlying asset.

43. Although some, like Miller (1994), counter that the derivatives markets are already adequately regulated.

firms, the suitability of derivatives for certain users, and the implications of derivatives for the stability of the financial system have manifested themselves in several studies by regulators, industry groups and Congress.[44] Predictably, most of these reports call for better-informed senior management, the resolution of legal and regulatory uncertainties regarding derivatives, better accounting, reporting, and tax treatment for derivatives, and better measurement and management of the various risks attending the dealing business.

Where the reports differ, again predictably, is in their recommendations about regulation. While the industry studies see little need for increased regulation, the Congressional studies recommend regulatory standards for a number of areas, including capital commitment, trading, disclosure, and stress-testing. But all the studies tend to agree that a central issue is whether the global over-the-counter derivatives markets pose new and significant risks to the financial system.

In a *perfect-markets* setting, the financial system (including derivatives) does not add risk to the economy; it merely facilitates the efficient allocation of existing risks associated with physical and human capital. With or without extensive risk allocation mechanisms, individuals ultimately bear all risks in the economy. The key issue is whether risks are being efficiently borne. Predictably organizations and mechanisms evolve to accommodate this latent demand for enhanced risk allocation.

Consider the creation of a market for the stock of an all-equity-financed firm. This market allows individuals to shed or acquire the traded stock's risk, which is not additional risk to the economy but simply a securitization of the business risk of the firm. Therefore the innovation of securitizing the firm does not add incremental risk to the economy, but makes individuals better-off because they are able to manage their risks more finely.

If the firm issues risky debt, and uses the proceeds to retire a portion of its equity, then the total risk of the firm is now borne by two classes of claimants, levered equity and risky debt, although the total risk associated with the firm is the same. The only difference is that, due to the revealed preferences of individuals, the risk is being borne in different securitized forms. If the firm borrows money from a bank to retire a portion of its equity, the total risk of the firm will be borne by the firm's levered equity holders, the bank's equity holders, and the bank's deposi-

---

44. See, for example, Bank for International Settlements (1990, 1992), "Derivatives . . ." (1993), Board of Governors of the Federal Reserve, Federal Deposit Insurance Corporation, and Office of Comptroller of the Currency (1993), Commodity Futures Trading Commission (1993), and House Banking Committee Minority Staff (1993).

tors (if uninsured) or the government (if the depositors are insured). The net result of these ever-finer partitionings of the firm's fundamental business risk is *not* to increase aggregate economic risk, but to allocate the firm's risk more efficiently.[45]

The firm could purchase fire insurance, in which case a part of the firm's total risk (the risk of the firm burning) is transferred from the firm's equity and debt holders to the equity and debt holders of the insurance company. And if there are multiple firms whose returns are not perfectly correlated, then risk-averse individuals could bear the collective risks of these firms more efficiently through some pooling mechanism such as a mutual fund. Again, aggregate economic uncertainty is unaffected by these innovations, which, in turn, promote the efficient allocation of risk in the economy.

But what if options, written on the equity of the firm, are introduced? A derivative viewed in isolation looks like a "created" risk visited on the economy. *Primary* securities, like equity and debt, represent the direct securitization of a real risk. *Derivatives,* on the other hand, are bilateral contracts that do not represent a direct securitization of a real risk. It is in this comparative sense that derivative markets are likened to casinos— the addition of unnecessary risk to the economy.

This is a flawed view of derivatives for several reasons. First, whether the derivative represents unnecessary or additional risk must be taken up in the context of the overall risk position. As is true for any security, the derivative when coupled with another risk can be risk-reducing to the individual or firm. Second, from an aggregate risk perspective, the risks associated with derivatives are zero–sum; in other words, the risk positions of buyers and sellers cancel out. Therefore the introduction of derivatives does not add to the total risk in a perfect economy.

If the point of the firm example is to underscore that financial innovation *per se*, including derivatives, does not add risk to the economy, what then are the "troublesome" risks associated with the derivatives business? Market, credit, and legal risks attend all financial securities, not just derivatives, so in this sense, there is nothing unique about derivatives markets.

Derivatives markets are global, rapidly growing, and relatively complex, and most important, a central part of the response to the fundamental demand for more efficient risk allocation. Financial contracting between global dealers and users has increased dramatically as a result of

---

45. Nor does aggregate risk decrease due to these partitionings of the firm's business risk. In this sense, the firm's business risk, from the standpoint of the economy, can be thought of like nuclear waste, i.e., "you can spread it around but you can't make it go away."

derivatives use. And while the extent and complexity of financial contracting in the economy will not approach that suggested by Arrow–Debreu, it is reasonable to ask if there are implications of this ever-expanding interconnectivity for the stability of the financial system.

Assessing credit risk can be more difficult, given increased financial contracting. Accounting standards and disclosure requirements for derivatives are crucial to the determination of the creditworthiness of both users and dealers. Any undue cost of obtaining credit information on counterparties undermines the real benefits of derivatives.[46] And legal risks are another implication of increased financial contracting. While it does not happen in a perfect market, there may be uncertainties and costs associated with the enforcement of contracts in an imperfect market. Again, these risks are not unique to derivatives, but are amplified by increased financial contracting.

Some critics have questioned the systemic implications of the market risks associated with dealer positions, given the comparison of the large notional amount of derivatives contracts outstanding to the capital of the dealer firms. Price discontinuities and lack of liquidity are, according to these observers, highly problematic for the implementation of proper risk management techniques in the derivatives dealing function. Dealers counter that their actual risk exposure to price discontinuities or illiquid markets is nothing like the notional amount of derivatives outstanding, and the risk of this nature that does exist is not large relative to their capital base.

Given their capital base, and risk management policies, dealers choose their level of market risk. In setting their level of market risk, however, it is doubtful that dealers internalize the systemic implications of the failure of their firms or the public cost associated with any implicit government "safety net." Some would argue that the mere presence of these externalities is sufficient to warrant some degree of explicit regulation of derivatives dealers.

Finally, there is both concern and confusion over the appropriateness of derivatives for certain users. As has been described, derivatives can be used to manage risks. But derivatives can also be an efficient means of speculating, given the cost and availability of leverage, transactions costs, and the tax, accounting, and regulatory treatment of the transaction. Whether a transaction should be viewed as speculative, or as a part of a risk management program, is often difficult to determine.

---

46. At the same time, it is not clear that derivatives involve as much credit risk as the next best alternative for accomplishing the same objectives, e.g., a foreign exchange swap versus a parallel loan.

Summary

The determination of whether derivatives markets are adding additional risk to the financial system must take into account the "unobserved alternative." That is, we know that individuals and firms will manage risks to benefit their economic interests. The question then is: What actions would individuals and firms take to manage their risks in the absence of derivative markets? Clearly individuals and firms would seek other (perhaps less efficient) means of risk management, including the use of private contracts and imprecise hedging instruments. It is not clear whether the degree of financial contracting under the next best alternative would be less "risky."

The global derivatives market is an example of innovating in one element of the financial system at a faster rate than in other elements. While the size, growth, and complexity of the derivatives market can strain some elements of the financial system, such as payments and settlements, and the cross-jurisdictional enforcement of contracts, this is not a reason to restrain the derivative markets. It is a reason to insist that other elements of the financial system keep pace in order not to impede the delivering of the real benefits of enhanced risk allocation.

Risk allocation is an important function of the financial system, and the derivatives markets are central to the risk management activities of both individuals and firms. Given the complexity of the issues we have discussed, policy decisions need to be informed by a clearer understanding of the costs and benefits associated with altering the pattern and practices of risk allocation in the economy. The implications of actions to regulate workings of the derivatives markets could be far-reaching.

References

Arrow, K.J. (1953), *"Le Rôle des Valeurs Boursières pour la Répartition la Meilleure des Risques,"* Econometrie Colloques Internationaux du Centre National de la Recherche Scientifique, XI: 41–47, Paris.

Bank for International Settlements (1990), "Report of the Committee on Interbank Netting Schemes" ("Lamfalussy Report"), Basle: Bank for International Settlements (November).

—— (1992), "Recent Developments in International Interbank Relations" ("Promisel Report"), Basle: Bank for International Settlement (October).

—— (1993), "Central Bank Survey of Foreign Exchange Market Activity in April, 1992," Basle: Bank for International Settlements (March).

Banz, R.W., and M.H. Miller (1978), "Prices for State-Contingent Claims: Some Estimates and Applications," *Journal of Business,* 51 (October): 653–672.

Black, F., and M. Scholes (1973), "The Pricing of Options and Corporate Liabilities," *Journal of Political Economy,* 81 (May–June): 637–654.

Board of Governors of the Federal Reserve System, Federal Deposit Insurance Corporation, Office of Comptroller of the Currency (1993), *Derivative Product Activities of Commercial Banks,* Washington, D.C.

Bodie, Z., and R.C. Merton (1992a), "Deposit Insurance Reform: A Functional Approach." Paper presented at Carnegie-Rochester Conference Series on Public Policy, April.

───── (1992b), "On the Management of Financial Guarantees," *Financial Management* (Winter): 86–109.

───── (1995), *Fundamentals of Finance,* Englewood Cliffs, NJ: Prentice Hall.

Breeden, D.T., and R.H. Litzenberger (1978), "Prices of State-Contingent Claims Implicit in Option Prices," *Journal of Business,* 51 (October): 621–652.

Breeden, D.T., and S. Viswanathan (1990), "Why Do Firms Hedge? An Asymmetric Information Model," Duke University.

Budget of the U.S. Government for Fiscal Year 1994 (1993), Office of Management and Budget, Washington, D.C.

Commodity Futures Trading Commission (1993), "OTC Derivative Markets and Their Regulation," Washington, D.C.: Commodity Futures Trading Commission (October).

Connolly, D.R. (1993), "Government Risk-Bearing: What Works and What Doesn't," in *Government Risk-Bearing: Proceedings of a Conference Held at the Federal Reserve Bank of Cleveland, May 1991,* M. Sniderman, ed. Boston: Kluwer Academic Publishers.

Damodaran, A., and M.G. Subrahmanyam (1992), "The Effects of Derivative Securities on the Markets for the Underlying Assets in the United States: A Survey," *Financial Markets, Institutions & Instruments,* 1: 1–21.

Darby, M.R. (1994), "Over-The-Counter Derivatives and Systemic Risk to the Global Financial System," NBER Working Paper 4801, Cambridge, MA.

Debreu, G. (1959), *Theory of Value,* New York: Wiley.

DeMarzo, P., and D. Duffie (1991), "Corporate Financial Hedging with Proprietary Information," *Journal of Economic Theory,* 53: 261–286.

"Derivatives: Practices and Principles" (1993), Global Derivatives Study Group, Washington, D.C.: The Group of Thirty (July).

Diamond, D.W., and R.E. Verrecchia (1987), "Constraints on Short Selling and Asset Price Adjustment to Private Information," *Journal of Financial Economics,* 18: 277–311.

Dodd, D. (1993), "Indiana Case May Have Big Impact on Corporate Hedging Decisions," *Corporate Financing Week,* January 18.

Froot, K., D. Scharfstein, and J. Stein (1993), "Risk Management: Coordinating Corporate Investment and Financing Policies," *Journal of Finance,* 5 (December): 1629–1658.

"Future Shock" (1993), *The Economist,* March 13.

Grossman, S.J. (1988), "An Analysis of the Implications for Stock and Futures Price Volatility of Program Trading and Dynamic Hedging Strategies," *Journal of Business* 61: 275–298.

Grundfest, J. (1990), "Lobbying into Limbo: The Political Ecology of the Savings and Loan Crisis," *Stanford Law and Policy Review,* 2 (Spring): 24–33.

Hakansson, N.M. (1976), "Purchasing Power Funds" *Financial Analysts Journal* 44 (3): 49–59.

House Banking Committee Minority Staff (1993), "Financial Derivatives," Washington, D.C.: U.S. Congress (November).

Lessard, D. (1990), "Global Competition and Corporate Finance in the 1990's," *Continental Bank Journal of Applied Corporate Finance,* 1: 59–72.

Lintner, J. (1965), "Security Prices, Risk and Maximal Gains from Diversification," *Journal of Finance,* 20 (December): 587–615.

Merton, R.C. (1973a), "Theory of Rational Option Pricing," *Bell Journal of Economics and Management Science,* 4 (Spring): 141–183.

———— (1973b), "An Intertemporal Capital Asset Pricing Model," *Econometrica,* 41 (September): 867–868.

———— (1975), "Theory of Finance from the Perspective of Continuous Time," *Journal of Financial and Quantitative Analysis,* 10 (November): 659–674.

———— (1977a), "On the Pricing of Contingent Claims and the Modigliani–Miller Theorem," *Journal of Financial Economics,* 5 (November): 241–249.

———— (1977b), "A Reexamination of the Capital Asset Pricing Model," in *Studies in Risk and Return,* I. Friend and J. Bicksler, eds., Volume I, Cambridge, MA: Ballinger.

———— (1990), "Financial Innovation and Economic Performance," *Journal of Financial Services Research,* 4 (December): 263–300.

Miller, M.H. (1994), "Do We Really Need More Regulation of Financial Derivatives?" Presented at client seminar of *Banco de Investimentos Garantia,* S.A., in Sao Paulo, Brazil, August 18.

Miller, M.H., and F. Modigliani (1961), "Dividend Policy, Growth and the Valuation of Shares," *Journal of Business,* 34 (October): 411–433.

Modigliani, F., and M.H. Miller (1958), "The Cost of Capital, Corporation Finance, and the Theory of Investment," *American Economic Review,* 48 (June): 261–297.

Mossin, J. (1966), "Equilibrium in a Capital Asset Market," *Econometrica,* 35 (October): 768–783.

Myers, S., and N. Majluf (1984), "Corporate Financing and Investment Decisions When Firms Have Information that Investors Do Not," *Journal of Financial Economics,* 13 (June): 187–221.

Perold, A. (1992), "BEA Associates: Enhanced Equity Index Funds," Harvard Business School, Case No. 293-024, Boston.

Phaup, M. (1993), "Recent Federal Efforts to Measure and Control Government Risk-Bearing," in *Government Risk-Bearing: Proceedings of a Conference Held at the Federal Reserve Bank of Cleveland, May 1991,* M. Sniderman, ed., Boston: Kluwer Academic Publishers.

Posner, R. (1974), "Theories of Economic Regulation," *Bell Journal of Economics and Management Science,* 5 (Autumn): 335–358.

Radner, R. (1972), "Existence of Plans, Prices and Price Expectations in a Sequence of Markets," *Econometrica,* 40 (March): 289–303.

Rawls, S., and C. Smithson (1990), "Strategic Risk Management," *Continental Bank Journal of Applied Corporate Finance,* 1: 6–18.

Ringleb, A.H., and S. Wiggins, "Institutional Control and Large-Scale, Long-Term Hazards," in *Government Risk-Bearing: Proceedings of a Conference Held at the Federal Reserve Bank of Cleveland, May 1991*, M. Sniderman, ed., Boston: Kluwer Academic Publishers.

Rodriguez, J., "Information and Incentives to Improve Government Risk-Bearing," in *Government Risk-Bearing Proceedings of a Conference Held at the Federal Reserve Bank of Cleveland, May 1991*, M. Sniderman, ed., Boston: Kluwer Academic Publishers.

Ross, S. (1976), "Options and Efficiency," *Quarterly Journal of Economics*, 90 (February): 75–89.

Rothschild, M., and J.E. Stiglitz (1970), "Increasing Risk I: A Definition," *Journal of Economic Theory*, 2 (September): 225–243.

——— (1971), "Increasing Risk I: Its Economic Consequences," *Journal of Economic Theory*, 3 (March): 66–84.

Sharpe, W.F. (1964), "Capital Asset Prices: A Theory of Market Equilibrium Under Conditions of Risk," *Journal of Finance*, 19 (September): 425–442.

Smith, C., C. Smithson, and S. Wilford (1990), *Managing Financial Risk*, New York: Harper Business.

Smith, C., and R. Stulz (1985), "The Determinants of Firms' Hedging Policies," *Journal of Financial and Quantitative Analysis*, 20 (December): 391–405.

Smithson, C., and C. Smith (1995), *Managing Financial Risk*, Baldwinsville, NY: Irwin.

Sniderman, M., ed. (1993), *Government Risk-Bearing: Proceedings of a Conference Held at the Federal Reserve Bank of Cleveland, May 1991*, Boston: Kluwer Academic Publishers.

Stein, J. (1988), "Informational Externalities and Welfare-Reducing Speculation," *Journal of Political Economy* 95: 1123–1145.

——— (1989), "Overreactions in the Options Market," *Journal of Finance*, 44: 1011–1023.

Stigler, G. (1971), "The Theory of Economic Regulation," *Bell Journal of Economics and Management Science*, 2 (1): 3–21.

Stiglitz, J.E. (1993), "Perspectives on the Role of Government Risk-Bearing within the Financial Sector," in *Government Risk-Bearing: Proceedings of a Conference Held at the Federal Reserve Bank of Cleveland, May 1991*, M. Sniderman, ed., Boston: Kluwer Academic Publishers.

Stulz, R. (1984), "Optimal Hedging Policies," *Journal of Financial and Quantitative Analysis*, 19 (June): 127–140.

Tobin, J. (1984), "On the Efficiency of the Financial System," *Lloyd's Bank Review* (July): 1–15.

Tufano, Peter (1993), "Liability Management at General Motors," Harvard Business School, Case No. 293-123, Boston.

Willman, John (1993), "Welfare versus Wealth of Nations," *Financial Times*, October 25.

CHAPTER SIX

The Informational Role of Asset Prices
The Case of Implied Volatility

ZVI BODIE AND ROBERT C. MERTON

An important function of the financial system is to serve as a key source of information that helps coordinate decentralized decision-making in various sectors of the economy. Households and investors use interest rates and asset prices observed in fixed-income and equity markets in making their consumption saving decisions and their portfolio allocation decisions. Interest rates and prices also provide important signals to managers of firms selecting investment projects and financing.

The informational role of asset prices has long been recognized. In his classic work on the theory of interest, Irving Fisher (1907, 1930) explains in detail how information extractable from competitive financial markets facilitates the efficient separation and decentralization of intertemporal consumption and production decisions, thereby improving social welfare.

Samuelson (1965) and Fama (1965) expanded Fisher's analysis by developing the efficient markets hypothesis, which holds that in a well-functioning and informed capital market, the best estimate of an asset's future price is the current price, adjusted for a "fair" expected rate of return. That is, an asset's current price fully reflects all publicly available information about future economic fundamentals affecting the asset's value.[1]

---

1. The reasoning behind the efficient markets hypothesis (EMH) is that if security prices are not informationally efficient, well-informed investors have opportunities to make

Information that is *reflected* in asset prices can, under certain circumstances, be *extracted* from those prices. That is the specific focus of this chapter: extracting information about the volatility of changes in stock, bond, currency, and commodity prices.

Volatility is a measure of the uncertainty about future changes in price or rate of return on assets. It is a fundamental measure used to quantify risk in modern finance theory, and a critical input for virtually all decisions relating to risk management and strategic financial planning.

Until 1973, volatility was generally estimated by using historical data. Since the appearance of exchange-traded options in 1973, the concurrent development of the theory of contingent claims pricing has made it possible to infer beliefs about the future volatility of an asset directly from the prices of options and other securities whose payoffs depend in a nonlinear way on the price of the underlying asset. The estimate extracted in this way is called *implied volatility*.

This chapter begins with a brief historical perspective on the informational role of bond prices. We then illustrate the general informational role of asset prices—both *spot* and *futures*—in contributing to efficient resource allocation. Our substantive focus is the use of security prices to derive estimates of asset return volatility. We show how information about asset price volatility can be extracted from option prices using models such as the one developed by Black and Scholes (1973). Extensions of this analysis indicate that we can use implied volatilities and prices of publicly traded securities to value *nontraded* firm liabilities (such as employee stock options).

The Yield Curve in Historical Perspective

Perhaps the most basic use of asset prices in informing financial decisions is the use of interest rates derived from the market prices of default-free bonds. The earliest recorded interest rates date from around 3000 B.C. in Mesopotamia, and the earliest prices of market-traded bonds date from Venice in the fourteenth century A.D.[2] Today, knowledge of the term structure of interest rates (also known as the yield curve) is the starting point for virtually any valuation model used in finance.

The most useful form in which to have this information is as a "dis-

---

"excess profits." Over time, competition leads to elimination of the excess profit opportunities, and asset prices become more reflective of the best available information about underlying fundamentals. For a review of the literature on the EMH, see Bodie, Kane, and Marcus (1993, Ch. 12).

2. See Homer (1977).

count function" giving the price of a unit of currency to be received at various dates in the future. Effectively, this means one would like to have the prices of zero-coupon bonds of all possible maturities. This form greatly facilitates valuation of all default-free fixed-income instruments promising any arbitrary temporal pattern of cash flows.

But until very recently, bond market price data rarely came in zero-coupon form. Even today the U.S. Treasury issues only two different security types: bills with maturities up to one year, which are issued in pure discount form, and notes and bonds with a semiannual coupon, which are usually issued at or close to par. For many years "implied" interest rates on zero-coupon bonds with maturities longer than one year could only be inferred from the observed prices of coupon bonds.

More recently, a secondary market has developed for U.S. Treasury strips created by investment banking firms. These firms buy U.S. Treasury bonds and sell off the component cash flows. By observing the market prices of the resulting U.S. Treasury strips, one can now have direct knowledge of the zero-coupon yield curve. Similarly, the development of a swap market in international bonds makes it possible to have direct knowledge of the yield curve in different currencies.

This improvement in the information provided by financial markets was not the intention of the firms that created the U.S. Treasury strips or the bond swaps, but rather is a by-product of their profit-making activities. As the markets for fixed-income securities and their derivatives continue to evolve, more and more information useful in valuing other fixed-income instruments will become available.

Financial institutions rarely have as their *manifest* function to provide information. The production of price information is more properly viewed as a *latent* function of the financial system.[3] In recent years, however, firms have emerged that specialize in gathering and analyzing asset price information.[4]

Futures Prices and the Efficient Storage of Commodities

The economics literature on the role of interest rates and asset prices in guiding resource allocation decisions is vast. Rather than attempt a survey, we instead offer a single example—*commodity futures*—to illustrate how the information that prices in the financial markets provide can enhance allocational efficiency.

---

3. That social behavior and organizations have manifest and latent functions is developed by R.K. Merton (1957, Ch. 1).
4. Prominent examples are Bloomberg and Reuters.

Commodity futures contracts are among the oldest financial instruments in existence. Futures contracts for rice were likely traded in ancient China.[5] While the manifest function of commodity futures markets is to facilitate the reallocation of exposure to commodity price risk among market participants, commodity futures prices also play an important informational role. *By providing a means to hedge the price risk associated with storing a commodity, futures contracts make it possible to separate the decision on whether to store a commodity physically from the decision to expose oneself financially to its price changes.*[6]

An example shows how this works. Suppose it is one month before the next harvest, and a wheat distributor has a ton of wheat in storage from the last harvest. The spot price of wheat is S, and the futures price for delivery a month from now (after the new crop has been harvested) is F. The distributor can hedge its exposure to price changes by either (1) selling the wheat in the spot market for S, and delivering it immediately, or (2) selling a futures contract short at a price of F, and delivering the wheat a month from now. In either case, the hedger has complete certainty about the price to be received for the wheat (assuming no risk of contract default).

Suppose a distributor's cost of physically storing the wheat, the "cost of carry," which includes interest, warehousing, and spoilage costs, is C. This distributor will choose alternative (2) and carry the ton of wheat for another month (i.e., past the next harvest) only if $F > S + C$. To put it slightly differently, the distributor will choose to carry the wheat for another month only if the cost of carrying it is less than the difference between the futures and the spot prices of wheat, (i.e., if $C < F - S$). Thus, the spread between the futures and the spot price governs how much wheat will be stored in aggregate and by whom: Wheat will be stored only by those distributors whose cost of carry is less than $F - S$.

Suppose now that the next wheat harvest is expected to be a bountiful one. In that case, the equilibrium futures price of wheat may well be lower than the current spot price ($F < S$), and it will not pay for anyone to store wheat from this growing season into the next, even if it costs nothing to do so (i.e., $C = 0$). The futures price of wheat conveys this information to all producers, distributors, and consumers of wheat, *including* those not transacting in the futures market.

To see how the futures market enhances allocational efficiency, consider what would happen in its absence. Now, every producer, distributor, and

---

5. For a brief review of the history of futures markets, see Miller (1990).
6. The decision to eliminate exposure to price changes is called "hedging."

consumer of wheat would have to rely on *forecasts* of the future spot price of wheat in deciding whether to store it for another month.[7] The futures market eliminates the need for *all* market participants to gather and process information in order to forecast the future spot price. Producers, distributors, and consumers of wheat may be in the best position to forecast future wheat prices (perhaps because they have low costs of gathering the relevant information), but others can also use the market. Competition among active forecasters in the futures markets will encourage those who have a comparative advantage in forecasting wheat prices to specialize in it.

Extracting Information from Asset Prices

Sometimes the information needed to make a particular financial decision is directly observable in the financial markets. If you are considering whether to refinance a mortgage, you can find out interest rates and other terms of the various financing alternatives directly and at low cost by looking in the newspaper or by calling a mortgage lender. Often, however, the information required to make a financial decision is not directly observable. It must be inferred or extracted from the prices you directly observe.

To extract information from the observed market prices of assets, an analyst must use a model that connects the information sought to the price. The analyst may have high or low confidence in the validity of the model as well as in the accuracy of the recorded market prices. Table 6-1 summarizes the possibilities.

Let us explore the implications of each of the four possible situations in Table 6-1. First, consider the cell labeled 1. If analysts are absolutely sure that the model used for extraction is correct, *and* that the observed prices are also correct, they can be certain that the information they are extracting is valid.

Suppose we want to obtain information about the current rate of exchange between the U.S. dollar and the British pound. We can observe only the rates of exchange between the U.S. dollar and the Japanese yen and between the pound and the yen.

Here the relevant model is based on the Law of One Price. This law holds that, in a competitive market, if two assets are functionally perfect

---

7. While the futures price "reflects" information about the future spot price, it is not necessarily an unbiased estimate of the future spot price, even in theory. For a discussion of the relation between futures prices and expected future spot prices of commodities, see Siegel and Siegel (1990).

Table 6-1 Matrix of Quality of Information Extraction

	Model Is Correct	Model Is Incorrect
Prices Are Correct	1	3
Prices Are Incorrect	2	4

substitutes, then they will have the same price. The Law of One Price is enforced by a trading process called *arbitrage*—the purchase and immediate sale of equivalent assets in order to earn a sure profit from a difference in their prices. When it is applied to currency exchange rates, the Law of One Price implies that, for any three currencies that are freely convertible in competitive markets, it is enough to observe the exchange rates between any two in order to infer a reliable value for the third.

In our case, suppose the dollar price of the yen is 1 cent per yen (or equivalently 100¥ to the dollar), and the price of the yen in terms of pounds is a half pence (£0.005) to the yen (or equivalently, ¥200 to the pound). Then, by the Law of One Price, one can infer that the dollar–pound exchange rate is $2 per pound (in the absence of taxes and transactions costs).

The reasoning behind this inference is as follows. There are two ways to buy pounds for dollars. One is *indirectly* through the yen market—by first buying yen for dollars, and then using the yen to buy pounds. Because one pound costs ¥200, and ¥200 costs $2.00, this indirect way costs $2.00 per pound. Another way is to purchase pounds *directly* with dollars. The direct purchase of pounds with dollars must cost the same as the indirect purchase of pounds with dollars because of the Law of One Price. If this equivalence is violated, there will be an arbitrage opportunity that cannot persist for very long.[8]

Suppose you believe the markets for all three currencies satisfy the conditions for being considered competitive, i.e., there are no impediments to the purchase or sale of any quantities of any of the three cur-

---

8. To see how the force of arbitrage works to uphold the Law of One Price in this example, let's look at what would happen if the price of the pound were $2.10 rather than $2.00. Suppose you walk into a bank in New York City, and you observe three exchange rates: 1 cent per yen, ¥200 per pound, and $2.10 per pound. Suppose there is one window for exchanging dollars and yen, another for exchanging yen and pounds, and a third window for exchanging dollars and pounds. Here is how you can make a $10 profit without leaving the confines of the bank:
1. At the dollar/yen window, convert $200 into ¥20,000.
2. At the yen/pound window, convert the ¥20,000 into £100.
3. At the dollar/pound window, convert the £100 into $210.

rencies. You are therefore very confident that the *no-arbitrage opportunities* model is correct and that the Law of One Price holds.

Now suppose you can also directly observe the dollar/pound market, and the exchange rate is $2.10 per pound. Then you must conclude either that the prices you observe are incorrect (i.e., cell 2 in Table 6-1), or that the model is incorrect (i.e., cell 3). There are two senses in which observed exchange rates can be incorrect. The first is that they are reported with error. That is, they all may not have been observed at the same time of day, or they are an average of the bid and asked prices rather than actual transaction prices. The second sense is that the data are genuinely synchronous transaction prices, but that the market is *mispricing* the three currencies.

The model may be incorrect because of some barrier to the operation of the force of arbitrage. For example, there may be government exchange controls or some other form of government intervention in one of the three markets. Yet, if you are truly confident that the model is correct and that the observed prices are genuine transaction prices, then you must conclude that an arbitrage opportunity exists. If you and others similarly informed proceed to exploit that opportunity, your trading activity will over time eliminate the arbitrage opportunity. Thus, such a situation is unstable and transitory, and eventually we will find ourselves in cell 1 of Table 6-1.

Of course, an analyst is almost never absolutely sure about both the validity of the model and of the observed prices. Each is believed with some degree of confidence that is less than 100%. Nevertheless, the underlying principle of inference illustrated here remains applicable. *No information extraction is possible without some model.*

A broad set of examples will clarify the process of information extraction and its uses.

Pure Default-Free Cash Flows

There is a form of "hierarchy" in the extraction of information from asset prices—a progression from the simple to the complex. We have already given an example of the simplest kind of extraction of information: computing the implied exchange rate between two currencies when the exchange rate cannot be observed directly. An example that raises the order of complexity is extracting information about the prices of pure default-free future cash flows, or, equivalently, extraction of the pure default-free term structure of interest rates.

To illustrate, suppose we have a pattern of cash flows denominated in U.S. dollars. The data used for valuing these flows are the prices of U.S.

Treasury bonds. As in the case of currencies, the basic model follows from the Law of One Price. Thus, we assume that inferences drawn from the prices of U.S. Treasury bonds are valid for *all* dollar-denominated cash flows that are free of default risk.

Let us first restrict the data to the prices of Treasury strips, which represent the value of a single cash payment on a specified maturity date. The objective is to use these Treasury strip prices to extract information about the prices for *all* possible maturity dates. Because there is a continuum of possible maturity dates, and strips are available for only a discrete number of maturity dates, additional assumptions are needed in order to infer the missing prices. One common approach is to assume that pure discount prices can be represented as a polynomial function of time to maturity. The model is calibrated by fitting its parameters to the observed prices. The estimated parameters are then used either to interpolate between observed maturity dates or to extrapolate beyond their range.

Even this relatively simple procedure of information extraction can give rise to both a difficulty and, perhaps, an opportunity: There may be more than one reported price for strips with the same maturity date. Different market prices for the same promised future cash flows can be the result of differences among bonds in liquidity, tax treatment, or other features such as call provisions. There are three ways to reconcile these differences:

- Explicitly incorporate the features that account for pricing differences by developing a more complex pricing model.

- Leave the features unspecified, assume they give rise to an "error term" that is uncorrelated with time to maturity, and use econometric methods to infer the hypothetical "pure" prices. This approach takes advantage of a powerful set of tools of statistical inference. Chief among these is the technique of multiple regression analysis.

- Conclude that there is a genuine arbitrage opportunity due to mispricing in the market for U.S. Treasury bonds and seek to exploit it.

These avenues to reconciliation of price differences are not mutually exclusive. The analyst typically pursues all three.

Nontraded Financial Assets

In many countries including the United States, regulatory bodies such as the Federal Reserve Board, rule-making bodies such as the Financial Accounting Standards Board, and guaranty agencies such as the Federal Deposit Insurance Corporation need information about the market values of the assets and liabilities of financial intermediaries. Such information is essential in monitoring the capital adequacy of banks, insurance companies, and pension funds.

The market prices of securities that are similar to the financial assets held by the intermediary can provide such information. Thus the prices of low-credit-quality "junk" bonds provide useful information for valuing the commercial loan portfolios of banks or the privately placed bond portfolios of insurance companies. This is sometimes called "pricing by analogy" or "matrix pricing."

As in the valuation of pure default-free cash flows, rarely does one find a traded security that is an exact analogue of the nontraded one. It is therefore necessary to resort to formal methods of inference such as pricing models to translate observed market prices into the desired valuations.

Residential Real Estate

It is a common practice in the United States that local governments levy taxes on the current market value of residential property. Because the vast majority of properties do not trade frequently, the typical practice is to infer their market values using a model calibrated to the observed prices of properties recently sold in arm's length transactions.

Models of real estate appraisal for tax purposes vary widely in their details. Generally, they invoke the Law of One Price and use multiple regression techniques. Observed transaction prices are regressed against a set of observable features of each property that should matter in valuation, such as the acreage and building size. A set of coefficients relating value to these features are estimated. The market values of all properties are then inferred from their observable features by applying the estimated coefficients from the regression model.

Credit Guarantees

A next-level increase of complexity in the hierarchy of information extraction provides that the output of one stage of extraction becomes the input in a subsequent stage. For example, suppose a firm is considering guaranteeing bonds issued by a certain corporation against default, and wants an estimate of the market value of such a guarantee.

The two-stage procedure first derives the prices of pure default-free cash flows from the prices of U.S. Treasury strips using the approach discussed above. Stage two then uses those prices to compute what corporate bonds would sell for if they were free of default risk. The difference between that computed default-free value and the actual market price of the corporate bonds is the *implied value* of the guarantee.[9]

Implied Tax Brackets

In many countries including the United States, income tax rates are progressive or "graduated." Private investors and tax authorities alike are interested in knowing the marginal tax bracket at which it becomes advantageous for investors to switch from holding taxable to tax-exempt securities. Market interest rates (computed from bond prices) provide one means of computing this implied "switch-over" tax bracket.

Implied tax brackets are useful in identifying and separating the effects of taxes from other factors that influence bond prices and yields. For example, the yield spread between corporate bonds and U.S. Treasury bonds can be attributed to three sources: liquidity differences, default risk, and the partially tax-exempt status of the government bonds.[10] The implied effect of this tax exemption can be extracted from the spread between high-grade corporates or U.S. government agency bonds and Treasury securities.

A Caveat

Even if information is perfectly and accurately reflected in asset prices, it may not be possible to extract that information from those prices. (In the language of mathematics, the "inverse function" may not exist.) To illustrate this point, suppose that the price of XYZ stock always accurately reflects investor expectations of XYZ's expected future earnings per share, E, discounted at a market capitalization rate, k. Thus $P = E/k$. Yet, neither E nor k is directly observable. One cannot extract the separate values of E and k from the observed price, P, without additional information. Establishing the conditions under which specific information can or cannot be extracted from prices is a particular instance of the general *identification problem* of statistics and econometrics.[11]

As a further demonstration of this central issue in information extraction, consider two typical examples.

Example 1: Extracting estimates of the expected future value of a stock index

---

9. Merton (1990) develops this procedure in detail and derives a set of guarantee values for low-credit-quality corporate bonds.

10. The interest earned on U.S. Treasury bonds is exempt from state and local income taxes. This exemption does not apply to debt issues of U.S. government agencies.

11. For a survey article on the identification problem in econometrics, see Hsiao (1983).

from the current futures price on that index. It can be tempting to believe that the futures price of a stock index is an indicator of its expected future spot price, and therefore that the creation of a financial futures market can provide information about investor expectations that is not extractable from spot market prices. However, the futures price of the index is related to the spot price through the arbitrage relation:

$$F = (1 + r - d)S$$

where F is the futures price, r is the risk-free interest rate, d is the dividend yield on the index portfolio, and S is the spot price of the index.

This relation does not produce a "perfect" arbitrage opportunity unless we know the dividend yield, d, with certainty.[12] Moreover, the expected future spot price of the index does not appear at all in this relation, and therefore no information about it can be extracted from the futures price that was not already extractable from the spot price.[13]

Example 2: Inferring the expected direction of change in a stock's price from the relative prices of puts and calls on the stock. It can be tempting to believe that the ratio of the price of a call to the price of a put on a particular stock can serve as an indicator of investor expectations about future stock price changes. Since a call pays off only if the stock price *rises above* its exercise price and a put only pays off if the stock price *falls below* its exercise, it would seem that the call–put ratio should be higher when investors are relatively "bullish" and lower when they are "bearish." Yet, no such inference is warranted.

The prices of puts and calls are related to the price of the underlying stock through an arbitrage relation that does not depend on the expected future price of the stock. In fact, the only incremental information reliably extractable from option prices is information about the *volatility* of the stock price, not about its expected return.[14]

---

12. The relation between the spot and futures prices and the risk-free interest rate can be used to estimate the dividend yield as:

$$d = r - \left(\frac{F}{S} - 1\right)$$

13. Indeed, the futures price is almost certainly a downward-biased estimate of the future spot value of the index, because the stock market offers a risk premium to investors.

14. Sprenkle (1961) provides an early attempt at a model to extract information about expected returns and investor risk preferences from option prices. Later research on option pricing shows that such inferences cannot be reliably identified [Merton (1992, p. 282].

What Is Volatility, and Why Is It Important?

Volatility is a measure of the uncertainty about future changes in an asset's price or its rate of return. Volatility is related to the *range* of possible rates of return from holding the security *and* to their likelihood of occurring. *A security's volatility is greater, the wider the range of possible outcomes, and the higher the probabilities of the returns at the extremes of the range.* The most common statistic used in finance to measure the volatility of a security's probability distribution of returns is *standard deviation—σ.* It is an indicator of deviations of per period rates of return from the expected rate of return weighted by their probabilities of occurring.[15]

Volatility is a fundamental variable in financial decision-making. Estimation of risk is essential for virtually every type of financial decision: whether capital investment and financing, asset allocation, buying or selling insurance and guarantees, or valuing risky debt and other corporate liabilities. In the absence of uncertainty, investment and financing decisions would simplify to a comparison of the present values of future cash flows discounted at observed interest rates. Portfolio selection rules would reduce to the simple imperative: Maximize the investor's return. There would be no need for insurance, and derivative security valuation would be a trivial matter.

To document the wide range of uses for volatility estimates in financial decision-making, we briefly describe applications in three broad categories: (1) financial services, (2) corporate finance, and (3) regulation.

Uses of Volatility Estimates in the Financial Services Industry

Portfolio selection. For more than forty years, starting with the pioneering work of Markowitz (1952), the portfolio optimization models used by professional investment managers have focused on estimating the *efficient portfolio frontier.*[16] The central idea is to find, for any given level of risk, the portfolio that maximizes the investor's expected rate of return.

---

15. Standard deviation is computed as follows:
 Standard Deviation (σ) = Square Root of the Sum of (Probability) × (Possible Return − Expected Return)^2

$$\sigma = \sqrt{\sum_{i=1}^{n} P_i(r_i - E(r))^2}$$

16. Markowitz received the 1990 Nobel Prize in Economics for this work.

These optimization models require return distribution information for all of the risky assets to be included in the investment portfolio. Specifically:

- Expected rates of return, which are derived from statistical analysis of historical data on asset returns and analyst assessments of future scenarios.[17]

- Estimates of rate of return volatilities including both *variances* and *covariances*, which until recently have been derived almost exclusively from historical analysis of past returns data.

Valuation.   Valuation is the lifeblood of firms engaged in investment banking activities. Firms that underwrite and sell corporate securities or arrange mergers and divestitures must have reliable valuation models if they are to remain competitive. Often the securities and other corporate liabilities that have to be evaluated are not traded in markets. Examples are executive stock options and unfunded pension liabilities. The modern technology for pricing these securities and contracts is *contingent claims analysis*, which requires estimates of the volatilities of the underlying economic variables.[18]

Risk management.   Firms that provide risk management services create customized contracts tailored to the unique circumstances of their clients. Examples are swaps, caps, collars, and floors contingent on interest rates, exchange rates, and commodity prices.[19] The models that financial intermediaries use in the production and pricing of these customized derivative securities require volatility estimates as inputs.

Uses of Volatility Estimates in Corporate Financial Management

Contingent claims analysis has been applied in capital budgeting decisions to explicitly recognize the value of flexibility in investment decisions.[20] For example, suppose a public utility is going to build a new power plant. It can choose between a less expensive, single-fuel plant that uses either only oil or only natural gas, or a more expensive, multi-fuel plant that can switch back and forth between oil and gas. In general, the value of fuel input type flexibility increases with increases in the uncertainty about

---

17. For a textbook exposition of how this is typically done, see, for example, Bodie, Kane, and Marcus (1993, pp. 894–900).
18. For development of contingent claims analysis and examples of its applications in security pricing, see Merton (1992, Chapters 11–13).
19. For a textbook introduction to these derivatives, see, for example, Hull (1993).
20. For a survey of the uses of contingent claims analysis in capital budgeting, see Merton (1992, pp. 425–427) and Dixit and Pindyck (1994).

the future relative prices of those fuels. Thus a critical consideration in the evaluation of these alternatives for a power plant is the volatility of the prices of gas and oil.

Financial contracting is an alternative that can substitute for such physical investments in plant and equipment that increase the firm's flexibility. If the utility wants the economic benefit of the ability to switch between two different types of fuel, it can enter into option-like contractual agreements that provide for cash compensation to the firm whenever the price of fuel it actually uses in its specialized plant exceeds the price of the alternative fuel. Similarly, a crude oil producer can create a "synthetic refinery," by entering into a cracking-spread contract for the firm to deliver crude oil and receive in return refined products such as gasoline and heating oil.

Uses of Volatility Estimates by Government Regulators

Financial guarantees. Governments all over the world provide financial guarantees either through specific guarantee programs such as deposit insurance or by providing credit directly. In the United States, for example, the federal government is the nation's largest underwriter of default risk. The U.S. Office of Management and Budget (OMB) estimates that three-fifths of all nonfederal credit outstanding in 1992 was assisted by federal credit programs, government-sponsored enterprises (such as the Federal National Mortgage Corporation), or deposit insurance.[21] OMB estimates the total present value of the costs of federal guarantees in force in 1992 at between $203 and $294 billion. Measurement and management of the government's exposure through these various guarantee programs requires estimates of volatilities of the underlying economic variables. [See Merton and Bodie (1992).]

Monetary and fiscal policy. The volatility of certain economic indicators such as the consumer price level, the growth rate of gross domestic product, or the unemployment rate is increasingly a target as well as an indicator of macroeconomic policy. For example, the long-standing issue of the trade-off between inflation and unemployment has been recast in terms of a trade-off between the *variabilities* of these two economic indicators.[22] In the United States, the Federal Reserve takes into account the volatility of stocks, bonds, currencies, and commodities in establishing monetary policy [See Nasar (1992)].

---

21. *Budget of the U.S. Government for Fiscal Year 1993,* Part One, Table 13-1, p. 267.
22. For example, see Taylor (1994).

Implied Volatility

Implied volatility is an estimate of σ that is extracted from the prices of options and other derivative securities with nonlinear payoff structures. The "watershed" date for implied volatility is 1973. In that year, two events occurred:

- Formal publication of the Black and Scholes option pricing model.
- Creation of an organized options exchange in the United States— the Chicago Board Options Exchange (CBOE).[23]

The basic insight underlying the Black–Scholes model is that a dynamic portfolio trading strategy in the stock can be found that will replicate the returns from an option on that stock. Hence, to avoid arbitrage opportunities, the option price must always equal the value of this replicating portfolio.

The Black–Scholes model characterizes a family of theoretical models of option pricing in which the only unobservable is σ, and the option pricing formula is monotonic in σ. Hence a unique solution for σ can be found that equates the market price of the option to the model's price.

The Black–Scholes formula for the price of a European call option on a nondividend-paying stock is:

$$C = N(d_1)S - N(d_2)Ee^{-rT}$$

$$d_1 = \frac{\ln(S/E) + (r - d + \sigma^2/2)T}{\sigma\sqrt{T}} \tag{1}$$

$$d_2 = d_1 - \sigma\sqrt{T}$$

where:

C = price of the call

$N(d)$ = the probability that a random draw from a standard normal distribution will be less than d

S = price of the stock

E = exercise price

---

23. Prior to establishment of the CBOE, options had been traded over the counter. The CBOE began trading the first listed options in the United States in April 1973, a month before official publication of the Black–Scholes model. By 1975, traders on the CBOE were using the model both to price and hedge their options positions. For a description of the story behind the development of the model and its impact on finance practice, see Bernstein (1992, Chapter 11).

e = the base of the natural log function (approximately 2.71828)

r = risk-free interest rate (the annualized continuously compounded rate on a safe asset with the same maturity as the option)

T = time to maturity of the option in years

ln = natural logarithm

σ = standard deviation of the annualized continuously compounded rate of return on the stock

The Black–Scholes formula has five parameters, four of them are directly observable: S, the price of the stock; E, the exercise price; r, the risk-free interest rate (the annualized continuously compounded rate on a safe asset with the same maturity as the option); and T, the time to maturity of the option. If we know the market price of an option, then the Black–Scholes formula can be used to derive a value for the unobservable σ that equates the price computed according to the Black–Scholes formula to the actual observed market price. This value of σ is called the *option's implied volatility* for the stock.[24]

The Black–Scholes model assumes that σ is a constant. Merton (1973) generalizes the model to allow for a time-varying, nonstochastic σ. Under this generalization, the implied volatility that is extracted from the Black–Scholes formula is the *average* σ over the life of the option.

Black and Scholes also assume that no dividends are paid during the life of the option. Merton (1973) generalizes the model to allow for a constant continuous dividend yield, d.[25] Merton's dividend-adjusted formula is:

$$C = N(d_1)Se^{-dT} - N(d_2)Ee^{-rT}$$

$$d_1 = \frac{\ln(S/E) + (r - d + \sigma^2/2)T}{\sigma\sqrt{T}} \qquad (2)$$

$$d_2 = d_1 - \sigma\sqrt{T}$$

---

24. Early academic work on implied volatility includes Latané and Rendleman (1976), Galai (1977), Chiras and Manaster (1978), Schmalensee and Trippi (1978), Beckers (1981), and Manaster and Koehler (1982). See also Jarrow and Wiggins (1989), Day and Lewis (1990), Lamoureux and Lastrapes (1993), Christensen and Prabhala (1994), and Bank of Japan (1995). For a recent survey of the academic literature, see Canina and Figlewski (1993). Discussion of implied volatilities among practitioners of risk management and derivatives trading is widespread and commonplace.

25. Merton's formula reduces to the Black–Scholes formula when $d = 0$. Whaley (1993) uses the cash-dividend-adjusted, Cox–Ross–Rubinstein (1979) binomial method to derive implied volatilities for the CBOE's index of implied volatility.

In the real world, both σ and d are rarely known with certainty and empirical evidence suggests that both vary stochastically over time. Models that incorporate these stochastic variations have been developed and are used in practice. Nonetheless, the implied volatility that is extracted from the dividend-adjusted Black–Scholes model can still serve as a reliable indicator (even if a biased one) of investor expectations for volatility over the life of the option.

As is evident by inspecting the Black–Scholes formula, investors who disagree about the expected return on an underlying security, but have the same estimate of σ, will agree on the "fair value" of the option. Therefore, option prices can reflect consensus views about σ even if there is no consensus about the expected return of the underlying stock.

Of course, there will not be a consensus among all investors about σ. Rather, the σ that is embodied in option prices is a weighted average of the σ used either explicitly or implicitly by option traders. Estimates of σ therefore form a distribution of values around the "true" value. If the observed *market* price of the option reflects an unbiased estimate of the Black–Scholes model price with stochastic volatility, then, because the Black–Scholes formula is *nonlinear* in σ, the implied value of σ derived from it will *not* generally be unbiased.

This bias can be minimized by selecting options with exercise prices equal to the forward price of the stock (that is, $E = Se^{rT}$). For such options, a *linear* approximation can be used for the values of both a European put and a European call on a nondividend-paying stock:[26]

$$C = P \approx \frac{1}{\sqrt{2\pi}} S\sigma\sqrt{T}$$

By inverting this equation, one can derive the implied volatility (i.e., σ) as a linear function of the option price and the underlying stock price:

$$\sigma = \frac{C\sqrt{2\pi}}{S\sqrt{T}}$$

The significance of this approximate linear relation is that implied volatility estimates derived from options whose exercise price equals the forward price will be nearly unbiased in a statistical sense.

The CBOE has constructed an implied volatility index (VIX) for the S&P 100 stock price index to be used as the basis for creating new futures and

---

26. See Brenner and Subrahmanyam (1988) or Feinstein (1988).

options contracts on implied volatility itself [see Whaley (1993, pp. 80–82)]. This implied volatility index is designed to minimize statistical bias while using information from the prices of eight S&P 100 index options with a maturity of approximately 30 days.

Figure 6-1 shows the value of the VIX over the period 1986–1993. It is evident that the implied volatility of the stock price index has fluctuated quite a bit. There was a huge "spike" at the time of the October 1987 stock market crash. Thereafter, implied volatility trended downward slowly as investors regained confidence in the future prospects for stocks. By the end of 1993, the level of the VIX was below 15%.

It is also evident from Figure 6-1 that implied volatility is affected by current political and economic developments.

Implied Volatility Versus Estimates from Historical Data

Instead of extracting volatility estimates from option prices, we can estimate volatility using the time series of past price changes. It has been shown [Merton (1980)] that, in estimating σ from past price data, the accuracy of the estimate increases with the number of observations for a given overall observation period. Therefore for a given calendar period (e.g., the last ten years), the estimates of volatility can be improved by moving from monthly to weekly or from weekly to daily data. In sharp contrast, the accuracy of the estimate of expected return increases only with the *length* of the observation period and not with the number of observations over a given period.

Estimates of σ derived *exclusively* from historical price data are by their nature unconditional forecasts. Such historical estimates thus do not exploit other publicly available information that would help forecast future volatility. For example, consider the period just before the outbreak of the Persian Gulf War in 1991. The United Nations on November 29, 1990, gave Iraq a deadline for removing Iraqi forces from Kuwait—January 15, 1991. Suppose at that time you wanted to estimate the volatility of stock or bond prices in the period between November 29, 1990, and January 15, 1991. An estimate of σ derived exclusively from past data clearly could not reflect the additional degree of uncertainty regarding future security prices engendered by uncertainty about the impending war.

Note that information about the possibility of war in the Persian Gulf was available to anyone who watched television news or read a newspaper. It was not insider information, and hence, was reflected in the prices of stocks and options. But an estimate of σ based exclusively on past data would not have picked up this information. One based on option prices (i.e., implied volatility) would have.

Figure 6-1 Implied Volatility: 1986–1993

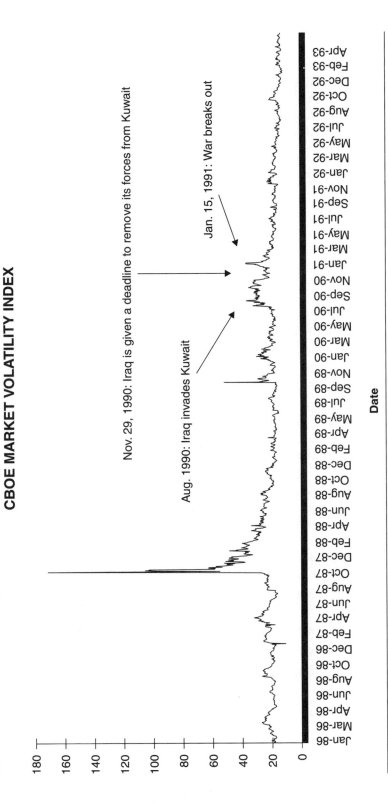

CBOE MARKET VOLATILITY INDEX

Nov. 29, 1990: Iraq is given a deadline to remove its forces from Kuwait

Jan. 15, 1991: War breaks out

Aug. 1990: Iraq invades Kuwait

Date

Another advantage of implied volatility over historical volatility stems from the *nonstationarity* of volatility. There is substantial empirical evidence that the volatilities of security prices, interest rates, exchange rates, and commodity prices are not constant over time.[27] Theoretical research on speculative prices also supports the hypothesis that volatility generally changes over time. There have been, and are sure to be in the future, periods of greater or lesser degrees of uncertainty regarding economic conditions, and those different degrees of uncertainty will be reflected in the volatility of financial markets. Volatility should not in general be modeled as a constant.

Nonstationarity complicates estimation of volatility from past data using standard statistical techniques. If volatility is "slowly" changing, one way to reduce the problem of nonstationarity of the volatility parameter is to use shorter time intervals (more frequent sampling) to achieve the same level of accuracy in estimating σ for a shorter overall observation period. Sophisticated econometric techniques, which allow for changing volatility (such as GARCH models), have had some success. As Black and Scholes (1972) conclude in the first empirical evaluation of their model, the best approach is to combine the information provided by implied volatility and historical volatility.[28]

The Term Structure of Implied Volatilities

The availability of government bond prices of different maturities makes it possible to derive an accurate term structure of interest rates. Just so, the availability of prices on multiple options with different maturities allows one to infer the term structure of volatility. In the exchange-traded options markets, there are different maturities for every strike price of an option. Implied volatilities can be computed from the prices of these different maturity options to yield a term structure of volatilities. The implied-volatility term structure is generally not flat, nor even monotonic.[29]

For example, Table 6-2 shows the term structure of volatility derived from options on the S&P 100 stock index (OEX) on December 3, 1990. Note that options maturing before the January 15, 1991, deadline for Iraq to leave Kuwait have an implied annualized volatility of 18.68%.[30] The

---

27. See the substantial literature on the ARCH and GARCH models for estimating dynamic changes in volatility. Engle, Kane, and Noh (1993) and Nelson (1991) are examples.
28. Brenner and Galai (1989) concur when they propose a standardized volatility index that is a weighted average of implied and historical volatility measures.
29. See, for example, Heynan, Kemna, and Vorst (1992).
30. The prospect of a "jump" distribution for nonlocal changes in stock prices when the

Table 6-2 Term Structure of Volatility on December 3, 1990

Contract and Maturity Date	Trading Days to Maturity	Price	Average Implied Volatility	Incremental Implied Volatility
Dec 1990 Call	15	$ 6.625	18.68%	NA
January 1991 Call	35	$11.250	20.45%	21.78%
February 1991 Put	55	$12.000	25.66%	34.38%

Note: Exercise price of all options is 305; Index closing value is 305.73; T-bill rate is 7.02% per year; number of assumed trading days in the year is 250. Historical annual σ estimated from daily data for the 30 days prior to December 3, 1990, was 17.38%.

implied volatility for options maturing after the deadline, in February 1991, is 25.66%. The "forward" or incremental annualized volatility over the added 30 days amounts to 34.38%. This sharp increase reflects the uncertainty associated with the war, which would likely be resolved only after the U.N. deadline, since negotiated solutions are rarely reached prior to such deadlines.

Implied Covariances

As in the case of default-free fixed-income securities, there is a "hierarchy" in the extraction of information from option prices—a progression from the simple to the complex. Thus, one can use a multi-step procedure to extract information not only about the volatilities (standard deviations) of economic variables, but also about their covariances with other economic variables.

For example, consider the simplest case of an option on a portfolio of two stocks. By definition, the variance of the rate of return on the portfolio is given by the formula:

$$\sigma^2 = w_A^2\sigma_A^2 + w_B^2\sigma_B^2 2w_Aw_B\sigma_{AB}$$

where w_A is the constant portfolio fraction in stock A, w_B is the fraction in stock B, and σ_{AB} is the covariance between the returns on stocks A and B.

From the prices of options on stock A and on stock B separately, one can infer the implied values of σ_A and σ_B. That is the first step. The price

uncertainty of war is resolved on the deadline date requires a modified version of the Black–Scholes model [see Merton (1976)]. Implied volatilities reported in Table 6-2, however, are computed using the standard formula.

of an option on a portfolio of stocks A and B can similarly be used to infer the implied variance of the portfolio, σ^2. Given the estimates for σ^2, σ_A, and σ_B, then, σ_{AB} is estimated by the formula:

$$\sigma_{AB} = \frac{\sigma^2 - w_A^2\sigma_A^2 - w_B^2\sigma_B^2}{2w_Aw_B}$$

Other examples of contingent claims models that permit similar extraction of information about covariances from derivative security prices can be found in Merton (1973), Margrabe (1978), Fischer (1978), and Stulz (1982).

Pricing Models for Fixed-Income Derivatives

During the 1980s and 1990s a host of new fixed-income derivatives—both standardized exchange-traded instruments such as puts and calls and customized contracts such as caps, floors, and collars—were created to help firms manage their interest rate risk exposures. To price and hedge these instruments, financial services firms have adopted generalized fixed-income models that are "matched" frequently to replicate both the observed term structure of interest rates and the term structure of interest rate volatilities.[31] The "implied" parameters of the models are "fitted" statically to the observed term structures in the same fashion that implied volatility is calculated in the Black–Scholes model. In practice, the models are recalibrated daily using the prices of publicly traded U.S. Treasury securities and standardized options on bond futures and swaps.

Applications of Implied Volatility

The prices of options on individual securities and on portfolios of securities can be used to infer the variance-covariance structure of returns on risky assets. These parameters can then be entered as inputs into Markowitz-type portfolio optimization models. Similarly, in corporate finance, one can also infer the parameters needed to make complex financial decisions from the prices of traded securities issued by the firm. As one example, consider the case of valuing executive stock options.

There has been considerable controversy in the United States over the recommendation that public corporations be required to report the value

---

31. Among the earliest stochastic interest rate models are ones by Vasicek (1977), and Cox, Ingersoll, and Ross (1985). More recently, the "matching" models are developed in Ho and Lee (1986), Black, Derman, and Toy (1990), and Heath, Jarrow, and Morton (1992). See Hull (1993, Chapter 15) for a survey description of all these models.

of stock options granted to employees as part of their compensation [see Financial Accounting Standards Board (1993)]. Since a market price for these options is not available, much of the debate surrounding the recommendation centers on the firm's ability to value them accurately. The exposure draft recommends two alternative valuation techniques that use option pricing models and volatilities estimated from historical price data.

Another alternative is to use contingent claims analysis and implied volatilities. To illustrate the procedure, suppose the ABC Corporation is a publicly held company. A contingent claims analysis starts by specifying the terms of each of the security types issued by the firm. Suppose that the securities issued by ABC Corporation are: (1) bonds maturing in one year with a face value of $100 million and a current market price of $85 million, (2) 1 million shares of common stock with a market price of $20 million, and (3) 100,000 employee stock options expiring in one year with an exercise price of $20 per share (and no market price). Thus, the options entitle their holders to buy 1/11 of the firm's value a year from now for a total price of $2 million. The risk-free interest rate r is 6% per year compounded continuously.

Consider the possible payoff pattern to the holders of ABC's debt at its maturity date one year from now. If the future value of ABC's assets exceeds the face value of its debt (i.e., if $V_1 >$ $100 million), the bondholders receive the promised payment of $100 million. If the value of the assets falls short of $100 million, however, the firm will default on the debt, and the bondholders will receive the firm's assets.

Now consider the payoffs to the optionholders. If the value of the firm's assets is less than $100 million a year from now, then neither the stockholders nor the optionholders get anything—the bondholders get it all. If the value of the firm's assets exceeds $100 million, the optionholders have the right to buy a fraction (1/11) of the firm's assets for $2 million. If they choose to exercise that option, they will have 1/11 of $(V_1 -$ $100 million $+$ $2 million). The value of V_1 at which it would just pay to exercise the option is therefore:

$$\$2 \text{ million} = (V_1 - \$100 \text{ million} + \$2 \text{ million})/11$$
$$V_1 = \$120 \text{ million}$$

Knowing the market value of the debt ($85 million) and the stock ($20 million), one can derive implied estimates both for the value of the entire firm (including the nontraded options) and for the future volatility of that firm value. As with standard implied volatility estimates, the market prices of the traded securities are assumed to satisfy the pricing formulas.

The equation for the market value of the bonds satisfies:[32]

$$85 = [1 - N(d_1)]V + N(d_2)100e^{-rT}$$

$$d_1 = \frac{\ln\left(\frac{V}{100}\right) + \left(r + \frac{\sigma^2}{2}\right)T}{\sigma\sqrt{T}}$$

$$d_2 = d_1 - \sigma\sqrt{T}$$

where $N(\ )$ is the cumulative normal density function; V is the (implicit) value of the firm as a whole (i.e., the combined total value of the bonds, the stocks, and the options), and σ is the volatility of this total combined value.

The equation for the market value of the stock satisfies:

$$20 = -N(d_1)V - 100N(d_2)e^{-rT} - \frac{1}{11}[N(d_3)V - 120N(d_4)e^{-rT}]$$

$$d_1 = \frac{\ln\left(\frac{V}{100}\right) + \left(r + \frac{\sigma^2}{2}\right)T}{\sigma\sqrt{T}}$$

$$d_2 = d_1 - \sigma\sqrt{T}$$

$$d_3 = \frac{\ln\left(\frac{V}{120}\right) + \left(r + \frac{\sigma^2}{2}\right)T}{\sigma\sqrt{T}}$$

$$d_4 = d_3 - \sigma\sqrt{T}$$

Solving these two equations simultaneously for V and σ, we get $V =$ $106.14 million and $\sigma = 0.3621$.[33] Therefore, the market value of the employee stock options is:

$$V - \text{Value of the Bonds} - \text{Value of the Stock} =$$
$$\$106.14 \text{ million} - \$85 \text{ million} - \$20 \text{ million} = \$1.14 \text{ million}$$

or $11.40 per option.

---

32. The contingent claims pricing formula for the debt is derived in Black and Scholes (1973) and Merton (1973, 1974, 1992).
33. The solution is found through an iterative procedure using the *Gauss* computer software program.

Information Extraction in the Future

As we have seen, the more complete and diverse the set of financial instruments traded in financial markets, the more information that can be extracted from their prices. Information extraction is an integral part of the financial-innovation spiral discussed in Chapter 1. The pace of financial innovation to manage risks, which accelerated in the 1970s and 1980s, is likely to continue into the future. As products such as futures, options, swaps, and securitized loans become standardized, and move from intermediaries to markets, the proliferation of new trading markets in those instruments facilitates the creation of new custom-designed financial products that improve "market completeness."

To hedge their exposures on those products, the producers (typically, financial intermediaries) trade in these new markets and volume expands. Increased volume reduces marginal transactions costs and thereby makes possible implementation of more new products and trading strategies by intermediaries, which in turn leads to still more volume. The success of these trading markets and custom products encourages investment in creating additional markets and products—so on it goes, spiraling toward the theoretically limiting case of zero marginal transactions costs and dynamically complete markets.

As new markets are created, they may not at first be informationally efficient. All the while, however, incentives are created for market participants to develop new or improved pricing models to exploit the profit opportunities created by any mispricing. Better models for valuing traded financial assets lead to more reliable information extraction, which in turn leads to better calibration of models for the pricing of new financial products. This richer information set will facilitate more efficient resource allocation decisions.

References

Beckers, S. (1981), "Standard Deviations Implied in Option Prices as Predictors of Future Stock Price Variability," *Journal of Banking and Finance*, 5 (September): 363–381.

Bernstein, P.L. (1992), *Capital Ideas: The Improbable Origins of Modern Wall Street*, New York: Free Press.

Black, F., E. Derman, and W. Toy (1990), "A One-Factor Model of Interest Rates and Its Application to Treasury Bond Options," *Financial Analysts Journal* (January/February): 33–39.

Black, F., and M. Scholes (1972), "The Valuation of Option Contracts in a Test of Market Efficiency," *Journal of Finance*, 27 (May): 399–418.

——— (1973), "The Pricing of Options and Corporate Liabilities," *Journal of Political Economy*, 81 (May/June): 637–654.

Bodie, Z., A. Kane, and A. Marcus (1993), *Investments*, second edition, Homewood, IL: Irwin.

Brenner, M., and D. Galai (1989), "New Financial Instruments for Hedging Changes in Volatility," *Financial Analysts Journal* (July/August): 61–65.

Brenner, M., and M. Subrahmanyam (1988), "A Simple Solution to Compute the Implied Standard Deviation," *Financial Analysts Journal* (September/October): 80–83.

Canina, L., and S. Figlewski (1993), "The Information Content of Implied Volatility," *Review of Financial Studies*, 6: 659–681.

Chiras, D.P., and S. Manaster (1978), "The Information Content of Option Prices and a Test of Market Efficiency," *Journal of Financial Economics*, 6 (June): 213–234.

Christensen, B.J., and N.R. Prabhala (1994), "On the Dynamics and Information Content of Implied Volatility: A Bivariate Time Series Perspective," Stern School of Business Working Paper S-94-25, New York University (November).

Cox, J.C., J.E. Ingersoll, and S.A. Ross (1985), "A Theory of the Term Structure of Interest Rates," *Econometrica*, 53: 385–407.

Cox, J.C., S.A. Ross, and M. Rubinstein (1979), "Option Pricing: A Simplified Approach," *Journal of Financial Economics*, 7 (September): 229–263.

Day, T.E., and C.M. Lewis (1990), "Stock Market Volatility and the Information Content of Stock Index Options," *Journal of Econometrics*, 52: 267–287.

Dixit, A.K., and R.S. Pindyck (1994), *Investment Under Uncertainty*, Princeton: Princeton University Press.

Engle, R.F., A. Kane, and J. Noh (1993), "Index-Option Pricing with Stochastic Volatility and the Value of Accurate Variance Forecasts," National Bureau of Economic Research Working Paper No. 4519.

Fama, E. (1965), "The Behavior of Stock Market Prices," *Journal of Business*, 38 (January): 34–105.

Feinstein, S. (1988), "A Source of Unbiased Implied Volatility Forecasts," *Federal Reserve Bank of Atlanta Bulletin*.

Financial Accounting Standards Board (1993), *Accounting for Stock-Based Compensation*, Exposure Draft No. 127-C, Norwalk, CT. (June).

Fischer, S. (1978), "Call Option Pricing When the Exercise Price Is Uncertain and the Valuation of Index Bonds," *Journal of Finance*, 33 (March): 169–176.

Fisher, I. (1907), *The Rate of Interest*, New York: Macmillan.

——— (1930), *The Theory of Interest*, New York: Macmillan.

Galai, D. (1977), "Tests of Market Efficiency of the Chicago Board Options Exchange," *Journal of Business*, 50: 167–197.

Heath, D., R. Jarrow, and A. Morton (1992), "Bond Pricing and the Term Structure of Interest Rates: A New Methodology for Contingent Claims Valuation," *Econometrica*, 60 (January): 77–105.

Heynan, R., A. Kemna, and T. Vorst (1992), "Analysis of the Term Structure of Implied Volatilities," Erasmus Center for Financial Research (August): Report 9206.

Ho, T.S., and S. Lee (1986), "Term Structure Movements and Pricing Interest Rate Contingent Claims," *Journal of Finance*, 41 (December): 1129–1142.

Homer, S. (1977), *A History of Interest Rates*, second edition, New Brunswick, NJ: Rutgers University Press.

Hsiao, C. (1983), "Identification," in *Handbook of Econometrics*, Z. Griliches and M. Intriligator, eds., Amsterdam: North Holland.

Hull, J. (1993), *Options, Futures, and Other Derivative Securities*, Englewood Cliffs, NJ: Prentice Hall.

Jarrow, R., and J.B. Wiggins (1989), "Option Pricing and Implicit Volatilities," *Journal of Economic Surveys*, 3: 59–81.

Lamoureux, C.G., and W.D. Lastrapes (1993), "Forecasting Stock Return Variance: Toward an Understanding of Stochastic Implied Volatilities," *Review of Financial Studies*, 6: 293–326.

Latané, H.A., and R.J. Rendleman, Jr. (1976), "Standard Deviations of Stock Price Ratios Implied in Option Prices," *Journal of Finance*, 31 (May): 369–382.

Manaster, S., and G. Koehler (1982), "The Calculation of Implied Variances from the Black–Scholes Model: A Note," *Journal of Finance*, 37 (March): 227–230.

Margrabe, W. (1978), "The Value of an Option to Exchange One Asset for Another," *Journal of Finance*, 37 (March): 227–230.

Markowitz, H. (1952), "Portfolio Selection," *Journal of Finance*, 7 (March): 77–91.

Merton, R.C. (1973), "Theory of Rational Option Pricing," *Bell Journal of Economics and Management Science*, 4 (Spring): 141–183.

——— (1974), "On the Pricing of Corporate Debt: The Risk Structure of Interest Rates," *Journal of Finance*, 29 (May): 449–470.

——— (1976), "Option Pricing When Underlying Stock Returns are Discontinuous," *Journal of Financial Economics*, 3 (January–March): 125–144.

——— (1980), "On Estimating the Expected Return on the Market: An Exploratory Investigation," *Journal of Financial Economics*, 8 (December): 323–361.

——— (1990), "The Financial System and Economic Performance," *Journal of Financial Services Research*, 4 (December): 263–300.

——— (1992), *Continuous-Time Finance*, revised edition, Oxford: Basil Blackwell.

Merton, R.C., and Z. Bodie (1992), "On the Management of Financial Guarantees," *Financial Management*, 22 (Winter): 87–109.

Merton, R.K. (1957), *Social Theory and Social Structure*, revised and enlarged edition, Glenco, IL: The Free Press.

Miller, M.H. (1990), "International Competitiveness of U.S. Futures Exchanges," *Journal of Financial Services Research*, 4 (December) 387–408.

Nasar, S. (1992), "For Fed, a New Set of Tea Leaves," *New York Times*, 5 July, sec. D:1.

Nelson, D. (1991), "Conditional Heteroskedasticity in Asset Returns: A New Approach," *Econometrica*, 59 (March): 347–370.

Samuelson, P.A. (1965), "Proof That Properly Anticipated Prices Fluctuate Randomly," *Industrial Management Review*, 6 (Spring): 41–49.

Schmalensee, R., and R.R. Trippi (1978), "Common Stock Volatility Expectations Implied by Option Premia," *Journal of Finance*, 33 (March): 129–147.

Siegel, D.R., and D.F. Siegel (1990), *Futures Markets*, Hinsdale, IL: Dryden Press.

Sprenkle, C.M. (1961), "Warrant Prices as Indicators of Expectations and Preferences," *Yale Economic Essays*, 1: 172–231.

Stulz, R.M. (1982), "Options on the Minimum or the Maximum of Two Risky Assets: Analysis and Applications," *Journal of Financial Economics*, 10 (July): 161–185.

Taylor, J.B. (1994), "The Inflation/Output Variability Trade-Off Revisited," in *Goals, Guidelines, and Constraints Facing Monetary Policymakers*, J.C. Fuhrer ed., Boston: Federal Reserve Bank (June): 21–38.

Vasicek, O. (1977), "An Equilibrium Characterization of the Term Structure," *Journal of Financial Economics* 5: 177–188.

Whaley, R.E. (1993), "Derivatives on Market Volatility: Hedging Tools Long Overdue," *Journal of Derivatives* (Fall): 71–84.

CHAPTER SEVEN

Incentive Problems in Financial Contracting

Impacts on Corporate Financing, Investment,
and Risk Management Policies

KENNETH A. FROOT

The functions discussed thus far in this volume are features of all financial systems. Even the perfectly frictionless, idealized systems that operate only in economists' models require the performance of these functions—the aggregation and disaggregation of wealth, the transfer of resources across time and space, the redistribution of risks, the accumulation and dissemination of information, and the settling and clearing of transactions. A perfectly efficient financial system by definition performs these functions costlessly. While perfection is impossible to accomplish in practice, advances in technology and communications may in the foreseeable future make the costs of performing these functions almost negligible.

Incentive problems are different. They are not features of a perfect financial system, but rather *barriers* to such perfection. Incentive problems arise because parties to financial contracts cannot easily observe or control one another, and because contractual enforcement mechanisms are not costless to invoke. Like transactions and communication costs—the other main barriers to a frictionless financial system—incentive problems associated with financial contracts can be attenuated through improvements in technology and contracting. However, unlike these frictional costs, incentive problems are fundamental. That is, even after technology has become so advanced as to make transactions and communications essentially costless, incentive problems will continue to impose major costs on the financial system and society. As a result, the mitigation of incentive problems will remain a major area for financial innovation.

We can liken the financial-contracting response to incentive problems to individuals' attempts to protect themselves against a social problem, such as theft. The prospect of theft induces people to purchase locks. It also influences their decisions about where to live, work, and recreate. Improvements in lock production technology can reduce costs and improve security, but locks will never provide complete protection against theft anywhere and anytime. Theft will remain a real and costly problem, and people will continue to alter their behavior in a myriad of ways (in addition to buying locks) to reduce the likelihood of theft.

The functional approach to the financial system interprets both incentive problems and the financial system's response to them as endogenous. To understand better the relationship between the financial system and incentive problems, this chapter focuses on one specific area of interaction: the contractual relationships between corporations and their capital providers. The discussion develops two basic points. The first is that the incentive problems that affect these relationships are pervasive in scope—their impacts are diffused into virtually all the financing and investment decisions firms make. Incentive issues affect the amount of external financing as well as its contractual nature; the benefits and goals of corporate risk management programs; the types and sizes of businesses in which firms invest; and the hurdle rates firms use for evaluating investments. Thus, as predicted by the functional approach, corporate financial policies can be interpreted as endogenous given the nature of incentive problems. This endogeneity has fundamental implications for corporate financing policies, investment policies, and risk management policies.

The second theme is that the reverse relationship is also very powerful—that the state of contracting and the financial system evolves endogenously in response to incentive problems. As the functional approach would predict, corporate securities and investment policies can be designed with incentive problems in mind. Derivative instruments, in particular, can be used to help firms deploy financial resources more effectively. Indeed, I argue that good financing, investment, and risk management policies go a long way toward reducing the costs of incentive problems (although they can rarely achieve first-best results). Because many of these policies would not be possible in the absence of derivatives and many new securities, the process of innovation has added considerable private value.[1]

This argument suggests not only that the corporate use of derivatives is likely to be a historically durable antidote to corporate financial contracting problems, but also that a motivating force behind the growth of derivatives is the need to reduce incentive problems. Furthermore, at the level of specific instrument innovation and design, there is evidence that incentive problems are an important driving force.

Take, as an example, convertible bonds. Convertibles have a long history of being issued by companies as a form of outside financing. Why have firms historically raised money in this way? After all, the returns on a convertible bond can in many circumstances be replicated by a portfolio of bonds and stock. The functional approach answers this question by showing how convertible bond financing can reduce incentive problems in a way that straight debt and equity cannot. This argument becomes particularly interesting in historical perspective. While convertibles have been around for a long time, I argue that there are a number of newer securities (such as put warrants) that also can reduce incentive problems. The functional approach predicts that the selection of such instruments will broaden as transactions costs fall and valuation technologies rise. This means that, both today and in the future, firms will have an increasingly flexible arsenal of securities, each of which can help reduce different mixtures of incentive problems.

Corporate Financing Policies in the Presence of Incentive Problems

Incentive problems have implications for capital structure and other corporate financing policies. We first focus on the determinant of "target" capital structure—i.e., the best long-run mix of debt and equity finance.

---

1. While this process of synergistic innovation has added considerable private value, its social rewards are harder to identify. Cost-reducing innovation, while good in the small, does not necessarily make the financial system better or more efficient. Indeed, in many instances rapid innovation by agents seeking and receiving private gain can destroy public goods, thereby possibly making society worse off. For example, medical insurance innovations that allow policyholders to pay less if they are healthy may be profitable for companies to offer. However, they also raise premiums for those who are sick. Taken to an extreme, this kind of innovation would clearly undercut the value of medical insurance. This chapter does not attempt to evaluate the impact that corporate financial innovation has on public goods, such as systemic stability and the institutional mechanisms through which managers communicate with capital providers.

We then examine how incentive problems generate a kind of dynamic trade-off between debt and equity. This dynamic trade-off can help explain why firms depart so persistently from their optimal "static" or target financing patterns. We then show how a variety of more complex financing instruments (e.g., convertibles, PERCs, put warrants) can be understood as helping to solve problems.

Optimal Capital Structure: The Static View

The static view of capital structure is a standard one in corporate finance. Assuming that markets are reasonably efficient, static trade-off theory says some combination of debt and equity is best for a given firm.[2] This static or "target" mix would trade off the benefits of debt (most commonly attributed to taxes and the discipline imposed upon management) against the costs of debt (usually financial distress).[3] Incentive issues help determine these benefits and costs.

Incentive problems and the benefits of leverage. Aside from generating tax shields, debt financing can be advantageous when there are conflicts of interest between owners and managers. For example, managers may have a tendency to divert the firm's discretionary funds, or "free cash flows," toward private perks, personal job entrenchment, or other activities that do not maximize firm value. Under such circumstances, debt can act as a disciplinary tool by helping to minimize funds that are at managers' discretion. Debt is "cheaper" than equity because it forces managers to pursue firm value maximization. Equity is more expensive because it gives managers the discretion to pursue goals other than value maximization. Thus, under the "free cash flow" view, the more equity a firm uses, the higher its average costs of capital will be.[4]

One problem with the free cash flow hypothesis is that managers themselves, and not owners, are usually responsible for choosing capital structure. If managers prefer not to maximize firm value in the absence of a disciplinary debt burden, it is not clear why they would choose to impose that burden on themselves in the first place. The free cash flow

---

2. See, for example, Brealey and Myers (1991).
3. There is evidence that supports the importance of these static trade-off forces. For example, firms that are less able to take advantage of interest tax shields appear to use less debt finance (see Mackie-Mason (1990) for evidence on tax loss carryforwards, and Froot and Hines (1994) for evidence on excess foreign tax credits). Schwartz and Aronson (1967) among others show that industry effects are important in explaining debt ratios: Companies with stable earnings use more debt financing than those with less stable earnings.
4. See Jensen (1986) for a discussion of the free cash flow hypothesis.

hypothesis therefore applies best to companies whose capital structures are determined by owners or corporate charters, rather than by incumbent managers.

Of course, incumbent managers *are* often partial owners, and this ownership pattern may itself help mitigate incentive problems. Managers who hold a large fraction of their wealth in their companies' stock are more likely to pursue value maximization. In such a case, debt can emerge as a relatively beneficial source of financing because it avoids managerial dilution. Thus, if inside equity funding is limited (because of managerial wealth constraints), and outside equity is costly (because it dilutes managerial incentives), debt can emerge as a relatively inexpensive source of funding.[5]

Costs of corporate leverage. Obviously, too much debt can be costly. Some of the costs associated with excessive leverage or financial distress are generated by incentive problems as well. These costs arise because financial distress creates conflicts of interest between capital providers, and these conflicts become incentive problems when they involve managers.

To see this, note that one implication of excessive leverage is a conflict of interest between capital providers. For example, in highly levered firms, underinvestment might occur if the interests of debt and equity holders conflict: Equity holders may refuse to contribute new funds for "good" investments, knowing that the proceeds of the investment will accrue not to them, but rather to the debt holders, who will see their "underwater" claims rise in value. Similarly, when leverage is high, some "bad" investments might be implemented. Equity holders may want to "roll the dice" by biasing investments toward unnecessarily risky projects. When the firm is highly levered, such investments may raise the value of equity, but only by diverting value from the debt.

To the extent that investment patterns lead to underinvestment in good projects or overinvestment in bad ones, they lower the value of the firm. This fall in value can be thought of as a cost of financial distress, even if the firm is neither in bankruptcy nor experiencing difficulties in servicing its debt. Underinvestment can occur any time a levered firm has a reasonable probability of defaulting on its remaining debt obligations. In this sense, some amount of financial distress costs are experienced by any firm issuing risky debt. Thus, externally sourced debt capital will tend to be

---

5. In the absence of incentive problems, a manager's only motivation for holding her own company's stock is as part of her diversified portfolio. Indeed, because managers' opportunities are already linked with their companies' success, they are already implicitly "long" their companies' stocks. In such a case, considerations of diversification would lead managers to go *short* their companies' stock in their financial portfolios.

"expensive" because of the implied costs of financial distress, which are generated by conflicts between capital providers.

Optimal Capital Structure: The Dynamic View

The static view of capital structure is useful for thinking about long-run target capital structures. But the static view is incomplete because it misses several important features of actual behavior. For example, the most important explanatory variable for the leverage ratio of a firm in a particular industry is past profitability.[6] The more profitable a firm has been, the lower its debt ratio, all else equal. Indeed, one study finds that firms resort almost *exclusively* to debt finance when they lose money.[7]

The relationship between cash flow and external finance. The sensitivity of leverage to profitability and cash flow suggests that the static optimal capital structure story is incomplete. Instead, it appears that firms deviate from their target capital structures, and that they do so for long periods of time. Furthermore, their deviations follow a kind of "pecking-order" pattern. That is, firms seem to build cash and/or pay down debt relative to their targets during times when they are profitable. They then draw on this buffer during leaner times. In other words, firms often pay for investments out of internally generated funds first, if such funds are available. Failing that, they tend to turn to outside debt next. Outside equity is typically used only as a last resort.

Indeed, it is striking how infrequent secondary equity offerings occur in comparison with net debt issues. Equity issues by mature corporations occur in only 2% of firm years, a very low rate of equity financing compared with that of debt.

Of course, the distance that firms stray from their target capital structure is not unlimited. Firms that earn less cash than their investments require may at first make up the shortfall with borrowing, but ultimately they must either cut back on investment or bite the bullet and issue equity. Similarly, firms that experience cash flows that are well above desired investment levels may at first delever. But over time, they also increase payouts to shareholders, either in the form of dividends or repurchases.[8] Thus, the static view is not irrelevant. But it is much less useful for explaining firm financing policies than it is for explaining long-run industry financing norms.[9]

As a consequence, most firm financing decisions fall squarely within

---

6. See, for example, Kester (1986) and Titman and Wessels (1988).
7. Shyam-Sunder and Myers (1993).
8. Marsh (1982) argues that the conditional probability of an equity issue rises with leverage.
9. In the original statements of the pecking-order hypothesis, Myers (1984) and Myers and

the pecking-order band. And there, financing patterns are very different from what the static trade-off would predict. Within the band, firms are happy to "strengthen" their balance sheets when they experience operating cash flows in excess of their investment needs. But they are much less willing to achieve the same amount of delevering through equity issuance. That is, under the dynamic view of capital structure, companies act as though there are two kinds of equity—retained funds and outside capital raised—to balance against debt. This is in contrast with the static capital structure view, which does not distinguish the source of a company's equity funds.

To understand what gives rise to pecking-order behavior, it is useful to appeal to a specific kind of incentive problem—that induced by informational asymmetries between value-maximizing managers and outside capital providers. Consider first why firms may be reluctant to adjust their capital structure by issuing equity. In an ideal world, companies would seek equity finance whenever they needed it; there would be no frictions (other than simple transactions costs) to prevent firms from keeping their capital structure at the static optimum. But when there are information asymmetries—i.e., when managers know more about their companies than outside investors do—there is a "lemons" problem that interferes with such easy recourse to the equity market.

This lemons problem occurs because outside investors cannot determine whether a given firm is relatively "good" or "bad." Yet firm insiders can. This means that, all else equal, the market will value the stock of the good and the bad firm at the same, intermediate price. In these circumstances, managers of bad firms will find their stock price to be above their perception of true value; managers of good firms will find their firm's stock prices too low. This leads to a kind of adverse selection in equity finance: Bad firms will rush to take advantage of outside equity, and good firms will hesitate. An equity issue is therefore perceived by the market at large as a negative signal, indicating that better-informed management is likely to view the stock price as too high.

This reasoning suggests that stock prices will fall upon announcement of an equity issue. The static trade-off theory, on the other hand, predicts the opposite: Since firms use equity to move back to their static optimums, the value of the firm should *rise* with the announcement of an equity issue.[10] The empirical evidence favors the lemons story. Specifically, announcement of a seasoned equity issue leads to a permanent stock price

---

Majluf (1984) argue that there is *no* optimal static capital structure. See also Shyam-Sunder and Myers (1993) who argue that the pecking-order model has greater explanatory power than a static trade-off model.

10. Note that static agency theory (in which managers hold equity to align their interests

fall of 3% on average.[11] Furthermore, the size of this decline seems to accord roughly with the degree of informational asymmetry. For example, the stock price decline for equity offerings by utilities and firms in other regulated industries (where the degree of public disclosure is unusually high) is much smaller.[12] The lemons story also applies to sales of equity by insiders, but not to block sales of shares by outsiders.[13] That is, the more informed the seller of equity appears to be, the larger the ultimate price effect.[14]

The case is different, of course, for debt finance. Debt issues do not create a "lemons" problem *per se*.[15] Indeed, for firms that initially have plenty of spare debt capacity, debt issuance sends a *positive* signal to the extent that it indicates an unwillingness to sell equity at prevailing prices. Increasingly high levels of debt, however, clearly raise the prospects of financial distress, which ultimately creates its own costs. Firms that have come down the pecking order by using up their preexisting debt capacity will find that *both* equity and additional debt finance are costly to use. That is, new creditors will anticipate the increased likelihood of distress, and will raise their premiums accordingly; new equity holders will lower their expectations of future performance and purchase the equity only at a lower price. Even if firms with high initial levels of indebtedness find additional debt finance to be cheaper than equity finance, they will find both considerably more expensive than internal funds.

These dynamic considerations can be summarized in a relatively simple maxim: Firms for the most part act as though external finance is more expensive than internal finance. Furthermore, as a firm relies on external financing to a relatively greater extent, the disparity between the cost of internal and external funds increases. This suggests a critical principle of the impact of information problems on corporate financing patterns:

---

with value maximization and use debt to support a substantial managerial ownership stake) also predicts that firm value should rise when an overlevered firm issues equity.

11. See, for example, Asquith and Mullins (1986). There is some evidence that the market does not fully comprehend just how negative a signal an equity issue is. Loughran and Ritter (1993) show that firms that make secondary equity offerings exhibit stock price underperformance over the subsequent five years of 20%–30%.

12. See Smith (1986) for details.

13. See Seyhun (1986).

14. Several papers find that trading by informed insiders moves stock prices by much more than trading by uninformed traders (see Meulbroek (1992)). The means by which the market *knows* these trades to originate with insiders is unclear.

15. The empirical evidence corresponds roughly with this hypothesis. There is no strong evidence that stock prices change at all when a debt issue is announced. As one might expect, announcement of issues of hybrid instruments (e.g., convertible bonds, preferred stock) result in a negative stock-price impact, with a magnitude in between that of straight debt and equity. See Smith (1986).

Principle 1: In the presence of informational asymmetries between managers and outsider capital providers, incentive problems exist. In these circumstances, the marginal cost of external finance is greater than that of internal finance, and is increasing in the amount of external finance raised.

I argue that this principle has surprisingly wide-ranging implications for corporate investment behavior, security innovation, and risk management policies, as well as for corporate financing patterns.[16]

What are the most important determinants of the cost of external funds? First, and probably foremost, is the degree of incentive problems a firm faces. In particular, companies that invest in "tangible," easy to evaluate assets (e.g., utilities) may find external finance relatively cheaper to access—their assets make better collateral for debt finance. Companies that invest in "intangible" assets may find external financing more costly. This is because the return on investments in intangible assets—such as price cutting for market share, R&D, or spending on human resources—is likely to be subject to large information asymmetries.

A second important influence on the marginal costs of external finance is a firm's preexisting capital structure. Firms that have large amounts of unused debt capacity will not find external debt finance very expensive. This is particularly true if the debt capacity arises from highly transparent assets. A firm that has already collateralized its transparent assets—and therefore has much less remaining debt capacity—will find that additional external funds are considerably more expensive than scarce internal funds. Thus, all else equal, leveraged firms will face higher marginal costs of external finance than less leveraged firms.

Security design. We have seen how incentive problems can help explain static and dynamic choices between debt and equity. Firms that follow pecking-order patterns of financing may be doing so in an effort to mitigate the costs of information problems, thereby raising firm value. Yet the implications of these problems do not end with the choice between debt and equity. Indeed, the presence of incentive problems (informational asymmetries in particular) helps us understand why specific instruments—even those that appear highly complex—add value.

a. Convertible Bonds. One example of a hybrid instrument that generates value through its effect on incentive problems is the convertible bond. The argument for convertibles comes from the same kind of informational asymmetries that give rise to the lemons problem.[17] To see this, recall that the lemons problem has good firms issuing debt and bad firms issuing

---

16. See Froot, Scharfstein, and Stein (1993) for the implications for risk management, and Stein (1992) for the implications for corporate security design.
17. Stein (1992) derives a formal "lemons" model of convertibles.

equity. Bad firms do not want to issue debt because additional leverage would generate potential costs of financial distress. Good firms can finance with debt without experiencing such potential distress costs, and in any case, they wish to avoid the bad signal associated with issuing equity.

Now add to this a third kind of firm, a medium firm—one that is known by managers (but not by outside investors) to have average future prospects. Its prospects may not be so good as to allow it to issue debt without incurring any potential costs of financial distress, as the good firm is able to do. So the medium firm is unlikely to want to mimic the behavior of the good firm by issuing debt. One the other hand, the strong negative signal sent by bad firms' equity issues would result in a low equity issue price, and therefore an aversion to issuing equity.

A convertible bond (or convertible preferred stock issue) provides the middle ground the medium firm is looking for. Managers' private knowledge may tell them that the stock price will soon rise sufficiently to allow the firm to call the bond and force its conversion to equity. Once the bond is converted, it cannot generate potential costs of financial distress. Also, its issuance does not send a strongly negative signal. This is because managers of bad firms would not expect to be able to convert the bond, and therefore would not choose it over equity. Thus, convertible bonds can allow the medium firm to economize on potential costs of financial distress by issuing a "backdoor" form of equity, which does not send the strong negative signal associated with a direct equity issue.[18]

As Stein (1992) argues, there is also empirical evidence for this interpretation of convertibles. First, surveys of managers suggest that the motivation for convertible issues is not so much to "sweeten" a regular bond, but to provide a mechanism for "delayed equity issue."[19] Managers therefore don't look to convertibles so much as bonds (which generate potential costs of financial distress), but more as indirect equity issues that help mitigate lemons problems.

Second, firms that issue convertibles and not stock presumably do so

---

18. Note that this medium signal cannot be replicated by a firm that issues a combination of debt and equity. To see this, compare a firm that issues a convertible with a firm that simultaneously issues both debt and equity. The downside signal for the former firm is obviously stronger, as it has been willing to commit to a larger debt downside. Thus a "bad" firm would prefer to issue a combination of debt and equity rather than a convertible. On the other hand, a "good" firm would also prefer to sell a combination of debt and equity (although it prefers a higher amount of debt in comparison with a bad firm) as, conditional on good news, the convertible is likely to sell off more of the firm. Thus it is more costly for other firms to mimic the medium firm by issuing a convertible, making the convertible a more reliable signal of medium firm status.

19. See, for example, Brigham (1966).

because they have trouble convincing the market that their prospects are brighter than those of the "bad" firm. This suggests that informational asymmetries are likely to be important for convertible issuers. While it is difficult to measure such asymmetries convincingly, there is evidence that firms with higher R&D/sales are, all else equal, more likely to issue convertibles. This seems consistent with the lemons theory of convertibles, at least to the extent that R&D quality is difficult to verify and its output hard to collateralize.

Third, the negative price shock associated with convertibles is considerably less than that for straight equity issues. Several studies have found that the average price reduction resulting from an equity announcement is about 3%, reducing firm value by an average of 30% of the equity issue amount.[20] For convertibles, the numbers are much smaller: Stock prices fall on average by about half as much, a reduction in value of somewhat under 10% of the convertible issue amount.[21]

MCI's classic experience with convertibles during the late 1970s and early 1980s demonstrates the lemons rationale.[22] In 1978, MCI had considerable opportunities to expand, yet had already built up a debt-to-capital ratio of over 80%. With such high preexisting leverage, the potential costs of financial distress associated with debt-financed expansion were high. The firm was also reluctant to issue equity, as such an issue would be a bad signal—the CFO stated that an equity issue would "knock the props out from under the stock." MCI thus turned toward convertible bonds and preferred stock. It managed five offerings without large negative stock price impacts, and was able to convert the issues into equity over time.[23]

b. PERCs Convertible bonds and preferreds are not the only kind of instruments whose value can be traced at least partially to incentive problems. Other examples are PERCs and put warrants.

Consider PERCs first. These are convertible preferred securities that convert into a fixed *dollar* amount of common stock if the stock price is above a given conversion price, and into a fixed *number* of common shares if the stock price falls below the conversion price. PERCs usually also

---

20. See, for example, Asquith and Mullins (1986) and Mikkelson and Partch (1986).
21. See, for example, Eckbo (1986).
22. Greenwald's (1986) case study depicts MCI's experience, and discusses the lemons rationale for issuing convertibles.
23. An additional pair of offerings in the mid-1980s did not convert, as MCI fared poorly in competition with AT&T. This negative change in opportunities then forced MCI to return to equity issuance those years. This demonstrates that the more positive signal of convertibles compared to equity comes with a potential cost: Potential financial distress costs remain.

carry higher dividend yields than the corresponding common stock. The higher yield could by itself generate a rationale for issuing PERCs if there is a clientele of investors who will pay more for a higher-yielding stock than a lower-yielding stock with the same total value.

But PERCs also may generate value for firms that face informational asymmetries. Like convertibles, PERCs generate near-term repayment requirements that trigger costs if they are not met.[24] This discourages firms with bad private information from issuing PERCs, which in turn makes a PERCs issue a relatively positive signal compared to a straight equity issue. As with convertibles, very good firms would prefer to issue debt rather than PERCs (since PERCs are still positively linked to equity performance). However, PERCs may work well for medium firms. These firms can signal that they wish to retain some upside in their common stock while committing to high preconversion dividend payments. Thus, PERCs, like convertibles, are a way of getting equity into the capital structure without sending the strong negative signal associated with an equity issue.[25]

c. Put Warrants   A very similar rationale exists for the issuance of put warrants. Put warrants are in a way the opposite of a convertible bond—that is, put warrants are to equity repurchases just as convertibles are to equity issues.

To understand how put warrants work, let us first consider stock repurchases. Stock repurchases send a good signal about firm prospects in much the same way that equity issues send a bad signal. That is, good firms are willing to sacrifice cash (or borrow) to purchase what managers perceive as undervalued shares; alternatively, bad firms' managers perceive the current stock price as too high, and in any case may not wish to return funds as quickly to shareholders because of concerns of financial distress.

The empirical evidence on stock repurchases is consistent with this signaling story. Tender offers to repurchase stock generate permanent stock price increases of approximately 20%. Tender offers have somewhat larger positive price impacts than other types of repurchases, such as Dutch auctions (in which potential sellers submit schedules of how much they would sell at different prices) or open-market repurchases (in which there is no public buyback announcement).

Different clienteles will have different preferences for one form of repurchase over another. From a long-run shareholder's perspective, the

---

24. If required PERC dividend payments are not made, they cumulate, and often permit holders to exercise greater control over management.
25. Tiemann (1989) explores the nature of PERCs.

firm should repurchase equity at the lowest possible price. This argues in favor of open-market repurchases and against splashy tender offers. However, short-run shareholders will have just the opposite preference, as they want to maximize short-term stock prices for given long-term value. In such instances, firms may choose tender offers as the preferred means of repurchasing equity.

Put warrants are simply a *conditional* equity repurchase. That is, put warrants commit a firm to repurchase a given quantity of shares, provided that at expiration the stock price is below the conversion price. If the stock price exceeds the conversion price, investors keep their shares, and the right to "put" them back to the company expires worthless.

Because put warrants result only in conditional future repurchases, they don't send as strong a positive signal as a direct repurchase. Like direct repurchases, however, they are unattractive to managers who anticipate firm performance poorer than that expected by the market. Managers of these firms will avoid issuing put warrants because they view the market price for the warrants as too low. Thus, put warrants are likely to be issued by medium firms, whose prospects aren't strong enough to merit the strong positive signal of an unconditional repurchase, but are good enough to risk the issue without excessively raising the potential costs of financial distress.[26]

Summary

I have argued that incentive problems make external finance costly. The more money firms must raise externally, and the more equity that they need to issue, the greater the perceived or actual deadweight costs of external finance are likely to be. Firms do not passively accept the additional costs of external finance: They alter their financing and investment policies as well as financial instrument selection in ways that help them mitigate the loss of value generated by these problems.

In spite of firms' ability to manage the costs of incentive problems, resort to innovative instruments may not be enough to eliminate altogether the deadweight costs of external finance. Convertible bonds, as we note above, are a "cheaper" financing alternative for medium firms than either debt or equity, although convertibles cannot fully eliminate deadweight financing costs as long as firms face costs of financial distress.

The fact that even innovative securities leave firms saddled with dead-

---

26. Intel Corporation's sale of put warrants on $1 billion worth of stock shows where signaling issues seem to have been at work. See Froot (1992) for a discussion of Intel's circumstances.

weight costs of external finance is important in two respects. First, it points toward the prospect of additional security innovation that might further minimize deadweight costs. It also gives a guide to criteria that will drive the innovation process. Securities that can solve or mitigate specific information or incentive problems along the lines we have discussed will raise firm value, and therefore should readily find niches in the global marketplace.

Second, financing and investment policies will generally be linked as long as external financing is costly. That is, the distortions that increase the cost of external finance will also raise (and otherwise alter) investment hurdle rates that firms should use in evaluating investment opportunities.

Corporate Investment Policy

The fact that, when incentive problems are present, firms are likely to find external financing costly has obvious implications for investment. High-cost financing will reduce the level of investment, and will also affect the mix of investments. The connection between financing and investment has implications for the performance of the macroeconomy as well as for the behavior of individual firms.

There are basically two ways incentive problems influence investment. The first mechanism occurs when incentive problems separate outside investors and managers, but managers nevertheless pursue firm value maximization. Under these conditions, managers will wish to pursue an investment policy in which all positive-net present value (NPV) investments are undertaken. However, the hurdle rates used to calculate NPV will not be determined entirely by systematic risk, as would be the case under traditional capital budgeting procedures. By raising hurdle rates above traditional levels, managers can increase firm value. But, incentive problems will give value-maximizing managers an incentive to *underinvest* compared to what would be optimal in the absence of such problems.

The second possible linkage between incentive problems and investment occurs when managers' objectives differ from those of shareholders. This may occur when managers are not compensated according to firm value—for example, when their salary and reputation grows with the size (rather than the total profitability) of the operations they oversee. Clearly, this can lead to *overinvestment* relative to what would maximize value. Overinvestment is likely to be more severe when firms have large amounts of discretionary free cash flow, and less of a problem when they are cash constrained.

At one level, these mechanisms have opposite implications for investment: One view predicts investment will be too high, while the other predicts investment will be too low. At another level, however, both mechanisms predict that investment will be "excessively" sensitive to cash flow and other measures of corporate liquidity. Capital spending will rise too quickly with increases in corporate liquidity, and fall too fast with decreases. Furthermore, both mechanisms lead to distortions in the mix of investment spending, as capital budgets will be skewed toward projects that help diversify corporate cash flows.

The "Underinvestment" Problem

We first consider the underinvestment problem, assuming for the time being that managers pursue the goal of value maximization. Because external finance is more expensive than internal finance, an increase in internal cash flow or corporate liquidity will reduce the cost of capital and increase investment, all else equal. In the extreme case, when a firm has *no* access to external finance, investment spending is capped by internal cash flow. Either way, firm value is reduced, and, if the effect on investment is sufficiently widespread, macroeconomic growth is reduced as well.[27]

This reasoning brings us to a second principle that follows from the presence of information asymmetries between managers and capital providers:

> *Principle 2: When external finance is more expensive than internal finance, investment spending will be excessively sensitive to internal cash flow, liquidity, and other measures of corporate financial slack.*

Principle 2 states that costly external finance generates a relationship between measures of corporate liquidity and investment spending. The scope of the principle is quite broad in two senses.

First, shortages in internal liquidity generate cutbacks in all kinds of corporate investments: purchases of fixed assets, inventory accumulation, and investments in worker training and employment, as well as basic strategic objectives. However, the precise nature of the cutbacks will differ by *type* of investment. For example, it may be relatively cheap for a firm to raise outside funds to purchase raw land or certain fixed assets that

---

27. The pecking-order theory does not imply that cash flow, *per se*, affects investment; rather it predicts that the tightness of financing constraints matters. A firm may find that it has expanded access to inexpensive debt finance when its stock price rises, due, say, to an increase in future expected cash flows on existing assets. Such an increase in financial slack will reduce borrowing costs, and therefore tend to increase investment spending. Changes in cash flow are often used because they are easily measured and a good proxy for changes in financial slack.

can be mortgaged or collateralized at relatively low cost. The key to low-cost collateralizability is that an asset be very "informationally unintensive"—that is, its value is beyond the control of firm managers, observable and verifiable by outside investors, and segregatable from the other assets of the firm.[28] "Informationally intensive" assets—such as R&D, investments in employee expertise, market share, etc.—are controlled and best observed by managers, hard to redeploy, often intangible, and, as a result, almost impossible to collateralize. This type of investment is therefore more costly to fund externally, so spending on it is likely to be more sensitive to fluctuations in internal funds than spending on readily collateralizable assets.

The second sense in which the principle is broad is in its reference to internal funds. In the narrowest sense, operating cash flows are the main source of internal finance. Yet changes in the value of a firm's easily collateralizable assets can be an important source of internal finance as well. For example, a firm that discovers oil on land that it owns will see that land increase in value. To the extent the land can be easily sold for a higher price or used more readily as collateral for funds, the need for costly external financing is decreased.[29]

If Principle 2 and its implications are correct, we should be able to find evidence that costly external finance exists and that it reduces investment. Testing this is tricky, however. Even in a perfect world—one that poses no incentive problems—a positive correlation between internal finance and investment is likely to emerge. That is, increases in cash flow are likely to be associated with increases in profitable investment *opportunities,* so it should not be surprising that investment spending increases, even in a perfect world. Thus, to construct a valid test of the underinvestment hypothesis, it is necessary to hold a firm's investment opportunities constant, and only then check for correlations between internal finance and investment.

An example of one such test appears in Lamont (1993). Lamont begins by looking at the oil price shock of 1986 and its effects on oil companies and their subsidiaries. When oil prices collapsed in early 1986, oil companies around the world cut back on their investment spending. Of

---

28. Note, however, that because many fixed assets are not easily redeployable, their liquidation values are far below their initial cost. This makes it more costly to collateralize these assets, and therefore increases the potential for underinvestment in them.
29. Of course, if *all* types of wealth could be costlessly converted into internal finance, there would be no distinction between external and internal financing costs. The point is that it is costly or impossible to raise funds with internal assets that are subject to incentive problems. For example, the entrepreneur who has an idea for a better widget cannot easily "collateralize" the idea by borrowing against its value.

course, oil investment opportunities probably fell with the price of oil, so the decline in oil investment cannot be attributed to costly external finance.

Lamont's innovation is to look at the *non-oil* subsidiaries of these oil companies. For example, Montgomery Ward is wholly owned by Mobil, relying on its parent to finance its investments. Lamont finds that the oil shock reduced Mobil's cash flows, and that this led to a decline in Montgomery Ward's investment spending. This decline in investment is unlikely to have been associated with a fall in MW's investment opportunities. Moreover, MW's product market competitors—who are *not* owned by oil companies—experienced no similar cutback in investment spending. The implication is that MW's decline in investment spending resulted from the decline in Mobil's internal cash flow. This implies that even a large firm like Mobil faces financing constraints that make external funds more expensive than internal funds. That is, if external funds were not costly, Mobil could have profitably funded MW's investments by raising external funds.

While this test of the underinvestment hypothesis is especially crisp, there is also evidence that suggests underinvestment is much more pervasive. For example, one study finds that the sensitivity of investment spending to fluctuations in cash flow is greater for low-dividend-paying firms than for high-dividend-paying firms.[30] Another study finds that the investment spending of Japanese firms associated with *keiretsus* is less sensitive to cash flow shocks than is the investment spending of firms that are not *keiretsu* members.[31]

Further evidence of the presence of financing constraints and their effects on investment comes from the literature on foreign direct investment. One paper finds that increases in financial slack, which can be driven by exchange rate changes or changes in stock market values, can give foreign firms an advantage in bidding against domestic rivals for domestic target companies.[32] Thus, for example, when the Japanese yen appreciated relative to the dollar in the late 1980s, Japanese firms more frequently outbid others in acquiring target companies. When the value of the Japanese stock market subsequently declined, the levels of foreign direct investment declined rapidly as well.

Finally, there is evidence that corporate financing constraints amplify the impact of monetary policy on economic activity and investment. That is, when a central bank contracts the supply of credit, interest rates rise,

---

30. See Fazarri, Hubbard, and Petersen (1988).
31. See Hoshi, Kashyap, and Scharfstein (1991).
32. See Froot and Stein (1991).

and bank lending typically contracts. In a world of perfect financial markets, any slowdown in activity from a monetary policy-induced increase in interest rates could be attributed only to the direct effect of higher interest rates on investment.

In a world where there are incentive problems, there are at least two other channels through which monetary policy affects the level of economic activity and investment. The first is the effect of higher interest rates on corporate cash flow and borrowing opportunities. That is, discretionary cash flows fall when interest rates rise, worsening the balance sheet and lowering the level of internal funds. Moreover, some borrowers may face quantity rationing constraints during monetary contractions. The rise in interest rates may accelerate expected net debt repayment schedules, thus intensifying the impact of monetary policy on cash flow. Note that this channel is not unique to monetary policy—any shock to corporate cash flow is likely to have similar kinds of effects on investment spending in the presence of incentive problems.[33] Note also that this monetary policy channel does not depend on whether companies use bank or capital market financing tools. As long as outside financing sources face some informational or agency disadvantage, this channel will be present.

The second monetary policy channel created by corporate incentive problems is known as the "credit" or "lending" channel, and it is specific to bank borrowings. The effect is that bank liquidity is reduced during monetary contractions, as the central bank forces banks to shift the mix of their assets toward government securities and away from loans.[34] This raises the cost or limits the supply of bank borrowing relative to capital market-based borrowing during monetary contractions. The implication is that firms that are bank-dependent for financing all, or part, of their balance sheet, will suffer additional adverse effects of a monetary policy contraction. In this sense, banks add an additional channel through which monetary policy impacts investment.

There is considerable evidence supporting the existence of these channels. First, the decline in bank lending during recessions does help to explain reductions in investment even after controlling for interest rates. This implies that there are at least some firms that find bank lending an imperfect substitute for other sources of finance. Indeed, those firms with access to commercial paper appear to *increase* their CP issuance when

---

33. This monetary-policy channel is discussed by a number of authors. See, for example, Bernanke and Gertler (1989), Calomiris and Hubbard (1990), and Greenwald and Stiglitz (1993).

34. See Kashyap, Stein, and Wilcox (1995).

bank-sourced financing dries up. That is, they substitute capital market financing for bank financing because bank borrowing becomes relatively more expensive or less available. Of course, those with little or no access to such markets have nowhere else to go. These latter firms—small firms in particular—witness the greatest declines in investment.[35]

The *mix* of reduced investment across different asset classes is also consistent with the presence of incentive problems. Take, for example, investment in inventories. Inventories appear to be disproportionately funded by bank loans in comparison with other assets on the balance sheet. Thus, one might expect the inventories of bank-dependent firms to decline more than the inventories of firms that have ready access to the commercial paper and other borrowing markets when monetary policy is tightened.

Kashyap, Lamont, and Stein (1992) show that this is indeed the case. They examine the behavior of inventories across firms during the monetary policy-induced recession of 1981–1982, and find that bank-dependent firms witnessed far greater declines in inventory holdings. To test whether this result is due to some other unobserved difference between bank-dependent and other firms, the authors compare their results with those from the 1985–1986 period of easy money. In the latter period, inventory behavior of bank-dependent firms is no different from that of other firms. This suggests that monetary contractions do indeed impact firms through a "credit" channel. It also suggests that, because inventory fluctuations are the single most important element of the business cycle, these effects are broadly important for the economy.

These examples suggest that a linkage between internal finance and investment, if it exists, may have important macroeconomic implications, not implications for just the financial system or a restricted group of nonfinancial corporations. To see this, note that if a decline in internal finance and availability of external finance triggers broad reductions in investment, there is likely to be a feedback effect as well: The fall in investment is likely to reduce the amount of internal finance further, both through a decline in economic activity and a fall in the value of easily collateralized assets.[36]

This leads to what Bernanke, Gertler, and Gilchrist (1993) call the "financial accelerator." The accelerator takes what would otherwise be small shocks to internal finance, and magnifies them into more major economic disturbances. This logic suggests that much of the amplitude of business cycle fluctuations could be attributable to incentive problems in

---

35. See Gertler and Gilchrist (1994).
36. Kashyap, Scharfstein, and Weil (1990) argue that this is the case for assets such as land.

corporate finance. In the absence of these problems, internal finance has no independent effect on investment spending, so the accelerator linkage would be broken.

Clearly, the potential costs of incentive problems for the entire economy can be very large. This suggests that the gains from security innovation, both from a micro- and macroeconomic perspective, can be large. Innovation in security design and intermediation practices helps to lower the costs of external finance, and thereby mitigates the effect of fluctuations in internal funds on investment.

One might argue that the financial system has already eliminated many of these effects, particularly for big companies that appear to have ready (and inexpensive) access to external markets. However, as the impact of oil price declines on Montgomery Ward's investment spending suggests, even big firms like Mobil continue to alter current investment on the basis of current cash flow. Incentive problems, which arise both between the firm and its investors as well as within the firm, may be too complex and ubiquitous to eliminate through financial innovation.

The "Overinvestment" Problem

It is not always the case that managers will underinvest when faced with costly external finance. As we mention above, managers may use investment to promote their own private objectives rather than the objective of value maximization. Such incentive problems may result in managers undertaking negative-NPV investments that help satisfy their private objectives. For example, managers may attempt to diversify their firms into unrelated industries in an attempt to provide corporate stability and expand the boundaries of their firm. To the extent that managers carry out these private agendas, corporate investment may be too high rather than too low.

The overinvestment view shares many predictions with the underinvestment view discussed above. For example, both views suggest that firms will exhibit a preference for internal over external funds. The two views do make different behavioral predictions in some cases. Consider, for example, firms that already have built up a very comfortable amount of financial slack. For such firms, the underinvestment view predicts that managers will return cash to shareholders in response to an unexpected increase in cash flow (with no change in investment opportunities). This would maximize firm value, because retaining the extra funds would only add another layer of taxation in comparison with a share repurchase. Alternatively, the overinvestment view predicts that managers will not return the funds to shareholders. Instead, they keep them within the firm under managerial control. In such a case, a cash windfall will not increase firm value one-for-one.

Blanchard, López-de-Silanes, and Shleifer (1993) try to distinguish between these two views.[37] They examine firms that had recently won lawsuits in lines of business from which they had previously exited. This particular group was selected because its investment opportunities are unlikely to be influenced by the cash awards. The authors find that firms did not typically return the cash to investors by paying down debt, increasing dividends, or repurchasing shares. Instead they tended to use the funds to make acquisitions, to continue existing loss-making operations, and to increase executive compensation. These results are inconsistent with the perfect capital markets model, which predicts that the cash should be paid out to investors. Given that the firms are small (and therefore likely to face financing constraints), the results appear to fit the overinvestment view.

Bernheim and Wantz (1992) succeed better in distinguishing between the over- and underinvestment views. They look at the effect of corporate dividend announcements on stock prices. Under the information/underinvestment view, announcement of a dividend increase raises stock prices because it signals higher expected future earnings. The higher the tax rate on dividend income, the more potent the signal. Thus, under the information view, higher tax rates should be associated with a greater sensitivity of stock prices to dividend announcements. Under the overinvestment view, on the other hand, higher dividends do not signal anything, so higher tax rates should *reduce* the sensitivity of stock prices to dividend announcements. That is, higher tax rates make dividends a more costly means of returning cash to shareholders (in comparison with repurchases) with no positive information effect to offset it. The empirical results for large numbers of firms strongly support the information/underinvestment view—investors treat dividend increases as conveying positive information about the company's prospects.

While the differences between these views are important for understanding the relative importance of incentive problems, the similarities are also important. For one thing, both views are consistent with Principle 2. That is, a reduction in cash flow will tend to reduce investment, whether on average investment is too low or too high. In this sense, the overinvestment and underinvestment views suggest very similar predictions about the correlation between cash flow and investment. They both,

---

37. They also distinguish both views from the perfect markets view, which says that firms *never* allow investment to be affected by cash windfalls, and use the windfalls instead to pay off debt and return cash to shareholders.

therefore, can give rise to financial accelerator models, in which financing imperfections are a major force behind firm-specific as well as economy-wide fluctuations in activity.

Furthermore, note that whether the average level of investment is too low or too high, *fluctuations* in investment spending are bad for shareholders. That is, the sensitivity of investment to cash flow lowers firm value *regardless* of under- or overinvestment. To see this, suppose that when cash flow is low, a firm will take its best investment project, one that provides a 20% internal rate of return. Suppose further that when cash flow is average, the firm will take this project plus the next best (equal-sized) project, which offers a 15% return. Finally, if cash flow is high, the firm will add the least desirable (again equal-sized) project to these, offering a 10% return. If the firm follows this rule, its investment spending is obviously sensitive to cash flow. To determine whether the firm is under- or overinvesting, we would need to know shareholders' hurdle rates for these investments. The firm would on average be under-investing relative to value maximization if the cost of internal funds is 10%, and overinvesting if the proper hurdle rate is 20%.

Either way, if cash flow is always at the average level, the firm would always take both the 15% and 20% projects, for a total dollar profit of 35% (relative to the cost of a single investment). If cash flow is low or high with equal probability, however, the firm would have a total profit of 20% when cash flow is low and 45% (20% + 15% + 10%) when cash flow is high. The average total profit from this latter investment strategy is 32.5% [(20 + 45)/2], as the two outcomes are equally likely. This is *less* than the 35% profit that results from steady investment spending. Higher profits therefore result from investment spending that remains steady and is not driven by fluctuations in internal cash. Furthermore, this is true whether the firm over- or underinvests (i.e., whether the appropriate hurdle rate for an individual project is 10% or 20%).

This argument implies that incentive problems, regardless of their precise manifestation, generate costs to individual firms and to the economy, and that these costs are related to the sensitivity of investment to cash flow and the availability of external finance.

The Investment "Project Mix" Problem

There is a third type of distortion in investment introduced by incentive problems: an inferior mix of investment activities. That is, compared to the optimal mix of investments chosen by a firm that faces no incentive problems, the mix of investments is inferior in the presence of these problems. Why would investment spending become distorted in such cases? When external funds are costly, investment policies that conserve on external funds are, all else equal, better than those that don't. By selecting their investments in certain ways, firms can mitigate the need for external funds and therefore raise firm value. This creates distortions:

Principle 3: In the presence of incentive problems, firms' optimal investment decisions mixes are biased in that they rationally: (1) value investments more highly, the less positively (more negatively) correlated their cash flows are with existing cash flows; and (2) value investments less highly, the greater the idiosyncratic risk of the cash flows. These biases become stronger as a company has less financial slack.

This proposition provides an economic rationale for the intuition of managers that investment projects with highly volatile returns ought to receive a higher hurdle rate, even if the volatility is purely nonsystematic. (The Capital Asset Pricing Model, CAPM, which is frequently used to determine hurdle rates, ignores the volatility of nonsystematic risks.)

Although the bias in investment is costly from the perfect markets perspective, it can be either a cost or a benefit once incentive problems are involved. If, for example, managers tend to be empire builders, investment mix distortions are bad for investors. They result from managers' ability to entrench themselves and pursue objectives other than value maximization.[38]

If managers are value maximizers, however, then outside investors prefer the distorted mix, which reduces the deadweight costs of external finance. To see this, suppose that outside debt finance is cheaper than outside equity, so that firms limit their leverage only because of the potential costs of financial distress. If a firm can reduce the volatility of its overall cash flows (through undertaking low-volatility and diversifying investments), it lowers the likelihood of financial distress. It can then finance itself more cheaply by using a higher fraction of debt finance. This in turn raises firm value.

This kind of argument provides a rationale for corporate insurance policies. Under the perfect markets paradigm, companies should be indifferent between self-insuring and buying fairly priced insurance (against fire, confiscation of assets, for example) through explicit policies. Of course, on average insurance premiums are set above fair value, since at a minimum insurance companies need to pay overhead expenses. Insur-

---

38. Corporate experiments with unrelated acquisitions of the 1960s and 1970s would seem an obvious example of the latter mechanism for distorted mix.

ance policies can therefore be thought of as an NPV-negative investment that is desirable because its payoffs are negatively correlated with cash flows net of investment. That is, when a profitable factory burns to the ground, the insurance contract removes the need to tap the costly outside funds needed to rebuild it.

Merton (1993), Froot and Stein (1994), and Merton and Perold (1993) discuss how value-maximizing firms would want to alter capital budgeting rules in the face of incentive problems. Froot and Stein derive a kind of multifactor pricing model to provide hurdle rates for such firms. The model says that the hurdle rate is a linear function of market risk and firm-specific risk. The market risk factor works exactly as it does in the CAPM—the price of risk is the expected return on the market, and the risk measure is the covariance of the asset's returns with that of the market. The firm-specific risk premium also contains a price of risk—the excess sensitivity of firm value to fluctuations in internal funds—and a quantity of risk—the covariance of new project cash flows with existing cash flows. All else equal, the greater this sensitivity, the more the value-maximizing firm should adjust hurdle rates as described in Principle 3.

We have noted that adjusting the level of investment as well as the mix of investment projects can help minimize fluctuations in internal funds. When access to external finance is costly, this form of internal funds management is valuable. Of course, investment policy is not the only way to manage internal funds. As we argue above, capital structure policies as well as security design can aid in efforts to align the supply of and demand for internal funds. Firms therefore have a variety of weapons that allow them to manage fluctuations in internal funds, thereby lowering the costs of external finance generated by incentive problems.

Risk Management

In addition to capital structure and investment policies, firms have a third means of mitigating costly fluctuations in internal funds—financial risk management programs. Corporations can use financial risk management instruments not simply to raise external funds, but also to shift the availability of internal funds from one possible future scenario to another. I argue that this motivation for risk management follows directly from the presence of incentive problems. Moreover, these problems also generate precise prescriptions about what and how much to hedge and about which derivative instruments to use.[39]

---

39. Portions of this section are taken from Froot, Scharfstein, and Stein (1993).

The Relation Between Risk Management and Incentive Problems

In practice, corporations take risk management very seriously. Recent surveys reveal that risk management is ranked by financial executives as one of their most important objectives.[40] Yet in spite of its practical prominence, there is little agreement on the rationale for undertaking corporate risk management. To some observers it may seem unnecessary to appeal to incentive problems to provide a motivation for corporate hedging. But given the proliferation of efficient, low-transactions cost markets, it is surprisingly difficult to come up with solid alternative rationales for corporate risk management.

Why do low-cost, efficient markets make corporate hedging harder to justify? The traditional argument is that, in such an environment, corporate shareholders can hedge themselves. As a result, they will not pay more for the stock of a company that has hedged for them. Indeed, investors may want to engage in hedging their portfolios regardless of what companies do. That is, it is unlikely that corporate risk management policies will result in aggregated stock portfolios that embody investors' preferred exposures to market risk variables. For example, if investors prefer to hold a certain amount of foreign exchange exposure in their portfolios, corporate hedging will eliminate the need for shareholder hedging only if the total portfolio exchange rate exposure happens to be exactly what shareholders desire.

By what mechanism, then, might corporate risk management add value? While there are undoubtedly many possible rationales for corporate hedging, we are particularly concerned here with arguments based on incentive problems. And indeed, these problems provide a convincing rationale—perhaps one of the most convincing—for the desirability of corporate hedging.

The reasoning goes as follows.[41] Because these problems make externally raised funds more expensive than internally generated funds, corporations can minimize their capital costs by generating *internally* the cash required to make positive-NPV investments. Often, however, corporations will generate surplus internal funds in some scenarios and face shortages of internal funds in other scenarios. Corporate risk management programs allow a firm to use its cash flow more effectively, by permitting it to shift the internal funds from excess scenarios toward deficit scenarios. This avoids the need in deficit scenarios either to raise

---

40. See Rawls and Smithson (1990).
41. This reasoning is spelled out in more detail in Froot, Scharfstein, and Stein (1993 and 1994).

Table 7-1　Value of Ajax's Investment Opportunities with No Hedging

	Internal Cash flow	Desired Investment	Actual Investment (no hedge)	NPV of Investment (no hedge)
Dollar Appreciation	$ 50	$100	$ 50	$30
Dollar Stable	$100	$100	$100	$45
Dollar Depreciation	$150	$100	$100	$45
Average Outcome	$100	$100	$ 83	$40

external funds or to cut investment spending, both of which are costly. Thus, by eliminating these costs, risk management programs can raise corporate values, locking in a firm's ability to undertake *all* its positive-NPV investments.[42]

An example.[43]　To see this argument more clearly, it is best to work with a hypothetical example, Ajax Inc. Let us assume that, to be competitive, Ajax must spend heavily on R&D, which it performs principally in the United States In the coming year, Ajax would like to spend $100 million, based on what it perceives to be positive-NPV opportunities for product development. Company analysts expect this spending to have a net present value of $45 million to shareholders. If Ajax is forced to cut back to $50 million of investment spending, the NPV would fall to $30 million; if it increases investment to $150 million, again the NPV would be only $30 million.

Of course, there are a number of things that could prevent Ajax from spending $100 million on R&D and realizing the (expected) NPV of $45 million. The corporation could be preempted by a competitor, lose a large lawsuit, or experience some natural disaster. Ajax buys insurance against some of these risks (fire, theft).

Ajax also faces foreign exchange risk, in that half of the company's sales occur abroad. An appreciation of the dollar would lead to a reduction in cash flow from $100 million to $50 million; a depreciation would increase cash flow to $150 million (see Table 7-1). Ajax's managers are concerned

---

42. An often-mentioned reason for corporate hedging is avoidance of bankruptcy. As long as bankruptcy is costly, such a rationale is legitimate. As discussed above, though, the costs of bankruptcy are, in many instances, a result of incentive barriers between outside capital providers and insider managers. Thus, hedging to avoid bankruptcy may be thought of as an example of hedging to reduce incentive problems.
43. This section draws on the discussion in Froot, Scharfstein, and Stein (1994).

Table 7-2 Value of Ajax's Investment Opportunities with Hedging

	Internal Cash flow	Desired Investment	Hedge Payout	NPV of Investment (with hedge)
Dollar Appreciation	$ 50	$100	+$50	$45
Dollar Stable	$100	$100	$ 0	$45
Dollar Depreciation	$150	$100	−$50	$45
Average Outcome	$100	$100	$ 0	$45

about the impact that dollar appreciation might have on R&D spending. They believe Ajax would be unable to borrow funds to finance the full desired R&D expenditure. They also think the board would be reluctant to issue equity to make up the difference.

Ajax in the past has not attempted to hedge its substantial currency risks, viewing such trading activity as "speculation." Some of its senior executives wonder whether this is the right decision. They argue that if the dollar appreciates, Ajax would have only $50 million of cash flow it could allocate to R&D, and that this would lower the NPV of the investment program by $15 million (from $45 to $30 million). A dollar depreciation, on the other hand, would not impair Ajax's ability to spend $100 million on R&D. Indeed, with a cash flow of $150 million, Ajax would wind up with surplus cash of $50 million (see Table 7-1).

If Ajax were to hedge away all of the foreign exchange risk imbedded in its cash flows, the company could lock in the ability to spend $100 million on R&D. It could do this by going long dollars (against a basket of foreign currencies). If the dollar appreciates, the hedge would bring in $50 million, just the amount needed to supplement Ajax's internal cash flow deficit of $50 million. If the dollar depreciates, the hedge would lose $50 million. Since the loss would come out of excess cash, Ajax will still have $100 million left for R&D. Thus, by buying additional cash flow in shortfall scenarios with excess cash elsewhere, Ajax can lock in its value-maximizing R&D expenditure of $100 million (see Table 7-2).

How much more valuable is it for Ajax—as opposed to its shareholders—to do the hedging? The answer can be found by comparing the last columns of Table 7-1 and Table 7-2. If Ajax hedges, shareholders receive the NPV of $45 million regardless of how the dollar turns out. This is $5 million more than if the firm does not hedge: The average no-hedging outcome is $40 million, reported in Table 7-1.

Figure 7-1 Ajax Inc.'s Hedging Strategy (fixed R&D investment)

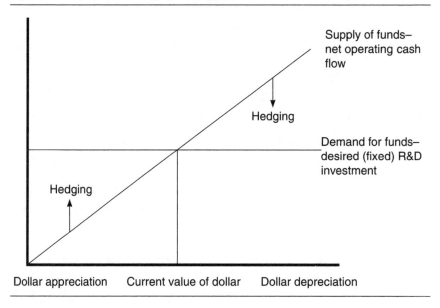

With this example in mind, we can summarize the role of risk management as:

Principle 4: When incentive problems make external finance more expensive than internal finance, risk management can add value to corporations through better alignment of the demand for funds with the internal supply of funds.

Figure 7-1 provides a graphical demonstration. As the dollar depreciates, the supply of internal funds—Ajax's cash flows—rises; this is the sloped line. The demand for funds—the desired level of investment—is fixed and independent of the exchange rate; this is the horizontal line. If Ajax doesn't hedge, the supply of and demand for funds are equal only if the dollar is stable. By hedging, Ajax reduces supply just when there is an excess, and supplements supply just when there is a deficit. The sloped line pivots clockwise. With proper hedging, the company has the funds precisely when it needs them.

This discussion shows generally how corporate risk management can add value. If fact, there are a number of more precise implications about hedging behavior that come out of the incentive approach.

Hedge ratios and hedging instruments. The Ajax example also provides a framework for evaluating what hedge ratios and types of instru-

Figure 7-2   Ajax Inc.'s Hedging Strategy (exchange rate-sensitive investment)

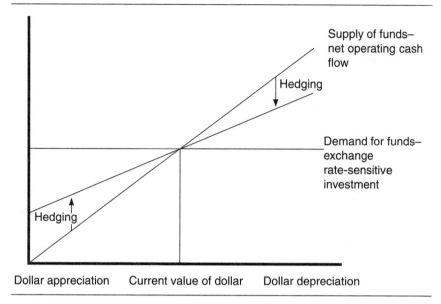

Supply of funds–
net operating cash
flow

Hedging

Demand for funds–
exchange
rate-sensitive
investment

Hedging

Dollar appreciation   Current value of dollar   Dollar depreciation

ments to use. First, let us look at how hedge ratios are determined. Suppose that, when the value of the dollar falls, Ajax's investment opportunities improve, as it is in a low-cost position vis-à-vis its foreign competitors. Similarly, if the dollar appreciates, Ajax's investment opportunities worsen. In view of this, suppose that Ajax will want to spend $125 million on R&D if the dollar depreciates and only $75 million if the dollar appreciates.

In this case, Ajax will not want to hedge as much as it did in the first example. That is, its "hedge ratio" will be reduced. Figure 7-2 provides a graphical depiction. As before, the supply of funds is upward-sloping, reflecting the sensitivity of Ajax's existing business to the value of the dollar. Now, however, the demand for funds is upward-sloping as well, reflecting the improvement in the value of Ajax's investment opportunities as the dollar declines. The net result is that the amount of hedging needed for Ajax to lock in its desired investment spending is reduced. Essentially, Ajax is naturally hedged to some extent because its investment opportunities are positively correlated with its currency cash flows.

Of course, Figures 7-1 and 7-2 show only two examples of the many possible configurations for demand and supply. For example, it is possible that the demand for funds is even more steeply sloped than the supply of funds in Figure 7-2. (This might be the case if Ajax were, say, an oil company, and the horizontal axis is the oil price—i.e., high oil prices could give rise to very large increases in the company's investment opportunities.) In that case, the best hedging program would have Ajax reversing the direction of its hedge, rotating the supply of funds in a *counter*clockwise direction.

In addition to saying something about the appropriate hedge ratio, the configuration of supply and demand may tell us something about the types of hedging instruments (options, futures, forwards) needed for an optimal hedge. In the examples above, aligning the supply of funds with the demand for funds involves a simple rotation of the supply-of-funds curve. Such rotations can be generated using foreign exchange futures or forward contracts. These contracts pay off in proportion to the change in the value of the risk variable from its initial position. Of course, it is not *necessary* to use forwards or futures to accomplish the rotation; by put–call parity, combinations of options can be used to replicate the behavior of a forward contract. But, in the Ajax example, futures or forwards would be enough to accomplish the rotation; options would not be required.

In other instances, a simple rotation of the supply-of-funds curve would not be enough to align it with the demand for funds. For example, the supply and demand curves may not be straight lines. In many instances, the upward-sloping demand-for-funds curve in Figure 7-2 would level off for large dollar appreciations, because a minimum amount of capital spending for repair and replacement purposes is always desirable if the firm is to maintain capacity. In such cases, the proper hedge will no longer need simply to rotate the supply-of-funds curve; it will have to change its shape as well. Forward and futures contracts, in any amount, will not be able to accomplish this. But options contracts (with strike prices at "kinks" in the demand-for-funds curve) can be used to align the two curves completely. With a complete set of options contracts available, a company can create a hedge portfolio to align *any* supply-of-funds curve with *any* demand-for-funds curve.

Hedging for "soft" versus "hard" investment spending. The example above uses investments in R&D as the investment expenditure. But the term "investment expenditure" should not be interpreted so narrowly to mean R&D or even capital expenditures in general. It applies to "softer" investments in intangible assets (even when they are expensed), such as a well-trained workforce, brand-name recognition, and market share.

In many instances, hedging will be most important for firms that invest more in intangibles than they do in plant and equipment. The reason is that capital-intensive companies can collateralize newly purchased plant and equipment. Service firms, on the other hand, will find it difficult to collateralize investments in human capital. These "soft" investments are subject to large incentive and information problems. This makes it especially expensive to use externally raised funds to finance hard-to-collateralize or "soft" assets.

Hedging and the elimination of risk. An important characteristic of risk management programs designed to mitigate the effects of expensive external funds is that they do not completely insulate the company from risk. That is, risk management programs that eliminate cash flow deficits and surpluses can be very different from those that attempt to insulate shareholders from risk.

To see this, consider Figure 7-2 again. In that case, Ajax wants investment opportunities that improve when the dollar depreciates, and worsen when the dollar appreciates. Ajax can undertake a hedge that locks in its desired investment spending, even though its investment opportunities still vary with the exchange rate. If the NPV of this investment program rises when the dollar falls (and vice versa), then Ajax's stock price should also rise when the dollar falls—even with the hedge in place. Basically, Ajax is in a poor competitive position when the dollar appreciates. The return on the basic business represented by the left-hand side of the balance sheet is low in that situation. There is nothing that clever financing can do to change this. All the hedging in the world won't make Ajax's business any better when its basic business prospects are poor.

Next note that a complete hedge—one that would fully insulate Ajax's market value from fluctuations in the dollar—would fail to align the supply of funds with the demand for funds. That is, an overly aggressive hedging program would reduce Ajax's value. To see this, note that a complete hedge could be achieved by making the supply-of-funds curve perfectly horizontal in every period; that way, Ajax's cash flows would be completely protected from exchange rate fluctuations. Yet, although Ajax's value would not fluctuate when the currency changes, its ability to meet its desired investment would. That is, with a horizontal supply-of-funds curve, Ajax will find it can invest up to only $100 million, regardless of the value of the dollar. (This is assuming that the company remains reluctant to issue equity.) This leaves it $25 million short of its desired investment spending when the dollar depreciates. Thus, a complete hedge would reduce the NPV of Ajax's investments below their opportunity values.

Summary

It should be clear that incentive problems create a number of motives for companies to manage risk actively. The basic goal of these risk management programs is to align a firm's supply of internal funds with the demand for internal funds. In this way, hedging will support a company's attempt to "do good investment," i.e., undertake all positive-NPV investment strategies that it finds.

I also argue that derivative instruments can increase firm value when used to help support a "do-all-good-investments" policy. Hedging creates value through the interaction of financing and investment, with fairly specific, and sometimes unexpected, implications for hedging programs.

For example, this paradigm would predict that a broker/dealer, like Goldman Sachs or Bankers Trust, might want to invest the company's capital in derivatives that are "long" volatility. Why does this constitute prudent risk management rather than outright "speculation"? Basically, dealers can trade on their own accounts more profitably when markets are volatile. This means that their investment opportunities expand when volatility is high. Thus, going long volatility may actually be a hedge for such dealers; it would deliver liquidity at just the moment when the profitable opportunities to use liquidity are greatest.

Putting Financing, Investment, and Risk Management Policies Together[44]

Thus far we have looked independently at three policy areas in which a firm can respond to the incentive problems it faces: financing policy, investment policy, and risk management policy. I argue that each set of policies can help reduce the burden created by incentive problems. But these policies also are not independent of one another—for example, the availability of sophisticated risk management tools may alter the financing and investment policies that a firm would otherwise wish to undertake. We need to explore this interdependence in order to understand more clearly how firms might create policies to minimize incentive costs.

As a first step, we need to distinguish between two broad classes of risks that companies face—what we call "marketable" risks and "nonmarketable" risks. Marketable risks are those that are exogenous to the firm, and observable and verifiable by market participants. In the case of Ajax Inc., the exchange rate clearly qualifies as a marketable risk. Other obvious marketable risks are exposure to fluctuations in commodity prices, interest rates, and aggregate stock indexes. Because these risk variables are exogenous and observable, investors and corporations have more or less equal access to knowledge about them. As a result, derivative financial instruments based on them can be created and traded, allowing investors to adjust their exposures as they see fit. Even risks that are not

---

44. This section draws on work from Froot and Stein (1994).

typically traded in financial markets—such as who will win the World Series—are, in principle, marketable, and therefore could be the basis for low-cost derivative financial contracts.

Nonmarketable risks, on the other hand, are risks that are not exogenous or observable by everyone. For example, in addition to facing exchange rate risk, Ajax Inc. is likely to face risks on the effectiveness of its new product pipeline, or of ongoing sales of its current products. Before sales or research results are announced to the public, managers will know much more about them than outsiders. As a result of this information asymmetry, derivative contracts based on nonmarketable risks are harder to trade; the playing field with respect to the risk variable is not level. For now, we can think of nonmarketable risks as those that are impossible (or prohibitively expensive) to write contracts on.[45]

With this distinction in mind, we can create a kind of hierarchical approach for mitigating the costs of incentive problems. The first step is that of risk management. Hedging techniques can be used to adjust the *marketable* risks of a firm's cash flows. As we argue above, the internal supply of funds should be aligned as much as possible with the demand for funds. If a firm faces *only* marketable risks—this is the case of Ajax, which we assume faces only exchange rate exposure—then risk management techniques allow the firm to align internal funds' supply and demand perfectly. Once this is accomplished, there are no occurrences of future cash shortfalls, and, therefore, the costs of incentive problems are eliminated.

> *Principle 5: If a firm faces only marketable risks, then it can completely eliminate the costs of incentive problems. In these instances cash flow supply and demand can be perfectly aligned in every state of nature using marketable derivative instruments (options, futures, swaps, etc.). Having eliminated incentive problems, the firm can go on to use standard capital budgeting techniques to determine the optimal amount and mix of investment.*

Principle 5 suggests that incentive problems need not spill over into suboptimal financing or investment policies. The distortion created by these problems can be nipped in the bud, if the risks are marketable and derivative instruments based on those risks are available. In these cir-

---

45. Of course, the distinction between marketable and nonmarketable is not so precise as this suggests. Many risks—such as individual employee disability—can be insured against despite having some nonmarketable characteristics. However, it may be "expensive" to insure against these risks, as insurers have to charge a premium to compensate for their inferior access to information.

cumstances, investment policy should mirror standard capital budgeting methods, which disregard both the volatility of an investment's cash flows and the correlation with firm cash flows. Similarly, financing policy need not hold in reserve additional debt capacity for cash shortfalls. If the prospect of these cash shortfalls can be eliminated by risk management techniques, then less of an equity buffer is needed.

Of course, in reality there are no firms that actually face only marketable risks. All firms face nonmarketable risks, although to greater or lesser extents. In such circumstances, while risk management cannot *perfectly* align supply and demand across all scenarios, it can remove the portions of nonmarketable risks that are *correlated* with marketable risks. This reduces, but can't eliminate, the costs of incentive problems.

To see this, consider again the example of Ajax. Suppose that, as in Figure 7-2, when the dollar depreciates, Ajax will need more cash to fund its investments *on average*. Of course, unrelated product market developments may lead to investment opportunities that turn out to be either above or below the average. The presence of these nonmarketable risks implies that Ajax will not be able to use exchange rate derivatives to avoid all cash shortfalls. Sometimes these shortfalls will occur, although not as a result of an exchange rate movement (against which the firm can hedge). Risk management will have helped Ajax eliminate the effects of the exchange rate on supply–demand alignment, but it will not be sufficient to eliminate the costs of incentive problems altogether.

In such a case, Ajax will wish to alter its capital budgeting rules and its financing patterns if it is to reduce incentive costs further. It will want to penalize investment projects that have very volatile returns by raising the hurdle rate such investments must meet. Similarly, Ajax will have a relative preference for "diversifying" investments, to include some whose payouts are not so highly correlated with existing cash flows. On the financing side, Ajax may wish to alter its target capital structure as a means of "hedging" against otherwise unhedgeable cash shortfalls. It might reserve some debt capacity for these shortfalls, employing a larger equity buffer that absorbs negative cash flow shocks. Overall, this implies:

> *Principle 6: Firms that face nonmarketable risks will not be able to eliminate incentive problems through risk management alone. These firms will wish to alter financing and investment policies as in Principles 2 and 3 in order to reduce the costs of these problems further.*

Clearly, firms in these circumstances will wish to adjust *both* investment and financing policies. How much they adjust each depends on their circumstances. For example, a firm that has little room to adjust investment cannot reduce its exposure to costly cash flow shortfall by changing the mix of investments. All else equal, this firm will wish to use a more conservative capital structure. On the other hand, firms that have little flexibility in choice of financing may place more emphasis on adjusting investment policies in order to reduce the risk of cash shortfalls. This implies:

> *Principle 7: Once a firm has used risk management techniques to remove the marketable portion of net cash flow risk, it should consider adjustments in financing policies (i.e., a less levered target capital structure) and investment policies (i.e., a risk-reducing mix of investments) as substitutes. These are adjustments that reduce the costs of incentive problems without the use of financial derivatives. They should be used only to offset nonmarketable risks. Marketable risks are better dealt with through the use of financial derivatives.*

Conclusions

This exploration of incentive problems for corporations that must rely on arm's length capital markets for financing indicates that these problems have a wide range of implications for corporate decisions: financing, investment, and risk management. Incentive problems have the effect of making external finance increasingly costly, the more is used. This in turn creates an incentive for firms to mitigate their use of equity financing and reduce the "lumpiness" of their external financial needs.

Innovations within the financial system have provided new ways of managing incentive problems. Firms today have at their disposal a wide variety of derivative instruments that allow for far better financial risk management. The result is that firms can reduce the frequency with which they raise external equity, at the same time as they maintain, or even increase, their use of debt. In this way, firms reduce their average cost of capital. Firms can also issue a range of securities that are designed to reduce incentive or information gaps between shareholders and managers. Both types of innovations help to eliminate the incentive barriers that separate management from the market.

References

Asquith, P., and D. Mullins (1986), "The Impact of Initiating Dividend Payments on Shareholder's Wealth," *Journal of Business*, 56: 77–96.

Bernanke, B., and M. Gertler (1989), "Agency Costs, Net Worth and Business Fluctuations," *American Economic Review*, 79: 14–31.

Bernanke, B., M. Gertler, and S. Gilchrist (1993), "The Financial Accelerator and the Flight to Quality," Working Paper, Princeton University, December.

Bernheim, B.D., and A. Wantz (1992), "A Tax-Based Test of the Dividend Signaling Hypothesis," NBER Working Paper No. 4244, December.

Blanchard, O.J., F. López-de-Silanes, and A. Shleifer (1993), "What Do Firms Do with Cash Windfalls?" NBER Working Paper No. 4258, January.

Brealey, R.A., and S.C. Myers (1991), *Principles of Corporate Finance,* fourth edition, New York: McGraw-Hill.

Brigham, E. (1966), "An Analysis of Convertibles: Theory and Some Empirical Evidence," *Journal of Finance,* 21: 35–54.

Calomiris, C., and R.G. Hubbard (1990), "Firm Heterogeneity, Internal Finance and Credit Rationing," *Economic Journal,* 50: 90–104.

Eckbo, B.E. (1986), "Valuation Effects of Corporate Debt Offerings," *Journal of Financial Economics,* 15: 119–152.

Fazzari, S., G. Hubbard, and B. Petersen (1988), "Financing Constraints and Corporate Investments," *Brookings Papers on Economic Activity,* 1: 141–206.

Froot, K. (1992), "Intel Corporation, 1992," Harvard Business School Case No. 292-106, Boston.

Froot, K., and J. Hines (1994), "Losing Interest: Interest Allocation Rules and the Cost of Debt Finance," Working Paper, Harvard University.

Froot, K., D. Scharfstein, and J. Stein (1993), "Risk Management: Coordinating Corporate Investment and Financing Policies," *Journal of Finance,* 48 (December): 1629–1658.

Froot, K., D. Scharfstein, and J. Stein (1994), "Developing a Risk Management Strategy," *Harvard Business Review,* 72 November/December: 91–102.

Froot, K., and J. Stein (1991), "Exchange Rates and Foreign Direct Investment: An Imperfect Markets Approach," *Quarterly Journal of Economics,* 56 (November): 1191–1219.

——— (1994), "Risk Management, Capital Budgeting, and Capital Structure Policy for Financial Institutions: An Integrated Approach," Working Paper, Harvard University.

Gertler, M., and S. Gilchrist (1994), "Monetary Policy, Business Cycles, and the Behavior of Small Manufacturing Firms," *Quarterly Journal of Economics,* 59: 309–340.

Greenwald, B. (1986), *"MCI Communications Corp., 1983,"* Harvard Business School Case No. 284-057, Boston.

Greenwald, B., and J. Stiglitz (1993), "Financial Market Imperfections and Business Cycles," *Quarterly Journal of Economics,* 58: 77–114.

Hoshi, T., A. Kashyap, and D. Scharfstein (1991), "Corporate Structure, Liquidity, and Investment: Evidence from Japanese Industrial Groups," *Quarterly Journal of Economics,* 56: 33–60.

Jensen, M. (1986), "Agency Costs of Free Cash Flow, Corporate Finance and Takeover," *American Economic Review,* 76 (May): 323–329.

Kashyap, A., O. Lamont, and J. Stein (1992), "Credit Conditions and the Cyclical Behavior of Inventories: A Case Study of the 1981–82 Recession," NBER Working Paper No. 4211, November.

Kashyap, A., D. Scharfstein, and D. Weil (1990), "The High Price of Land and the Low Cost of Capital: Evidence from Japan," Working Paper, MIT.

Kashyap, A., J. Stein, and D. Wilcox (1995), "Monetary Policy and Credit Conditions: Evidence from the Composition of External Finance," *American Economic Review*.

Kester, W.C. (1986), "Capital and Ownership Structure: A Comparison of United States and Japanese Manufacturing Corporations," *Financial Management*, 15: 97–113.

Lamont, O (1993), "Corporate Liquidity and Investment: Evidence from Internal Capital Markets," Working Paper, MIT.

Loughran, T., and J.R. Ritter (1993), "The Timing and Subsequent Performance of New Issues," Working Paper, University of Illinois, November.

Mackie-Mason, J. (1990), "Do Taxes Affect Corporate Financing Decisions?," *Journal of Finance*, 45 (December): 1471–1494.

Marsh, P. (1982), "The Choice Between Equity and Debt: An Empirical Study," *Journal of Finance*, 37 (March): 121–144.

Merton, R.C. (1993), "Operation and Regulation in Financial Intermediation: A Functional Perspective," Harvard University Working Paper No. 93-020, July.

Merton, R.C., and A. Perold (1993), "Theory of Risk Capital in Financial Firms," *Journal of Applied Corporate Finance*, 6 (Fall): 16–33.

Meulbroek, L. (1992), "An Empirical Analysis of Illegal Insider Trading," *Journal of Finance*, 47 (December): 1661–1700.

Mikkelson, W., and M. Partch (1986), "Valuation Effects of Security Offerings and the Issuance Process," *Journal of Financial Economics*, 15: 31–60.

Myers, S.C. (1984), "The Capital Structure Puzzle," *Journal of Finance*, 39 (July): 575–592.

Myers, S.C., and N. Majluf (1984), "Corporate Financing and Investment Decisions When Firms Have Information Investors Do Not Have," *Journal of Financial Economics*, 13 (June): 187–221.

Rawls, W.S., and C.W. Smithson (1990), "Strategic Risk Management," *Continental Bank Journal of Applied Corporate Finance*, 1: 6–18.

Schwartz, E., and R. Aronson (1967), "Some Surrogate Evidence in Support of the Concept of Optimal Financial Structure," *Journal of Finance*, 22 (March): 10–18.

Seyhun, H.N. (1986), "Insiders' Profits, Costs of Trading, and Market Efficiency," *Journal of Financial Economics*, 16: 189–212.

Shyam-Sunder, L., and S. Myers (1993), "Testing Static Trade-off Against Pecking Order Models of Capital Structure," Working Paper, MIT, March.

Smith, C.W., Jr. (1986), "Alternative Methods for Raising Capital–Rights Versus Underwritten Offerings," *Journal of Financial Economics*, 5: 273–307.

Stein, J. (1992), "Convertible Bonds as 'Backdoor' Equity Financing," *Journal of Financial Economics*, 32 (August): 3–22.

Tiemann, J. (1989), "Avon Products," Harvard Business School Case No. 289-049, Boston.

Titman, S., and R. Wessels (1988), "The Determinants of Capital Structure Choice," *Journal of Finance*, 43 (March): 1–19.

CHAPTER EIGHT

Financial Infrastructure and Public Policy
A Functional Perspective

ROBERT C. MERTON AND ZVI BODIE

The central theme of this book is that the basic functions performed by the financial system are stable across time and place, but the institutional ways that they are performed are not. Over time, institutional form follows function, as innovation and competition lead to greater efficiency in the performance of the functions. Therefore, an integrated understanding of the changing global financial system is facilitated by using the financial function as the focus of analysis instead of the financial institution. The preceding chapters offered specific analyses and illustrations of this theme.

This chapter begins with highlights of the key points raised in these chapters, and it then explores the changes in financial infrastructure and regulation that may be necessary to support further improvements. It focuses on the need for vastly upgraded accounting systems that results from the cumulative innovations in financial contracting and trading practices developed over the past few decades. It also shows how a functional perspective on regulation can help to address some of the key

This chapter is a synthesis and extension of work presented in Merton (1989, 1993, 1995), Merton and Bodie (1992, 1993) and Bodie and Merton (1993).

public policy concerns that have arisen regarding these financial innovations. The chapter concludes by applying the functional perspective to take a prospective look at major trends and policy issues that may affect the financial system in the future.

Highlights of Preceding Chapters

Chapter 2 makes the case that the vast majority of payments volume today is related to securities transactions, and that derivative instruments have come to serve as an important extension of the clearing and settlement process for such transactions. A key insight into the increased use of derivatives is that fund transfers are more frequent, but also smaller than in the past, and therefore derivative securities can actually reduce the risk of systemic disruption to the payments system that a single large default would produce.

Chapter 3 shows how pooling is accomplished both through financial intermediaries, such as banks, and through financial contracting, such as issuing securities. It examines how the process of securitization has fostered the growth of new forms of pooling by removing nontraded assets from the balance sheets of financial intermediaries and packaging them in more convenient forms for investors to hold. As illustrated in both the mortgage-backed securities market and the commercial-paper market, securitization has made possible the direct purchase of new financial instruments by households and supported the growth of mutual fund companies.

Chapter 4, which discusses the transfer of economic resources, illustrates how subdividing financial activities along functional lines can enhance efficiency in the performance of the separate functions. Specifically, it shows that by separating the lending activity into a resource transfer function and a credit insurance function, lending can be more efficiently performed in some important instances. This separation of functions has been accomplished through a combination of securitization of debt contracts and new institutional arrangements designed to guarantee contract performance. In this manner, the United States residential mortgage market has been transformed from a highly local market to an international market.

Chapter 5 investigates the essential function of risk management and transfer. It has parallels with the analysis in Chapter 4 when it examines how the development of derivative securities has facilitated the separation of the risk management function from the resource transfer function. It also explores the impact of this development on the stability of the financial system and the possible need for regulation of derivatives trading.

Chapter 6 illustrates the way the increased diversity of financial markets during the past two decades has expanded the opportunities to extract useful information from the prices of financial instruments. It shows in particular how information about the volatility of future changes in security, currency, and commodity prices can be extracted from options and option-like securities.

Chapter 7 shows how recent innovations in financial contracting such as the use of derivatives within corporate risk management programs can reduce the costs of dealing with incentive problems. Because incentive problems make it more costly for companies to raise external capital than to use internal capital, they affect corporate investment, financing, and risk management policies. By materially reducing the costs of solving incentive problems, financial innovation can thus have fundamental effects on these policies.

Infrastructure and Regulation

The financial infrastructure consists of the legal and accounting procedures, the organization of trading and clearing facilities, and the regulatory structures that govern the relations among the users of the financial system. From a long historical perspective of several centuries, the evolution of the infrastructure of the financial system has been identified as perhaps the key to understanding economic development.[1] In particular, the emergence of England as the first industrialized nation in the world during the eighteenth and nineteenth centuries has been attributed to the creation of the necessary financial infrastructure during the latter part of the seventeenth and early eighteenth centuries.[2]

An important challenge for public policy is explicit recognition of the interdependence between product and infrastructure innovations and acknowledgment of the inevitable conflicts that arise between the two. To call up a simple analogy, consider the creation of a high-speed passenger train, surely a beneficial product innovation.[3] Suppose, however, that the tracks of the rail system are inadequate to handle such high speeds. Without any rules, the innovator, whether through ignorance or a willingness to take risk, might choose to run the train at high speed anyway.

If the train crashes, it is, of course, true that the innovator and the passengers will pay dearly. But if in the process the track is also destroyed, those who use the system for a different purpose, such as freight opera-

---

1. See North (1994, pp. 258–260).
2. See Dickson (1967) and North (1994, p. 263).
3. This analogy is taken from Merton (1989).

tors, will also be harmed. Hence the need for policy to safeguard the system.

A simple policy that meets that objective is to mandate a safe, but low speed limit. Of course, this narrowly focused policy has the unfortunate consequence that the benefits of innovation will never be realized. A better, if more complex, policy solution is to upgrade the track, and in the meantime set temporary limits on speed, while there is a technological imbalance between the product and its infrastructure.

As in this hypothetical rail system, the financial system is used by many for a variety of purposes. Separate and discrete financial innovations in products and services can be implemented in an entrepreneurial way and rather quickly. Innovations in financial infrastructure, however, must be more coordinated; they therefore take longer to implement and will occur more gradually.

Successful public policy depends importantly on recognizing the limits of what government can do to improve efficiency and on recognizing when government *inaction* is the best choice. Government regulatory actions can do much to either mitigate or aggravate the dysfunctional aspects of financial innovations. By analogy again, hurricanes are inevitable, but government policy can either reduce their devastation by encouraging early warning systems or it can aggravate the damage by encouraging the building of housing in locations that are especially vulnerable to such storms. Similarly, well-intentioned government policies aimed at reducing the systemic risks of a crisis in the global financial system may have the unintended and perverse consequence of actually increasing the risk of such a crisis.

Risk Accounting

A fundamental part of the infrastructure that will require significant changes to accommodate future financial innovation is the financial accounting system. Traditionally, accounting focuses on value allocations. For this purpose it is generally effective. We need not distinguish here between book or market valuation, because the point is that the accounting system basically looks only at value allocations. It is therefore an ineffective structure for identifying risk allocations.

To illustrate this point, suppose a hypothetical savings bank has fixed-rate mortgages as assets, floating-rate deposit liabilities, and equity. The accounting system indicates the value of assets (the fixed-rate mortgages) on the left-hand side, and on the right-hand side it tells us the value of deposits as well as the value of the bank's equity.

Suppose that this bank now enters into a swap in which it agrees to receive the floating interest rate and pay the fixed rate. What is the impact of this transaction? The objective, of course, is to match the risk of interest rate exposure of its assets and liabilities by transforming floating-rate financing into fixed-rate financing, or equivalently in this case by transforming fixed-rate returns into floating-rate returns.

But where does that drastic change in the risk exposure of the equity appear in the balance sheet? The current financial accounting structure with its focus on valuation has no place for it. The reason is that the value of a swap is typically zero when the institution enters into it. It thus can be listed neither as a liability nor as an asset.

Much is written and said today about the large and varied exposures that are "off-the-balance-sheet" of banks and other financial institutions. It is even suggested that firms that use those swaps or other off-balance sheet contractual arrangements do so to hide information from outsiders. At times and for some firms, disguise may be a primary motive, but the more frequent and widespread reason that these "zero-value" contractuals are off-balance-sheet is simply that the accounting system does not have a place to put them.

Although contracts like interest rate swaps and futures contracts have no initial value, they can have an immediate and significant impact on the risk exposure of the various assets and liabilities that are on the balance sheet. It is precisely in this sense that accounting can be said to do a good job at valuation but that it is totally inadequate to deal with risk allocation.

Major changes in accounting structure and methodology are required to address this inadequacy. In particular, financial accounting needs fundamental revisions to develop a specialized new branch called "risk accounting." The prospect for such development is not just prospective and theoretical. Pressed by the reality of need, financial firms that deal extensively in complex securities have already developed risk accounting protocols as part of their internal management systems. With the benefits of real-world experience, these protocols could serve as prototypes for standardized risk accounting.[4]

An Example: Regulation of OTC Derivatives

Chapters 1, 2, and 5 call attention to the extraordinary growth in the trading of derivatives since the mid-1980s. Driving this growth is the vast savings in transactions costs from their use. The most recent growth has

---

4. For generic examples, see Hindy (1995) and Merton (1989, pp. 242–247; 1992b, pp. 450–457).

been focused in over-the-counter (OTC) derivatives. These contracts are transacted away from a central market, putting greater pressure on the intermediary issuing them to price them correctly and to manage their risk.

Much has been written on whether it is time for governments to take strong steps to protect against increases in systemic risk arising from the use of OTC derivatives.[5] Yet, as discussed in Chapters 1, 2, and 5, the use of OTC derivatives can just as well be framed as reducing systemic risks.[6] Resolving this issue therefore rests on the empirical evidence. Thus a key question in the debate becomes how to measure the risk exposure created by derivatives.

The contribution to systemic risk exposure from OTC derivatives must be measured relative to the risk exposure contribution of the financial structure that they replace, and not in some abstract, absolute terms as if there were no systemic risk exposure prior to their introduction. For example, the over-the-counter options market for foreign exchange (forex) is in part a substitute for interbank forex market trades. The exposure to contract default on OTC options is related to the *difference* between the principal amount and the strike price. In the forex market, principal amounts are exchanged, so the default exposure is the *total* principal amount. Therefore, although the options surely have exposure to contract default, their use as a substitute for the standard forex transaction actually reduces the magnitude of systemic exposure.[7]

Prior to the widespread development of swaps, parallel loans were used to achieve similar results. The systemic exposure of these loans includes the principal and gross interest payments on *each* loan. The swap, by contrast, involves no principal amount exposure; it has exposure only to net interest payments. Yet public debate on the systemic risk of swaps and other derivatives is often clouded by the nearly universal practice of citing the notional principal amount of swaps outstanding, and treating that number as if it were the amount at risk.

To facilitate measurement, financial accounting must undergo funda-mental revisions in the long run. In our opinion, central to those revisions

---

5. Most recently in the United States, the General Accounting Office 1994 report and the Global Derivatives Study Group (1993). See also Darby (1994), Freeman (1993), Miller (1994b), and Paré (1994).

6. The focus on increasing systemic risk is all the more perplexing because derivative securities have long been integral parts of the financial system. As discussed in Merton (1992a), options, forward contracts, and futures have been around since the seventeenth and eighteenth centuries in Europe, the United States, and Japan. Among the earliest derivative securities were bank currencies (money), which "derived" their value from their convertibility into the underlying gold held in depositories.

7. Chapter 2 makes the same point for the Rolling Spot forex futures contract traded on the Chicago Mercantile Exchange with respect to the length of the settlement period.

is the creation of a specialized new branch dealing with risk accounting. Until a system of risk accounting is in place, truly effective regulation will be difficult to implement.

Functional Regulation

As discussed in Chapter 1, increasingly more sophisticated trading technologies, together with low transactions cost markets to implement them, tend to blur the lines among financial products and services. The existence of these technologies and markets also implies easier entry into the financial services. As a result, distinctions between financial institutions are likely to become even less clear in the future.

For example, insurance companies now offer U.S. Treasury money market funds with check writing, while banks use options and futures markets transactions to provide stock-and-bond-value insurance that guarantees a minimum return on customer portfolios. Credit subsidiaries of major manufacturing firms no longer serve only the single, specialized function of providing financing for customers of their parents; they now offer services ranging from merchant banking for takeovers and restructurings to equity-indexed mutual funds sold to retail investors. Electronics also makes the meaning of "the location of the vendor" of these products ambiguous. Therefore, whatever the change in the degree of regulation in the future, a major change in the format of regulation from *institutional* to *functional* seems inevitable.

The approach generally adopted by regulators is to treat the existing institutional structure as given, and to view the objective of public policy as helping the institutions currently in place to survive and flourish.[8] In contrast, the functional perspective takes as given the functions to be performed, and asks instead what the best institutional structure is to perform those functions.

Functional regulation promises more consistent treatment for all providers of functionally equivalent products or services and thereby reduces the opportunities for rent-seeking and regulatory capture. Furthermore, functional regulation can facilitate necessary changes in institutional structures by not requiring a simultaneous revision of the regulations or the regulatory bodies surrounding them as is often required with an institutionally based regulatory structure.[9]

---

8. The thrust of policymaker thinking is perhaps reflected in the titles given to government reports. For instance, the U.S. Treasury entitled its February 1991 detailed proposals for financial system reform, *Modernizing the Financial System: Recommendations for Safer, More Competitive Banks.*
9. See Chicago Mercantile Exchange (1993) for an example of a model for a more function-

The case of regulating OTC derivatives provides an illustration of a major advantage of functional regulation. To be effective and avoid unintended consequences, policy implementation must be comprehensive and include similar treatment of economically equivalent transactions. For example, a proposed regulation to force marked-to-market collateral requirements on OTC derivatives, but not on loans and other "traditional" investments, could actually cause a shift back toward structures (like parallel loans) that actually increase the systemic exposure of the system.

Implementation of comprehensive regulations, however, will be quite difficult. To underscore the point, we repeat the example from Chapter 1 of the varied ways to take a levered position in the Standard & Poor's 500 stocks:

1. You can buy each stock individually on margin in the cash stock market.
2. You can invest in an S&P 500 Index fund and borrow from a bank to finance it.
3. You can go long a futures contract on the S&P 500.
4. You can go long an OTC forward contract on the S&P 500.
5. You can enter into a swap contract to receive the total return on the S&P 500 and pay LIBOR or some other standard interest rate.
6. You can go long exchange-traded calls and short puts on the S&P 500.
7. You can go long OTC calls and short puts.
8. You can purchase an equity-linked note that pays on the basis of the S&P 500 and finance it by a repurchase agreement.
9. You can purchase from a bank a certificate of deposit with its payments linked to the return on the S&P 500.
10. You can either buy on margin or purchase the capital appreciation component of a unit investment trust (examples are Super Shares or SPDRs) that holds the S&P 500.
11. You can borrow to buy a variable-rate annuity contract with its return linked to the S&P 500.

In the United States alone, the types of institutions involved in these equivalent trades include brokers, mutual funds, investment banks, commercial banks, insurance companies, and exchanges. The regulatory authorities involved include the Securities and Exchange Commission, the Com-

---

ally oriented regulatory structure. See also the National Commission on Financial Institution Reform, Recovery, and Enforcement (1993), Pierce (1993), and Miller (1994b).

modity Futures Trading Commission, the Board of Governors of the Federal Reserve System, the Comptroller of the Currency, and state insurance commissions. One need hardly mention that, in the real world, attempts to regulate just two or three of the eleven ways of doing an equivalent thing are not going to be effective.

Looking Ahead

As we look into the future, there are a number of areas where a functional perspective on regulation seems to offer the potential for improved policy options. Let us consider some of them.

Regulation of Banks

First, consider commercial banks in the United States.[10] Since the 1930s they have performed traditionally two main economic activities: They make loans (including guarantees of loans) to businesses, households, and governments, and they take deposits from customers. The loans and guarantees made by banks are risky and tend to require careful monitoring. Thus, bank loans are relatively "opaque" assets.[11] On the other hand, bank deposits are expected by customers to be safe and liquid.

Government insurance through the Federal Deposit Insurance Corporation (FDIC) is the principal means to assure safety of customer deposits. It is the fundamental mismatch between bank demand-deposit liabilities insured by the government and the illiquid, risky, and opaque loans collateralizing those insured deposits that gives rise to the deposit insurance problem.[12]

Even if historically there were efficiency gains from using insured deposits as the primary source to finance the commercial lending activities of banks, there is no evidence that such benefits exist today.[13] We argue

---

10. Merton and Bodie (1993) and Pierce (1993) present an explicitly functional approach to the subject of bank regulation in the United States While their analysis focuses specifically on the U.S. experience, it also applies to many other countries with a similar structure.
11. We use the term "opaque" here in the sense developed by Ross (1989).
12. In discussions of deposit insurance, it is common practice to use the cost to the U.S. taxpayer of bailing out the depositors of failed depository institutions as the measure of the problem. The true cost to society, however, is the misallocation of investment and the unintended redistribution of income and wealth caused by the current system. The current deposit insurance system, accounting rules, and regulatory procedures can encourage excessive risk-taking.
13. Gorton and Pennacchi (1991) present several "agency cost" arguments for using very short-term debt to finance in large part those specialized institutions that make opaque and illiquid loans. They show, however, that there is no need for this short-term debt to take the form of insured demand deposits that are part of the payments system.

elsewhere (1993) that by changing the institutional structure of commercial banking—through separating banks' lending and loan guarantee activities from their deposit-taking activities—it is possible to achieve potentially large social benefits with no apparent offsetting costs. We are therefore led to agree with Black (1985), Kareken (1986), Litan (1987), Pierce (1991, 1993), and Tobin (1985, 1987) that deposit insurance can be effectively reformed by this separated structure. As discussed in Merton and Bodie (1993), this separation can be achieved by simply requiring that federally insured deposits be fully collateralized with the equivalent of U.S. Treasury bills.[14]

This proposed solution to the structural problem of deposit insurance, however, does not require a so-called narrow-bank structure that prohibits institutions that take transactions deposits from engaging in other financial activities, including risky lending. Indeed, under these collateral conditions, there is no danger to the safety of deposits from depository firms offering other financial services. Thus, this proposal does not eliminate any opportunities for economies of scope or scale from "one-stop shopping" for consumers of financial services.

Once the lending and loan-guarantee activities of banks are separated from insured deposits as the funding source, lending could be carried on with many fewer government restrictions and strict capital requirements designed to protect the FDIC. The financing of these lending activities would probably evolve to some combination of common and preferred stock, long-term and short-term debt, and convertible securities, as determined by competitive market forces. If, as some have suggested, government intervention is required in the area of commercial lending to over-

---

Indeed, Merton and Bodie (1993) argue that financing with *insured* deposits would defeat the agency purpose of short-term debt because the holders of that debt would no longer have an incentive to monitor the firm in making their decision whether to "roll over" the debt and continue to finance the firm.

Benston and Kaufman (1988) argue that if the same institution that holds a customer's deposits also grants loans to that customer, economies of scale and scope can be achieved. Black (1975) and Fama (1985) appear to make similar claims, although Black (1985) later seems to reject such synergies. In these times, it is rare that either a business or an individual carries all its financial accounts including credit cards with a single bank. Moreover, we are unaware of any widespread practice to induce this behavior by offering significantly better loan terms to those who would do so. If, however, such potential efficiency gains are really there, the Merton and Bodie (1993) proposal for reform does not rule out lending and deposit-taking activities within the same company, provided that the loans do not serve as collateral for deposits.

In summary, we know of no study showing direct synergistic benefits from having risky loans serve as the collateral for insured demand deposits.

14. The idea of requiring interest-earning obligations of the U.S. government as 100 percent reserves against bank demand deposits was proposed by Friedman (1960). His proposal, however, is motivated by the objective of achieving more effective control of the money supply.

come private market failures, that intervention can surely be made more efficient if it is not complicated by the existence of government-insured demand deposits.

The proposed reform also readily permits other institutions, such as mutual funds, to compete with depository banks in offering insured deposits to their customers. As long as these other institutions maintain the required collateral and follow the same reporting procedures, a level playing field is created for all providers of safe and liquid transactions deposits.

In this new environment, is there still a role for deposit insurance? Reasons given for deposit insurance tend to fall into five categories:

- To encourage and enhance a safe and convenient form of investment for small savers.
- To ensure an adequate and stable supply of credit to worthy borrowers who would not otherwise have access to the nation's supply of capital.
- To facilitate the creation of liquidity.
- To prevent a run on the banking system that might destabilize the macroeconomy.
- To enhance the efficiency of the payments system.

In our opinion, only the last of the five actually requires deposit insurance for efficiency. The other four are better served by alternative means.

Deposit insurance enhances the efficiency of the payments system by eliminating unnecessary monitoring costs. If demand deposits are subject to default risk on the part of the bank, then sellers of goods seeking to verify the ability of buyers to make good on their promises to pay would have to verify not only that the buyer has enough money in an account, but also that the bank in which the account is held is solvent. Similarly, buyers who want the convenience of writing default-free checks would have to monitor the solvency of the bank in which they have their account. Uncertainty about the ability of the bank to make good on its deposit liabilities thus creates deadweight losses. The system of collateralized demand deposits we advocate eliminates this deadweight loss for all parties at minimal cost. The role of the FDIC in this system is simply to confirm to the public that sufficient collateral is there and that, if it is not, the FDIC will make good on the payment.

Regulatory Cooperation and Competition

The blurring of distinctions among financial intermediaries and markets might seem to support a broader case for widespread coordination, and even standardization, of financial regulations, both domestically and across national borders. However, such extrapolation is valid *only if* the coordinated regulatory policies chosen are socially optimal. The reduction in regulatory diversification that by necessity occurs with more effective coordination will accentuate the social losses if the common policies chosen are suboptimal.[15]

A related question is whether imposition of a single regulator for all providers of a particular financial function has the unintended consequence of actually inducing a new systemic risk component that did not exist before. Put differently: Do multiple types of institutions and regulators serving a particular financial function create multiple channels of service, which thereby serve to reduce systemic exposure?

As an analogy, consider an instance from transportation.[16] The objective is to assure travel from England across the Channel to France. Suppose that only one institutional form of transportation across the Channel is available, flight by airplane. Assume further a single regulator for air transportation. In this structure, foggy weather, which is known to happen in England, becomes a systemic event that can shut down transportation.

Because nothing is going to fly, it does not matter how many different airlines there are. Moreover, if the single regulator decides that planes should not fly because it thinks there is bad weather coming, and the forecast happens to be wrong, then the single regulator actually induces the systemic event. Why not allow the Channel tunnel as another way of getting across? With a different regulator, it is in every dimension a different way to cross. Systemic risk is reduced by this diversification. But the tunnel too could block up. So why not a third way such as a hovercraft that can go across the surface? The likelihood that all three ways would fail simultaneously is probably quite small. Hence, the presence of multiple modes of transportation with different structures reduces the systemic risk of complete breakdown in ability to cross the Channel.

As with transportation, so with financial services. We acknowledge that regulating a particular financial function is more complicated when there are multiple channels of providers, because a regulator has to deal with many different kinds of institutions. But the end objective should not be what is easiest for regulators, but what is best for the end users of the financial system.

Pension Reform and Privatization

Financial innovation can facilitate the achievement of some nonfinancial goals of public policy. Pension reform and privatization of state-owned

---

15. White (1993) makes a similar point.
16. This analogy is taken from Merton (1995).

enterprises are examples. These two objectives are high on the list of many countries, including Argentina, Brazil, Chile, the Czech Republic, Hungary, Israel, and Italy.[17] The idea of linking the implementation of policies to achieve both of these objectives simultaneously provides an occasion to illustrate application of the functional perspective to public policy regarding the financial system.

Privatization in its most general sense means transferring responsibility for performing some economic function from the government to the private sector. In the context of pension reform, privatization has come to mean less reliance on the government-run part of the pension system, which is typically a pay-as-you-go system, and greater reliance on employer-provided pensions and specially designated private retirement accounts.

But, privatization also means the transfer of the ownership and control of state-owned enterprises to the private sector. In many countries, privatization in this sense is under consideration as a mechanism for improving the way business firms are managed and scarce capital resources are allocated among those firms. It is believed that by encouraging the creation of competitive securities markets and by finding structures that make managers more accountable to the owners of these securities, the most competent managers will rise to the top, and resources will be allocated more efficiently.

Reform of a country's pension system and privatization of state-owned enterprises are quite separate financial matters. Nonetheless, under certain circumstances, combining the two may make it easier to resolve problems that arise in trying to implement each separately. For example, a major element in switching from a government-run pay-as-you-go retirement income system to a funded private pension system is providing both financial instruments for pension funds to invest in and liquid markets in which to trade them. Similarly, privatization of industry is greatly facilitated by having an array of securities markets to absorb the stocks and bonds issued by newly privatized firms. Undertaking pension reform and privatization of industry at the same time permits a more balanced growth in securities markets by simultaneously developing the demand (by pension funds) and the supply (by privatized firms).

In implementing pension reform, financial managers in both the private and public sectors can exploit the global financial network discussed in Chapter 1 to avoid conflict with other policies. For example, swaps can

---

17. A recent World Bank study (1994) documents many of these efforts. In particular, Chile's experience since 1981 has been closely studied as a possible model for other countries. See Myers (1991, 1992) for details about the Chilean experience. See Bodie and Merton (1992) on Israel; Diamond (1992) on Poland, and Hanke (1991) on the former Communist countries of Eastern Europe.

be used to allow local firms and individuals to diversify internationally without exposing the country to the problem of "capital flight."[18] As an illustration, consider an international equity swap contract between a small-country pension fund and a foreign institution on a notional or principal amount of $1 billion. In the proposed swap, the total return per dollar on the small-country's domestic stock market is exchanged annually for the total return per dollar on a market-value weighted average of the major world stock markets. Trading and ownership of actual shares remain with small-country investors.

The swap agreement effectively transfers the risk of the small-country stock market to foreign investors and provides the domestic investors with the risk return pattern of a well-diversified world portfolio. Since there are no initial payments between parties, there are no initial capital flows in or out of the country. Subsequent payments, which may be either inflows or outflows, involve only the difference between the returns on the two stock market indexes, and no "principal" amounts flow.

Foreign investors benefit from the swap by avoiding the costs of trading in individual securities in the small-country market and by avoiding some potential tax complications that often arise with cross-border investments. Furthermore, they avoid the problems of corporate governance issues that arise when foreigners acquire large ownership positions in domestic companies. Unlike standard cash investments in equities, debt, or real property, the custodial-default risk or expropriation exposure of foreign investors is limited to the difference in returns instead of the total gross return plus principal.

The risks of default are further reduced when the small country party to the swap is a pension fund with its assets invested in the small-country stock market as a hedge. The foreign counterparty to the swap could, of course, also be a pension fund with its assets invested in the world stock market portfolio.

Equity-return swaps based on the returns of major stock markets are common today. Although we are unaware of their explicit application to stock markets in countries with capital controls, given the current rate of innovation, we would not be surprised to see such a development soon. More generally, customized private financial contracting is now available in world capital markets on a large enough scale to accommodate the needs of national governments. As illustrated by our hypothetical swap example, such contracting often makes possible low-cost elimination (or at least reduction) of unintended and undesirable side effects of public financial policies without interfering with the intended objectives of these policies.

---

18. Merton (1992a) develops this idea in detail.

Stabilization Policy

Chapter 1 briefly discusses the ways that financial innovation can affect central bank activities designed to stabilize the macroeconomy. Without taking a position on whether governments should pursue stabilization, we believe that if stabilization remains an objective of government policy in the future, central banks will almost surely use derivative instruments to help implement it.

For an example of how derivatives could be used in the future, consider the German government's issue in 1990 of a sizable private placement of ten-year *Schuldscheine* bonds with put option provisions.[19] The securities are just like standard ten-year government bonds, except they have the feature that the holders can put them back to the government for a fixed price.

By issuing these bonds, the German government in effect introduced a preprogrammed stabilization policy. How is that? Suppose it had issued a standard ten-year bond instead. Suppose further that afterward interest rates start to rise, and therefore, that bond prices fall. Normal ten-year bonds would fall in price in line with interest rate rises.

But what happens to the bonds with the put option? The put bonds will not decline as much as the normal ten-year. Furthermore, the rate of decline in the put bonds becomes less and less until they cease to decline at all. At that point, the bonds will actually begin to behave just like a short-term money instrument. If interest rates were to fall and bond prices to rise, the puts would become more out-of-the-money, and the effective outstanding bond exposure held by investors would increase, which is effectively the same as the government's issuing more bonds.

Note that the decrease or increase in the equivalent bond exposure takes place immediately as interest rates change, without requiring that the bonds actually be put back to the government. It is unlikely that stabilization was the original intent of the German government. Nevertheless, by issuing the put bonds, the government in effect put into place an automatic stabilizer to the extent that "stabilization" means to "lean" against market movements; that is, to buy bonds when bond prices go down, and sell bonds when they go up. The put bonds thus function as the equivalent of a dynamic, open-market trading operation without any need for actual transactions.[20]

---

19. We are indebted to Peter Hancock and the J.P. Morgan Global Research Group for alerting us to the existence of the *Schuldscheine* bonds with put options.
20. In the usual applications, the contingent-claim instrument is given, and a dynamic trading strategy is derived that replicates the payoffs to the claim. Here, we start with

The put bonds achieve more than that because their issue also in effect announces a prescribed open-market policy. If the market believes that issuance is a systematic part of policy, then by looking at the size and terms of government put issues, the market can figure out the implied stabilization policy. In comparison to traditional open-market activity, the put option bond automatically kicks in as soon as events occur because that feature is built into the structure of the securities. Therefore the securities add value because on weekends, non-trading days, and during crashes, the central bank need not be on the scene to implement the open-market operations.

The stated interest rate to be paid by the government on these put bonds is lower than on a standard ten-year bond because the price of the bond includes the value of the put. This provides another difference between selling put bonds to the market and undertaking a traditional open-market stabilization policy. The government in effect charges for the stabilization insurance because the private sector pays for the put option rather than receiving it for free.[21]

To charge explicitly for stabilization may or may not be an objective that policymakers want to achieve. It is, however, now feasible to charge the private sector for interest rate insurance in an efficient way. By issuing the bonds, the government effectly gives the private sector a positive supply of interest rate insurance, which can then be distributed by the private sector.

As noted, none of this is likely to have been the conscious intent of the German government in the case of the *Schuldscheine* bonds. The action nonetheless provides an alternative to traditional stabilization policies, and thus it is an early instance of a class of new techniques for dealing with a low-friction, global financial system. It should be evident that this same approach to automatic stabilizers could also be applied to automatic intervention programs for currencies.

Summary and Conclusion

This book assumes that the functions of the financial system are stable, but that the ways in which functions are performed are not. Accordingly, it introduces an analytical framework that relies on functions rather than on institutions as its conceptual anchor. From our perspective on the financial system, institutional form follows its function.

---

a trading strategy and derive the contingent claim that replicates the payoffs from the strategy. This reverse approach is used by Cox and Huang (1989) to solve the lifetime consumption problem. See also Merton (1992b, pp. 457–467).

21. Of course, it is not really "free," since taxpayers pay for it.

From the most aggregated level of the single primary function of resource allocation, six core functions performed by the financial system are identified:

- To provide ways of *clearing and settling payments* to facilitate trade.
- To provide a mechanism for the *pooling of resources* and for the *subdividing* of shares in various enterprises.
- To provide ways to *transfer economic resources* through time, across borders, and among industries.
- To provide ways of *managing risk.*
- To provide *price information* to help coordinate decentralized decision-making in various sectors of the economy.
- To provide ways of *dealing with the incentive problems* created when one party to a transaction has information that the other party does not or when one party acts as agent for another.

Chapters 2 through 7 describe these six functions. Each chapter connects financial innovation with major improvements in the performance of financial functions. Specific instances include:

- Trading in derivative instruments has substituted in a variety of ways for trading in underlying securities, thereby providing an alternative mechanism for the clearing and settling of transactions.
- Securitization has made it possible for institutions such as mutual funds to flourish, thereby facilitating the pooling of resources and the subdividing of shares.
- Improved techniques for collateralization, credit enhancement, and financial contracting using derivatives have made it possible to overcome some traditional incentive problems, thereby enhancing the transfer of capital resources around the world and the global allocation of risks.
- Expansion of the number and diversity of financial markets creates more opportunities to extract useful information from the prices of financial instruments.

Chapter 8 has considered the changes in financial infrastructure and regulation necessary to support further improvements. Among these is the need to develop a new branch of accounting to measure the exposure of firms to the risk of unanticipated changes in the economic environment. Effective regulation is impossible without such an accounting system.

In the future, public sector managers are likely to become increasingly familiar with financial engineering, derivatives, and the advanced financial technology and concepts currently used in the private sector. They must do so not only so they can understand the parts of the financial system they regulate, but also to execute their own functions more effectively. We harbor the hope that the functional perspective we have set forth can help with the efficient evolution of the system by providing a single framework of analysis shared by both public sector and private sector managers.

References

Benston, G., and G. Kaufman (1988), "Risk and Solvency Regulation of Depository Institutions: Past Policies and Current Options," New York: Salomon Brothers Center Monograph Series in Finance and Economics, Monograph 1.

Black, F. (1975), "Bank Funds Management in an Efficient Market," *Journal of Financial Economics*, 2 (December): 323–339.

—— (1985), "The Future for Financial Services," Chapter 8 in *Managing the Service Economy*, R.P. Inman, ed., Cambridge: Cambridge University Press.

Bodie, Z., and R.C. Merton (1992), "Pension Reform and Privatization in International Perspective: The Case of Israel," Harvard Business School Working Paper No. 92-082, Boston (May). Also published in Hebrew, *The Economics Quarterly*, August 1992, 152.

—— (1993), "Pension Benefit Guarantees in the United States: A Functional Analysis," in *The Future of Pensions in the United States*, R. Shmitt, ed., Philadelphia: University of Pennsylvania Press.

Chicago Mercantile Exchange (1993), "A Blueprint for Reform of the Financial Regulatory Structure."

Commodity Futures Trading Commission (1993), *The Report of the Commodity Futures Trading Commission: OTC Derivative Markets and Their Regulation*, Washington, D.C. (October).

Cox, J.C., and C. Huang (1989), "Optimum Consumption and Portfolio Policies When Asset Prices Follow a Diffusion Process," *Journal of Economic Theory*, 49 (October): 33–83.

Darby, M. (1994), "OTC Derivatives and Systemic Risk," National Bureau of Economic Research Working Paper 4801, Cambridge, MA.

Diamond, P. (1992), "Pension Reform in a Transition Economy: Notes on Poland and Chile," Paper prepared for NBER Conference on Industrial Restructuring in Eastern Europe (February).

Dickson, P.G.M. (1967), *The Financial Revolution in England*, New York: St. Martin's Press.

Fama, E. (1985), "What's Different About Banks?" *Journal of Monetary Economics*, 15 (January): 29–39.

Freeman, A. (1993), "A Survey of International Banking: New Tricks to Learn," *The Economist*, April 10: 1–37.

Friedman, M. (1960), *A Program for Monetary Stability*, New York: Fordham University Press.

General Accounting Office (1994), *Financial Derivatives: Actions Needed to Protect the Financial System,* Report GAO/GGD-94-133, Washington, D.C. (May).

Global Derivatives Study Group (1993), *Derivatives: Practices and Principles,* Washington, D.C.: The Group of Thirty (July).

Gorton, G., and G. Pennacchi (1991), "Financial Innovation and the Provision of Liquidity Services," in *Reform of Deposit Insurance and the Regulation of Depository Institutions in the 1990s,* D. Brumbaugh, ed., Grand Rapids, MI: Harper Business.

Hanke, S.H. (1991), "Private Social Security: The Key to Reform in Eastern Europe," *Contingencies* (July/August): 18–21.

Hindy, A. (1995), "Elements of Quantitative Risk Management," in *Risk Management: Problems & Solutions,* W.H. Beaver and G. Parker, eds., New York: McGraw-Hill.

Kareken, J.H. (1986), "Federal Bank Regulatory Policy: A Description and Some Observations," *Journal of Business,* 59 (January): 3–48.

Litan, R.E. (1987), *What Should Banks Do?* Washington: The Brookings Institution.

Merton, R.C. (1989), "On the Application of the Continuous-Time Theory of Finance to Financial Intermediation and Insurance," *Geneva Papers on Risk and Insurance,* 14 (July): 225–262.

———— (1992a), "Financial Innovation and Economic Performance," *Journal of Applied Corporate Finance,* 4 (Winter): 12–22.

———— (1992b), *Continuous-Time Finance,* revised edition, Oxford: Basil Blackwell.

———— (1993), "Operation and Regulation in Financial Intermediation: A Functional Perspective," in *Operation and Regulation of Financial Markets,* P. Englund, ed., Stockholm: The Economic Council.

———— (1995), "Financial Innovation and the Management and Regulation of Financial Institutions," *Journal of Banking and Finance,* 19 (July): 461–482.

Merton, R.C., and Z. Bodie (1992), "On the Management of Financial Guarantees," *Financial Management,* 22 (Winter): 87–109.

———— (1993), "Deposit Insurance Reform: A Functional Approach" in *Carnegie-Rochester Conference Series on Public Policy,* A. Meltzer and C. Plosser, eds., 38 (June).

Miller, M.H. (1994a), "Functional Regulation," *Pacific-Basin Finance Journal,* 2 (May): 91–106.

———— (1994b), "Do We Really Need More Regulation of Financial Derivatives?" Banco de Investimentos Garantia, Sao Paulo, Brazil (August).

Myers, R.J. (1991), "Privatizing Social Security: It's Not Exactly One Size Fits All," *Contingencies* (November/December): 9–11.

———— (1992), "Chile's Social Security Reform After Ten Years," *Benefits Quarterly,* 1 (Third Quarter): 6–20.

National Commission on Financial Institution Reform, Recovery, and Enforcement (1993), *Origins and Causes of the S&L Debacle: A Blueprint for Reform,* Washington, D.C.: Government Printing Office, (July).

North, D.C. (1994), "The Evolution of Efficient Markets in History," Chapter 11 in *Capitalism in Context,* J.A. James and M. Thomas, eds., Chicago: University of Chicago Press.

Paré, T.P. (1994), "Learning to Live with Derivatives," *Fortune,* July 25: 106–116.

Pierce, J.L. (1991), *The Future of Banking*, New Haven, CT: Yale University Press.

―――― (1993), "The Functional Approach to Deposit Insurance and Regulation," in *Safeguarding the Banking System in an Environment of Financial Cycles*, R.E. Randall, ed., Proceedings of a Symposium of the Federal Reserve Bank of Boston (November): 111–130.

Ross, S.A. (1989), "Institutional Markets, Financial Marketing, and Financial Innovation," *Journal of Finance*, 44 (July): 541–556.

Tobin, J. (1985), "Financial Innovation and Deregulation in Perspective," *Bank of Japan Monetary and Economic Studies*, v. 3, no. 2, (September): 19–29. Reprinted in Y. Suzuki and H. Yomo, eds., (1986), *Financial Innovation and Monetary Policy: Asia and the West*, Tokyo: University of Tokyo Press, 31–42.

―――― (1987), "The Case for Preserving Regulatory Distinctions," in *Restructuring the Financial System*, Federal Reserve Bank of Kansas City.

White, L.J. (1993), "Competition versus Harmonization: An Overview of International Regulation of Financial Services," New York University Salomon Center Working Paper S-93-58.

World Bank (1994), "Averting the Old Age Crisis: Policies to Protect the Old and Promote Growth," Policy Research Report (June).

ABOUT THE CONTRIBUTORS

Dwight B. Crane is the George Gund Professor of Finance and Banking at the Harvard Business School. His current research, part of a continuing project by the Global Financial System Project at Harvard, focuses on the future role and structure of financial institutions. Professor Crane has written several articles on the management of customer relationships and the impact of bank mergers as well as other topics. His most recent book (as co-author) is *Doing Deals: Investment Banks at Work.*

Kenneth A. Froot is a professor at the Harvard Business School, where he teaches corporate finance and international finance courses. He has published articles in a wide variety of financial journals and edited a number of books, most recently *The Transition in Eastern Europe.* He is also editor of the *Journal of International Financial Management and Accounting* and the *Journal of International Economics.*

Scott P. Mason is the Edmund Cogswell Converse Professor of Finance and Banking at the Harvard Business School and currently chairs the finance department. His research interests include such capital markets issues as valuation, risk management, and financial engineering. Professor Mason has authored articles for the *Journal of Financial Economics* and the *Journal of Finance* and is a co-author of *Cases in Financial Engineering: Applied Studies of Financial Innovations.*

André F. Perold is the Sylvan C. Coleman Professor of Financial Management at the Harvard Business School where he specializes in capital markets and investment management. His recent research concerns derivative instruments and their relation to the payment system, and risk management and capital allocation within principal financial firms. Implementation costs within investment organizations, management of currency stock, and stock market efficiency and liquidity. Perold is a co-author of *Cases in Financial Engineering: Applied Studies of Financial Innovation*, and is the developer of a widely-used software package for portfolio construction. He serves on the editorial board of the *Financial Analysts Journal*.

Robert C. Merton is the George F. Baker Professor of Business Administration at the Harvard Business School. A past president of the American Finance Association, he is a Senior Fellow of the International Association of Financial Engineers and a principal in Long-Term Capital Management, L.P. His fields of expertise include risk management, capital asset pricing, pricing of options, risky debt, loan guarantees, and complex derivative securities. Professor Merton has written extensively on the operation and regulation of financial institutions and is the author of *Continuous-Time Finance*.

Zvi Bodie, a visiting professor at the Harvard Business School, is on the faculty of Boston University's School of Management. Professor Bodie has published widely on pension finance and on hedging against inflation. He is a consultant on pension issues to the U.S. Department of Labor, Israel, as well as to several pension asset management firms. He has written and edited several books, most recently *Securing Employer-Based Pensions*.

Erik R. Sirri is an assistant professor at Babson College. His research focuses on the design of securities exchanges, risk management, and the economics of the mutual fund industry. As a consultant, he has worked with securities firms, investment advisors, and market makers.

Peter Tufano is an associate professor at the Harvard Business School. His current research focuses on innovative financial products, the use of financial engineering techniques by corporations and product-level competition in financial markets. Professor Tufano's research has been brought into the MBA Classroom through his course, Corporate Financial Engineering. He is a co-author of *Cases in Financial Engineering: Applied Studies in Financial Innovation*.

INDEX

Countrywide Credit Industries, Inc.
(mortgage banking firm), 140
Currency hedging, 67

D
Debreu, G., 160
Delivery-versus-payment (DVP), 49–50
Derivative instruments. *See also* specific
instruments
cash market volume and derivatives
volume, 68–71
concerns about, 188
currency hedging, 67
exchange-for-physicals (EFP), 68
fixed-income, 218
futures contracts, 61–62
growth in trading of, 264, 267–268
impact on financial system, 153, 183,
187–192
to increase firm value, 256
information from, 16
interest rate swaps, 60–61, 167, 266–267
options and other contingent claim
securities, 64–66
and payment system risk, 75
payment systems and, 13, 38, 56–60
possible regulation of, 188–189, 267–269
risk management and, 15, 153, 187–192
as speculative, 191
stabilization policy and, 277–278
stock index futures, 62–64, 206–207
as substitutes for trading in physical
securities, 60–68
types of, 157
Discount function, 198–199
Diversification, 15, 101–108
efficiency gains due to, 169, 171–172, 173
example: reduced risk for ship owners,
168–171
and lowered risk, 101, 103, 168–172
minimum efficient scale for, 103
partial, cost of, 106–107
and transaction costs, 102, 104–105, 107
DVP. *See* Delivery-versus-payment

E
Efficient markets hypothesis, 197
Efficient portfolio frontier, 208
EFP. *See* Exchange-for-physicals
Equity capital, 23
Esty, B., 114
Eurobond market, 37
Euroclear, 34, 37, 55
Eurodollar futures market, 21–22
Exchange-for-physicals (EFP), 68

F
Fama, E., 197
Federal Deposit Insurance Corporation
(FDIC), 158, 271–273
Federal Deposit Insurance Corporation
Improvement Act (FDICIA), 51
Federal Home Loan Mortgage Association
(Freddie Mac), 139
Federal Housing Administration (FHA),
formation of, 138
Federal National Mortgage Association
(Fannie Mae), 138–139
FedWire, 39, 50–51
Finality of settlement, 50–52
"Financial accelerator" models, 243, 246
Financial contracting, 210
Financial engineering technology, pooling
and, 120
Financial firms
creditworthiness, importance of, 181–183
risk management of, 176, 181–183
Financial infrastructure and public policy,
263–282
functional regulation, and potential
applications, 269–278
infrastructure and regulation, 265–266
pension reform and privatization, 274–276
regulation of banks, 271–273
regulatory cooperation and competition,
273–274
risk accounting, 266–267
stabilization policy, derivatives and,
277–278
Financial-innovation spiral. *See* Innovation
spiral
Finnerty, J.D., 20
Firm, as legal entity, 82–83
Firm size
and auto industry, 94
and economies of scale, 84–85
and family wealth, 88–91, 92
and international family wealth, 94–95
Fischer, S., 218
Fisher, I., 197
FLEX options, 53
Foreign & Colonial Government Trust, 130
Forex market, options market for, 268
Forward agreement, contract
example of, 165–166
global daily turnover, 165
as hedging mechanism, 162, 165–167
settlement lag as, 56–59
Free cash flow hypothesis, 228–229
Fremont Financial Corporation, 148
securitization of mid-market loans,
145–146
structure and rating, 146

Incentive problems *(cont.)*
  investment "project mix" problem,
      246–248
  in lending, 133–135, 145
  marketable and non-marketable risks,
      256–259
  and monetary policy channels, 242–
      243
  optimal capital structure: dynamic view,
      230–237
  optimal capital structure: static view,
      228–230
  "overinvestment" problem, 244–246
  and PERCs, 235–236
  potential cost for entire economy,
      243–244
  and put warrants, 236–237
  and risk management, 248–256. *See also*
      Hedging; Risk management
  and security design, 233–237
  "underinvestment" problem, 239–244
Index futures, 62–64
Informational role of asset prices. *See* Price
      information
Information asymmetries, 16
  and incentive problems, 133–135, 147,
      231–235
  in middle-market lending, 144–147
  multiple bilateral contracts and, 97
  and transaction costs, 179–180
Innovation spiral, 4, 6
  information extraction as part of, 221
  product migration from intermediaries
      to markets, 20–22
  in types of pooling, 100
Institutional perspective, 10–11, 263
Insurance, 15
  actuarial, 172–174
  firms as mortgage providers, 137–138
  guarantees, 174
  options, 174–175
  and risk management, 172–176
  role of diversification in, 172–173
Interest Equalization Tax, 37
Interest rate swaps, 60–61, 167, 266–267
International Finance Corporation (IFC), 99
Intertemporal transfer of resources, 18
Investment management services, pooling
      and, 111–115
  advantages of intermediate pooling,
      112–114
  costs of intermediate pooling, 114–115
Ippolito, R., 114

J
Jensen, M.C., 109

K
Kareken, J.H., 272
Kashyap, A., 243
Kyrillos, B., 113

L
Lamont, O., 240–241, 243
Lamoreaux, N., 110
Law of One Price, 201–204
  applied to currency exchange rates,
      201–203
"Lemons" problem, 102, 109, 231–232
  lemon theory of convertibles, 235
LIBOR (London Interbank Offered Rate),
      21–22, 143–144
"Life-cycle" funds, 113
Life-cycle needs, 129
Liquidity, 27–28
  vs. certainty of payment, 27
  defined, 27, 108
  and pooling, 108–109, 117
Liquidity stripping, 116, 118
Litan, R.E., 272
López-de-Silanes, F., 245

M
Margrabe, W., 218
Market completeness, 21, 221
Markowitz, H., 208
Matrix pricing, 205
MBS Clearing Corporation (MBSCC), 48
MCI, experience with convertible bonds,
      235
Meckling, W.H., 109
Merton, R.C., 97, 115, 212, 214, 218, 248, 272
  dividend-adjusted Black-Scholes
      formula, 212–213
  version of Arrow-Debreu model, 161
Middle-market lending, 144–147
  barriers to change, 147–148
  Fremont Financial Corporation, case of,
      145–146
  motivations for securitization, 148–149
  nationwide companies, 146–147
  role of institutions in, 150
  securitization, 145–146, 147–150
  standardization and, 148–149
Minimum efficient scale (MES), 84
  cross-industry study of, 85–86
  for diversified portfolio, 103
Mobil, cash flow and investment level,
      241, 244
Monitoring
  costs of, 145
  and pooling, 109–110

Mont Blanc Capital Corporation (MBCC), 143
Montgomery Ward, influence of Mobil's cash flow decline, 241, 244
Moral-hazard problems, 16, 97, 141
  examples of, 134, 145
  and government risk-bearing, 185–186
Mortgage-backed securities, 18, 58, 83–84. *See also* specific agencies
  description of, 116
  development of, 138–140
  early interregional lending, 137–138
  government sponsored, 139
  impact of, 140–141
  as long-distance transfer, 132
  ownership of, 141
  private securitization, 139
Multilateral netting, 46–47, 73–74
Multi-seller conduit
  advantages of, 144
  cost structure, 143–144
  securitizing receivables, 143
Municipal bond insurance, 19
Mutual funds, 14, 120, 273
  and cost of diversification, 106, 108
  managers' access to information, 113
  as multilateral contracts, 83, 112
  risk-pooling benefits of, 168, 171

N
Nasar, S., 210
National Securities Clearing Corporation (NSCC), 47, 51
Neoclassical economics perspective, 10–11
Netting, 46–49
  benefits of, 47–48
  bilateral, 47
  clearinghouse, 47
  FDICIA and legal integrity of, 51
  multilateral, 46–47, 73–74
  potential problems, 49–52
Netting over time, in forward market, 58, 59
Netting ratios, 47–49
No-arbitrage opportunities model, 203
NSCC. *See* National Securities Clearing Corporation

O
Opaque assets, 271
Opaque intermediaries, 112
Options, 64–66, 71, 190
  exchange-traded, 15, 175, 198
  over-the-counter, 175, 268
  put-call parity, 254
  puts and calls, 69, 174–175

revision frequency, 65–66
  volatility of stock price and price of, 207
OTC derivatives, regulation of, 267–269
"Overinvestment" problem, 244–246
Oxford Provident Building Association, 133

P
Payment system, 5, 12–13, 33–79
  cash market volume and derivatives volume, 68–71
  delivery-versus-payment, 49–50
  and derivative instruments, 13, 38, 56–71. *See also* Derivative instruments
  design and efficiency, 56
  extension of credit, 54–55
  finality of settlement, 50–52
  and funds transfer systems, 39
  immobilization, 45–46
  netting, 46–49
  operational aspects of clearing, 44–45
  payments volume in U.S., 35–37, 41
  performance guarantees, by clearinghouses, 52–53
  settlement problem in foreign exchange, 71–75
  sketch of, 39–43
  systems for clearing and settlement, 40–56
  transaction risks and costs, 33–34
  volume growth and structural change, 37
Penn Square Bank debacle, 131
Pension Benefit Guarantee Corporation (PBGC), 158
Pension reform, 7–8, 274–276
PERCs, 235–236
Perfect markets economy, 159, 189, 247
Perold, A., 23, 248
Pierce, J.L., 272
Pooling resources, 5, 13–14, 81–127
  alternative forms of pooling capital, 97–101
  and asset securitization, 115–118
  and banking, 110
  capital structure, 100
  in communist and socialist regimes, 99–100
  costs of, 97, 114–115
  demand by enterprises: scale economies, 84–101
  demand by households: liquidity and diversification, 101–111. *See also* Diversification; Liquidity
  effect of technologies on, 84
  effect on social and private welfare, 92–97